More
Than It Seems

More
Than It Seems

HOUSEHOLD WORK AND LIFELONG LEARNING

by
Margrit Eichler, Patrizia Albanese,
Susan Ferguson, Nicky Hyndman,
Lichun Willa Liu, and Ann Matthews

Women's Press
Toronto

More Than It Seems
Margrit Eichler, Patrizia Albanese, Susan Ferguson, Nicky Hyndman, Lichun Willa Liu, and Ann Matthews

First published in 2010 by
Women's Press, an imprint of Canadian Scholars' Press Inc.
180 Bloor Street West, Suite 801
Toronto, Ontario
M5S 2V6

www.womenspress.ca

Canadian Scholars' Press Inc./Women's Press gratefully acknowledges financial support for our publishing activities from the the Government of Canada through the Book Publishing Industry Development Program (BPIDP) and the Government of Ontario.

Library and Archives Canada Cataloguing in Publication

More than it seems : household work and lifelong learning / Margrit Eichler ... [et al.].

Includes bibliographical references.
ISBN 978-0-88961-481-9

1. Stay-at-home mothers—Canada—Case studies.
2. Wives—Canada—Case studies. 3. Households—Canada—Case studies. 4. Housekeeping—Canada—Case studies. 5. Adult learning—Canada—Case studies. I. Eichler, Margrit

HQ759.46.M67 2010   306.874'30971   C2010-902980-1

Text design by Colleen Wormald.
Cover design by EmDash Designs.

09 10 11 12 13   5 4 3 2 1

Printed and bound in Canada by Marquis Book Printing, Inc.

Canadä

Table of Contents

FOREWORD

More Than It Seems is an apt title for this groundbreaking work that explores connections between lifelong learning and household work.

Although the fields of adult education and lifelong learning explore learning in a wide range of contexts, one place that has been consistently overlooked as an important site of adult learning experiences is the home. In my own research, I have long argued that in order to understand gender differences in learning experiences and to appreciate fully the expansiveness, complexity, and potential richness of the concept of lifelong learning, we cannot continue to ignore or devalue learning that occurs in the homeplace.

I am therefore delighted to have the opportunity to provide a foreword to a book that takes up provocative and insightful issues around lifelong learning in connection to household work—work that is centred in the home. This study began in the early 2000s when Dr. Margrit Eichler, a respected feminist scholar, was invited by Dr. David Livingstone, to join the Changing Nature of Work and Lifelong Learning (WALL), a project designed to investigate diverse forms of lifelong learning and work, including unpaid labour such as household work. She invited her colleague, Dr. Patrizia Albanese to join her, and together with contributions from a team of graduate students, they have written a book that is a varied, multi-layered, and thoroughly engaging read.

One of the main challenges in discussing learning and household labour is that people often struggle with language to name their experiences, because unpaid work in the home is often treated as an invisible activity, not worthy of acknowledgement, and the processes of informal learning are often difficult to identify and describe. Deciding what gets counted as work and what gets acknowledged as learning reveals the ways in which our understanding of the world and our experiences within it are shaped and constrained by larger social, political, cultural, and economic structures. Probing beneath the surface of seemingly mundane activities such as cooking, taking a shower, or sending a child off to school can deepen our understanding of informal learning in everyday contexts. Thus, when a man talks about learning to take over cooking responsibilities since coming to Canada, gender dynamics are revealed when it becomes clear that his wife still chops the vegetables and cleans up afterwards. Understanding the notion of self-care as a form of work and learning becomes more apparent after reading about the struggles of doing daily tasks such as bathing after the onset of a physical disability. The ways in which globalization impacts upon the home become more obvious when thinking about a nanny who waves goodbye to another woman's children each morning at the bus stop, all the while thinking about her own child being raised by her mother in her country of origin, thousands of kilometres away.

The six authors of *More Than It Seems* have done a remarkable job pulling together a book that is scholarly and rich in empirical data, but also very accessible in its writing style. Readers will connect with the learners whose stories are told through brief but often poignant vignettes at the start of each chapter. Throughout the book, insightful analysis and explanation of policies and research are interwoven with quotes from the many different participants. Eichler, Albanese, and the others do not gloss over the difficulties that many of these learners must address. They point out that while there are people who learn positive things through household work, there are also people who resist learning, sometimes with tragic consequences, and many "things people should not have to learn," such as adaptation to poverty. The chapters on immigrant experiences and learning associated with disabilities provide important contributions to areas that have not been researched adequately.

This book establishes a solid beginning for empirical research that links lifelong learning with the home by examining experiences around learning and household work. It is to be hoped that other researchers will see the need to build on this work in the future. But for now, Eichler, Albanese, and the others have made a substantive contribution to the field of lifelong learning by writing a richly textured book that provides numerous critical insights into the challenges that people face in their everyday learning contexts within the home. Enjoy the read!

Patricia Gouthro
Mount Saint Vincent University
Halifax, Nova Scotia

Introduction
MORE THAN IT SEEMS:
HOUSEHOLD WORK AND LIFELONG LEARNING
Patrizia Albanese

Introduction: The Elephant in the Room

This old Hindu tale has been retold many times and in many versions over the past few centuries, and while perhaps overused, it seems to have great bearing on what we are about to embark on in this book. The story—or at least one variant—goes as follows.

A group of blindfolded men (or men in the dark, but still men!) stand at different ends of an elephant and begin to touch the part of the elephant that is directly in front of them to learn what it is like. Each one touches a different part, but only that one part, and begins speculating on what this animal looks like. One touches a tusk, another its trunk, another the tail, and so on. They start discussing what they touched, comparing what each came to believe the animal looked like. Inevitably, they were all in complete disagreement, and were particularly off the mark with regard to its immense size and extraordinary shape.

This parable has been used around the world to indicate that reality may be viewed differently depending upon one's perspective. It suggests that what seems to be an absolute truth, based on tangible observations may, in fact, be relative or incomplete because each observer has looked at only part of the object under study or because of the ideology regarding it. It's also about the oversimplification or trivialization of complex things.

This book is about a colossal elephant—household work—and a seemingly growing body of facts and fictions on what it *might* look and feel like. We aim to show that each of the many hands that have touched this elephant have felt only a part. And that our often fixed ideas about work and learning; about their nature, scope, and practice; about money-earning, skills, and power; about private and public; and about gender have not allowed us to feel the whole elephant and understand its magnitude and social worth.

While seeking to lift the cloak on the nature, scope, and social relations that household work includes, we also sought to understand the type and amount of learning involved in performing household work. Neither was an easy task. We anticipated that it would be difficult to make visible the work involved in household work, even to the people who performed it. We knew it would be even more difficult to expose the learning it involved.

We found that with each probe, we encountered preconceived notions that prevented individuals from seeing the work and learning parts of our elephant (household work). When we touched upon the work involved, many people could not, at first, get past ingrained or superficial ideas about all work being paid work. With subtle and not so subtle nudges and probes, rich discussion about household work as work ensued.

When we touched upon the learning, again, many could not at first identify the array of informal learning—unstructured and at times unintended knowledge and skills that people acquire incidentally through everyday experiences—that is part of their household work, and that lies alongside and behind formal learning in their lives. We also hit deeply rooted ideas about formal and informal learning as happening mostly (or only) through, around, and for paid work. Through discussion and probes, however, most people we spoke to came to recognize and talk about a great deal of learning they experienced in the course of their daily household work.

We found that to help shed light on the work and learning that are so much a part of household work, we had to touch (and get others to touch) more than the one part of the elephant before us. We decided to do this by integrating carework into our understanding of household work and exploring the experiences of recent immigrants from China,[1] nannies, people with disabilities, and others who had experienced important life changes. These became lenses through which we could expose and magnify often ignored aspects of household work and learning. We believe that seeing household work and learning through these underutilized lenses can help us challenge some of the pre-set thinking that so often acts as a barrier to a greater understanding of household work and learning.

This book sets out to show that what we as a society conceptualize as work, for the most part, often excludes unpaid household work or addresses only part of it. As such, we continue to undervalue its contribution to society and the weight of its continued burden on the backs of individuals (still, for the most part, women) who perform it. The growing volume of data and research on unpaid household work worldwide is impressive. However, national statistical agencies and researchers, as we will see in this book, collect these data in a variety of ways using a range of techniques and schemes. This book does not challenge the importance and necessity of this work and this counting, but it does question whether we are counting the whole thing and in the right way. We wonder out loud how something so large, like our elephant in the room, could be rendered so invisible? We asked and we probed about what else household work includes, who else it involves, and where it takes place. We asked how it changed throughout the life course, and how it was affected by specific life events (loss of a partner, a change in jobs, migration, disability, etc.). Following this, we spent a considerable amount of time focusing on the learning that happens through household work. We spoke to and surveyed people of different ages, classes, abilities, educational backgrounds, genders, races, and household configurations; newcomers, Aboriginals, and those in between. We wondered how household work is affected by being differently located in the world: as a Black woman, an Aboriginal woman, a White man, by being young or old, for instance. Their thoughts and voices helped shed new and more light on different parts of our elephant.

The Project

SOME BACKGROUND

This book is the outcome of a four-year study on unpaid household work and lifelong learning (see Appendix 1 for more details). It is the result of team-work that began in the early 2000s when David Livingstone invited Margrit Eichler to become part of a new research initiative on Work and Lifelong Learning (WALL—see Appendix 2 for more details). Margrit approached a feminist organization that deals with housework and motherwork—Mothers Are Women (MAW—see Appendix 3 for more details), and who were familiar with some of her work; they agreed to join the research project as our community partner. When the project was funded, Margrit invited Patrizia Albanese, a friend and colleague from Ryerson University, to join her. Together they devised the first questionnaire, to be distributed to MAW and other women's groups. This was Phase 1 of a four-phase project.

THE FOUR PHASES

Phase 1 involved mailing a questionnaire to members of women's groups, asking them what housework and carework they perform and what they learn through it. Our intent was to establish to what degree people (and particularly women who were already part of awareness-raising groups) are conscious of performing mental and emotional functions when engaging in unpaid household work.

Phase 2 involved a total of 11 focus groups comprised of 66 participants in three Canadian cities: three groups consisted of White women only, diverse in age and socio-economic status; two groups of Black women; one group of Aboriginal women; one group of White disabled women; one group of racialized disabled women;[2] one group of Chinese women; and two groups of men, all of whom were White except for one Chinese man. There was also one online discussion group with 20 disabled women. Our goal in this phase was to explore the range of activities the participants actually did, and specifically to probe for mental and emotional functions associated with housework. We also wanted to see whether participants considered engaging in these activities as work. Finally, we wanted to know if and how their unpaid housework changed over time, what they had to learn to adjust to these changes, and how they learned.

Phase 3 involved in-depth interviews with 75 individuals,[3] who had participated in the larger national WALL survey, with respect to the learning associated with the unpaid housework they have done in the past five years. The WALL respondents we followed up with had all gone through a major life change (lost a paid job, gained a new paid job, acquired a child, lost a partner, emigrated from China, or had a disability). In this phase, we were interested in how this major life change affected the housework and carework they do, or no longer do. We hypothesized that a significant life change would require them to learn new skills, knowledge, and understanding, and possibly unlearn others.

Phase 4 involved in-depth interviews with 10 paid housecleaners and 10 nannies. We were interested in understanding the experiences of women who do the same job for pay and without pay, and specifically about their work and learning. Our goal was to determine if housework, carework, and learning are experienced differently when they are done for pay.

A WORD ON NOMENCLATURE AND OUR USE OF THE TERM "HOUSE-HOLD WORK"

Originally we intended to discuss only housework in our study. It was our community partner, MAW, who insisted that we insert a separate question on carework into the questionnaire (Phase 1). Our data were richer for having asked a separate question, but also a lot more unwieldy. Given that we had asked open-ended questions, we needed to develop a coding system for both housework and carework. This did not prove to be easy. Some people included carework under housework and others did not. After trying to develop separate codes for housework and carework, we gave this up as not only useless but theoretically unwarranted and confusing. We eventually developed a single coding system for housework and carework. If people simply noted that they performed one of the activities, regardless of the question under which they recorded this, we coded it as housework. If they listed it as an activity they had performed on behalf of someone, including themselves, we coded it as carework. On the basis of our data we came to the conclusion that housework and carework are two sides of the same coin: Both involve the same work, but when categorizing the work as housework, it is the activity that is emphasized, while carework puts the stress on the relational aspect of the work. For example, if someone wrote: "I cleaned the bathroom and baked two cakes," we coded it as housework, but if she wrote "I cleaned the bathroom and baked two cakes for my dad," it was coded as carework (Eichler 2008a). We then decided that the term "household work" better described all this than the term "housework." As a result, this study and book, for the most part, use the term "household work" instead of "housework."[4]

OUR GOALS, APPROACH, AND CONTRIBUTIONS TO THE FIELD

One of our key contributions to this area of study is our new definition of household work, which we believe best reflects the complexity of this work. In this definition we identify four dimensions of household work that emerged from the study: (1) physical, (2) mental, (3) emotional, and (4) spiritual. Each of these dimensions of household work, and the learning associated with it, will be presented and discussed in more detail throughout the chapters in this book. We have defined household work as follows:

> Household work consists of the sum of all physical, mental, emotional, and spiritual tasks that are performed for one's own or someone else's household and that maintain the daily life of those for whom one has responsibility.

But defining household work was just a first step. We also aimed to show that household work *is* work because, for the most part, people still equate work with paid work. This is evident in the way we speak about it. For example, we say, "She's a working woman" when she has a paid job, but not when she performs unpaid work at home. Or if someone asks, "What does your mother do for a living?" the answer might be "Nothing, she's just a housewife." Similarly, much scholarship talks about the conflict between "family and work," as if no work takes place within families. Through this project, we proceeded on the assumption that paid and unpaid work are mutually interdependent even though people continue to see some unpaid household activities as non-work. Working on the assumption that household work is work helps us begin to address the question of what people learn from it.

Throughout this book, we aim to contribute to a body of knowledge on lifelong learning, which contains within itself an incomparably smaller body of literature on the lifelong learning that takes place within household work. Together with others, we help challenge ideas that continue to promote paid work as publicly valuable and involving a great deal of skills and learning, and unpaid work, in contrast, as less socially valuable, private, "natural" to women, and involving little or no skills and learning. We seek to show the fluidity and ongoing interaction between paid and unpaid work by revealing (and making more visible) household work's magnitude and value, and the abundance of informal learning it involves. Through this research we and the study participants came to rethink the household work we do, why we do it, where, how, for whom, what it involves, its significance and value, and the learning it entails. We hope the same happens for you.

The Research Team and the Writing and Structure of This Book

The project team has ballooned and shrunk depending on the phase of the research. Many have contributed to the diverse phases and stages,[5] but, for the most part, the team has been made up of two professors (Dr. Margrit Eichler, Principal Investigator, Ontario Institute for Studies in Education/ University of Toronto, and Dr. Patrizia Albanese, Ryerson University), graduate students (Ann Matthews, Lichun Willa Liu, Susan Ferguson, and Nicky Hyndman), and one community partner (Kathryn Spracklin, Mothers Are Women). This book is the result of our co-operative efforts in data collection, analysis, and writing.

This book is like many others, and then again it's not. Typically, team research produces co-authored books, in which at least in theory, all parts of a book are written by everyone collectively, or it produces edited books, in which each team member writes a chapter or two, with a bridging introduction and conclusion. This book involves a bit of both. We each took responsibility for specific chapters, but shared information across chapters. We read, reflected upon, and commented on each other's work, recommending literature, restructuring and rewording where we felt it would enrich the chapter. There were times when seeds were planted by some and nurtured by others. We struggled collectively and grew individually. As a result, each chapter shares certain elements, yet has its own voice.

Chapters in this book are separated by a one-page portrait profiling the experiences of one study participant whose story is linked to the contents of the upcoming chapter. We decided to do this in order to help bring the material to life. Each chapter then has a detailed chapter introduction that begins with a personal narrative or reflection by the author aimed at setting the stage. Each chapter also draws upon data from one or more phases of the project outlined above. Whenever possible and to bring some of the findings to life, we included direct quotes from individual participants. Some of the quotes in the book have involved minor editing for grammar and clarity, and to capture the spirit and intent of the original quote. A few quotes were translated from Chinese by Lichun Willa Liu. All the names of participants, as well as other potentially identifying information, have been changed to help protect their identity and ensure confidentiality.

AN INTRODUCTORY WORD ON WORK (A LOOK TOWARD CHAPTER 1)

Household work has been treated as a private affair, done *by* private individuals (mostly women) *for* private individuals within private households. In doing this, household work has been, for the most part, invisible and viewed as personal—a "labour of love"—and not necessarily as *socially* valuable. Only recently, as a result of women's movements organizing, have governments and international bodies started paying attention to household work as socially relevant, recognizing, for example, that the monetary and social devaluation of unpaid household work is connected to the systemic undervaluation of women's work in general.

A few decades ago Canada was seen as an international leader in the measurement and valuation of unpaid household work (Colman 1998), as Statistics Canada released its first data on unpaid work in the 1970s (Hamdad 2003). In 1994, Canada hosted an International Conference on the Measurement and Valuation of Unpaid Work, and in 1996 the first Canadian Census collected data on unpaid work (Statistics Canada 1996). Since then, Statistics Canada has released and made publicly available volumes of data and dozens of studies on the number of hours spent doing unpaid housework, its measurement and valuation, on converging gender roles, on the division of household labour in dual-earner households, etc. But have all these data actually changed social attitudes, unmasked its social worth, and captured the full range of work it involves and the learning that inevitably comes with it? Chapter 1 explores these and related questions in more detail. It begins by asking the questions: What is household work? Where is it performed, by whom, and how? It also asks what makes work *work*, and why household work so often fails to be seen as such.

Chapter 1 presents some of our current research and thinking about household work, and identifies some of the key shortcomings in two bodies of literature on work and housework. It also presents an alternative way of thinking about housework, which includes our new definition and household work's multiple dimensions.

AN INTRODUCTORY WORD ON LEARNING (A LOOK TOWARD CHAPTER 2)
While the measurement, valuation, research, and theorizing regarding household work is abundant (although often very limited, as we see in Chapter 1), the recognition and measurement of the learning associated with it is almost completely unexplored. So often, when we think about learning, we think about formal schooling or the kinds of skills we seek

and acquire to allow us to do our paid work. We very often overlook the skills and abilities we develop and use when we do unpaid work. Chapter 2 discusses this second invisibility—the type and abundance of learning that so often accompanies and occurs through household work.

Ironically, as a society, we recognize that children learn a great deal at home and in *informal* settings (see Maddock 2006), but we then assume, or by the absence of research and theorizing, imply that adults do not. We know children are socialized in the home (to be punctual, organized, co-operative, healthy, accommodating, etc.) by watching, imitating, and being guided by parents and other adults. Like Gouthro (2005) and Livingstone (2001), we believed that the home (and daily life) is an important site of learning, and that household work is a way through which many people develop and use a number of often unacknowledged skills. Chapter 2 discusses this in more detail.

When we began working in this area, we assumed that the literature on lifelong learning would shed some light on the learning associated with household work. We were, for the most part, disappointed. Since the 1970s, there has been an international movement afoot promoting the notion of education and learning for life ("skills for life"). Subsequently, there has been a growing body of literature and policy stressing the importance of developing and recognizing opportunities for ongoing, lifelong acquisition of knowledge. The notion of lifelong learning grew in prominence, particularly in light of changing and globalizing economies and the promise of the coming of a knowledge-based society. In this changing economic context, rather than recognizing the broad array of learning and skills development that takes place throughout the life course and in various places, spaces, and social contexts (including the home), lifelong learning, for the most part, came to mean a drive for lifelong *formal* education/schooling and skills (re)training, particularly following job losses, the rise in non-standard jobs, and cuts to social spending (Appleby and Bathmaker, 2006; Hughes, Blaxter, Brine, and Jackson 2006; Cruickshank 2002). Chapter 2 outlines our efforts and approach to reclaiming the notion of lifelong learning by bringing to the fore the learner, self-initiated informal learning, and households as sites of learning. In doing this, we find ourselves part of a small body of scholars (Gouthro 2005; Gerzer-Sass 2004; Livingstone 2001; Butler 1993; Hart 1992) who are working toward reclaiming the concept of lifelong learning to include learning that is truly lifelong—from the cradle to the grave—and life-wide, across life's spaces, including the home. By looking at the learning associated with household work, we seek to contribute to a body of literature on what lifelong learning *is*, and what lifelong learning *can be*.

Chapters 1 and 2 outline and critique what has been done in the areas of work and learning. They also set the stage for the remaining chapters, which take our new definition, approach, and dimensions of work and learning into often overlooked areas and sets of experiences. The experiences of people with disabilities, recent immigrants from China, those who engage in unpaid carework, and nannies who do this for pay become lenses (we recognize that there are many others) that help amplify and allow us to see more clearly the often invisible and taken-for-granted aspects of work and learning that make up household work. Toward the end, each chapter also makes reference to what people should not have to learn, but do as a result of their social circumstances (Pratt 2008).

UNDERSTANDING HOUSEHOLD WORK AND LEARNING THROUGH DISABILITY (CHAPTER 3)

Many of us take our bodies for granted. We often engage in activities, including household work, without thinking about why and how. Chapter 3 shows us that given our current social conditions and the dominance of the medical model for understanding disability, having or acquiring a disability forces individuals to plan and think through what, how much, with whom, and how to do some of the things many of us take for granted on a daily basis. In Chapter 3, individuals share their experiences of having to learn (unlearn and relearn) many skills needed to perform household work. In particular, the chapter focuses on an often overlooked part of this work—self-care—and the learning that goes along with it. The chapter first presents many things that participants learned through self-care. It goes on to outline and explain how they learned, and what they should not have had to learn. In using self-care as a lens, the chapter makes more visible the various dimensions of this work and learning. It contests typical notions of self-care, which often emphasize rehabilitative activities focused on returning the body to "normal" functioning and productivity. It also challenges the dichotomizing of independence and dependence, and normative notions of care that represent people with disabilities as only ever the recipients of care provided by others.

UNDERSTANDING HOUSEHOLD WORK AND LEARNING THROUGH EXPERIENCES OF RECENT IMMIGRANTS FROM CHINA (CHAPTER 4)

Chapter 4, on the experiences of recent immigrants from China, sheds light on the work and learning that becomes visible because it is performed differently in a different country under different circumstances. This chapter looks at the profound changes and learning done by Chinese immigrants, particularly as this relates to food and cooking.

The chapter shows us that through food work, Chinese immigrants learn Canadian norms, values, and practices. We see that they develop their language skills, social networks, and a better understanding of Canadian society through their food-related household work. Indeed, through the immigrant lens, we are reminded that the unpaid work we do within and across households reinforces (for better or worse) certain kinds of social order and sets of relations and roles. We also see how some of these relations and roles are disrupted with changes in how we do household work.

UNDERSTANDING HOUSEHOLD WORK AND LEARNING THROUGH CAREWORK (CHAPTER 5)

The household work we do on a daily basis is often done for the self (as we see in Chapter 3) and others, and can thus be considered carework. Chapter 5 begins by showing us this. It also reminds us that much of this work is overlooked, undervalued, and deemed "natural" to women—a labour of love, with little or no broader social value.

Canadian feminist Meg Luxton (1980/2009) and others have shown us that so much of the carework performed mostly by women helps to maintain family members—keeping them fed, healthy, rested, and ready for paid work—which, in turn, helps to maintain capitalism. And for about a century before this, socialist literature has talked about household work, particularly carework, as an important part of social reproduction (Delphy 1984).[6]

This chapter shows that carework involves a great deal of learning, and thus is not merely "natural" to women. It also shows that carework takes many forms and involves a wide range of relationships and responsibilities. It is complex and fluid, particularly given the changing nature of global economies and the ongoing retrenchment of states from the provision of a range of social services. Through a gender analysis, the chapter uncovers a great deal of learning that happens through carework, and concludes with a detailed discussion of what people should not have to learn when performing unpaid carework.

UNDERSTANDING HOUSEHOLD WORK AND LEARNING THROUGH NANNIES' EXPERIENCES (CHAPTER 6)

Chapter 6 shifts the focus of the book from unpaid household work and learning to carework done for pay by nannies. The chapter notes that the work of nannies in general, through the Live-in Caregiver Program in particular, has been used to shift some of the burden of care off women with higher incomes onto often marginalized women, further passing the invisibility of carework onto paid work. It also shows that much of the work done by nannies for pay involves formal learning, built into immigration policies and requirements, as well as self- and other-directed (and at times coerced) informal learning linked to emotion work, motherwork, and care. Chapter 6 presents details about the large amount of work and learning experienced by nannies, which remains undervalued, even when done for pay.

THE REMAINING PARTS OF THE BOOK

The conclusion of this book presents an overview of the main findings and highlights the book's contribution to a more nuanced understanding of household work through a unique dual focus on household work and learning. The chapter ends with a section on the project's policy implications and suggestions for future research. All this is followed by a methodological appendix, outlining in more detail the approach, decisions, and some of the challenges faced when collecting, analyzing, and disseminating findings from this project (Appendix 1), its link to the larger WALL study (Appendix 2), and a description of our community partner, MAW (Appendix 3).

In doing all this, we do not seek to glorify household work and its daily drudgery. Instead we hope to reveal its magnitude, and then shed light on how its changing nature forces adults, most often women, to learn, relearn, and unlearn, almost on a daily basis. This book also highlights some of the things people *should not have to learn* but do because of structural inequalities and power relations at the societal level.

While we do not profess to have revealed the whole elephant, we believe that each of the chapters sheds light on another, often unacknowledged part of the elephant. Through the application of our new definition of household work, which includes four dimensions of work and learning, we are able to explore more of the complexities of this work. Examining household work through learning, and learning through household work, we hope to open the way for others to continue to tackle elements of this work and learning that may still remain in the dark.

If upon reading some parts you end up with more questions than answers, we consider this project a success as another one of our goals has been to challenge and disrupt simplistic ways of thinking about both work and learning. To help make more visible some of the invisible, we have also put together a documentary DVD based on this research.

MORE THAN IT SEEMS: A DOCUMENTARY DVD

As part of this project, we collaborated on the creation of a documentary film/DVD to highlight some of the project's key findings. The DVD contains four thematic segments: "What's It Worth?," "More Than It Seems,"

"Parents and Children," and "Barriers to Paid Work." It also contains six portraits of individuals who recount some of their journey through their understanding of household work and learning. The DVD comes with a teacher's guide, created by teachers, with the classroom and curriculum in mind. This is available and included on CD.[7]

Chapter 1
WHAT IS HOUSEWORK?
Margrit Eichler

About five years ago, Patrizia Albanese and I sat in my dining room, the table covered with large sheets of paper. We were discussing how to formulate questions for a questionnaire on housework that we were planning to give to members of various women's groups. How could we make it interesting and get at what we wanted to get at, so that people would fill out this questionnaire?

As we were debating what to ask and how to ask it, there was loud laughter from the kitchen. My husband Don and our cleaning woman Lucille[1] were listening to the two of us, while doing the things that we were talking about. Which of us was working?

For Patrizia and me, both professors, conducting research and publishing are part of our job description. Constructing a question-naire, even on as unlikely an issue as housework, was thus a legiti-mate aspect of our paid work. On the other hand, we were having a lot of fun, and much preferred thinking about housework to actually doing it. Were we really working as we sat there debating issues and drinking coffee? Lucille was getting paid, so cleaning the kitchen was part of her job. Don, working along with her, was not getting paid.

All four of us were working at home, but with very different connotations. For Patrizia and me, it simply denoted the location where we carried out part of our jobs. Lucille was working for pay in a private home that was not her own, and Don was working without pay in his own home.

Did we all experience our various activities as work? Why or why not? How does most research deal with the activities we were engaged in?

Introduction

Asking people[1] to describe what housework they have done is a bit like asking people to describe how they breathe. Without breathing, we would be dead, but describing the process is pretty complicated, and not something most people spend their time analyzing. In many ways, unpaid household work is indeed like breathing. It needs to be done for individuals to live and for societies to survive, but we tend to be consciously aware of it only when something has gone wrong—when the fridge is empty, when there is no one at home to look after the newly discharged patient, when the child is neglected, or the elder is abused. And if the focus is on learning, things become even more complicated. One can be aware of having learned to do something or from having done something only when one is aware of having done it, and when people are unaware of many aspects of the household work they perform, this makes verbalizing the learning very complicated.

This is a key issue this book addresses. It simultaneously requires making people aware of the household work they do at present and what they have done in the past, how the work has changed over the past five years, what they learned in doing the work, and how they learned what they learned. By looking specifically at what we learn through household work, both the work itself and the learning come into sharp focus.

In this chapter, I tell the story of how we explored the meaning of household work and arrived at a new definition. I also reflect on how this relates to the current literature on the topic. In the next chapter, we tell the story of what this expanded view of household work means for our understanding of lifelong learning.

How Is Household Work Currently Seen?

The funny thing is that we know quite a bit about household work, even as we choose to ignore it. Almost everybody does some, although across the world, women do significantly more of it than men. Statistics Canada tells us that in Canada, women perform on average 4.3 hours per day on household work, and men 2.5 hours per day (Marshall 2006).[2] This is a large chunk of time, and the calculation is based on a restricted definition that, we will show, excludes significant aspects of household work.

While much household work is unpaid, economists have calculated its economic value in dollar terms. There are different methods of assessing the value that household work contributes to the economy of a country. One method is to calculate the replacement value of the work: In other words, what would a person pay if she was to buy the work she performs within her own household by hiring someone to do it for her?[3]

Using this method, and taking only the restricted definition of housework that he used in his study, Chandler (1994: 3.5) estimated that in Canada, housework would constitute 41.4 percent of the gross domestic product (GDP). By contrast, Ironmonger (1996), an Australian economist, argues that we need to calculate the dollar value of unpaid housework in exactly the same manner as we calculate the market activities that make up the GDP: by taking the capital goods used in household production (housing, vehicles, and domestic appliances) into account along with the value of unpaid labour. He concludes that in such a case, the total household value is about equivalent to the total market value, i.e., the GDP. Again, he arrives at this conclusion by taking only a restricted set of activities into account. If economists were to adopt our definition of household work, which includes a much wider range of activities, it is reasonable to expect that they would arrive at the conclusion that the dollar value of unpaid household work exceeds the total value of all market activities.

Whichever calculation we adopt, unpaid household work is obviously extremely valuable. Nevertheless, it is ignored in national budgets (Waring 1988) and hence is not taken into account in policies. Because it is not visible, it is treated as if it were valueless. Because it is seen as valueless, the people who do this work—which today is most, if not all of us—are not seen as workers when doing this type of work. We count as workers only if we are paid for the work we do. Hence there are no entitlements to holidays, health insurance, pensions, or other statutory fringe benefits associated with performing this work.

When it comes to unpaid carework, even using a very restrictive definition,[4] Statistics Canada put its value at $50.9 billion in 1998, noting that: "this is more than the labour income ... generated by the health care and social assistance industry ($42.1 billion), education services ($40.1 billion) or the finance, insurance and real estate industry ($43.4 billion)" (Zukewich 2003: 18). Beyond these figures, unpaid carework also reproduces the paid labour force insofar as individual participation in paid work rests upon the considerable amount of caring labour that takes place primarily without pay and primarily within the sphere of private households. As Meg Luxton notes:

> The organization of daily life in capitalist societies such as Canada depends significantly on the unpaid and unrecognized labour of adults who manage their own day-to-day subsistence and provide care for their children, partners, and other family members. (Luxton 2006: 287)

The pervasive invisibility of unpaid household work maintains some of the fictions on which neo-liberal agendas rest. It allows for the justification of cutting social services, which is a prominent aspect of neo-liberal politics.

These actions are viewed as something that saves "us" money and are treated as an unmitigated good, without concern for the terrible consequences this has for many people. Since the unpaid household work performed in individual homes is invisible, the fact that the downloading of work previously provided by service agencies needs to be taken up by individual families (which, in turn, means mostly by women) also remains invisible. Counter to the rhetoric, however, families become less able to help their members the fewer social services and resources are provided (Noce 2005).

Dealing with things that have so far been invisible usually interests people—raising a sunken ship, identifying a new gene, finding a new mine are usually perceived as intriguing—but doing research about household work? And learning? What can one possibly learn from doing something that comes seemingly just naturally? The invisibility of household work is a peculiar one. We do know it needs to be done, and often we do it ourselves, but we have trained ourselves not to recognize all we do.

Household Work and Gender

Household work is one of the most gendered activities in the world. Across the globe, women do a lot more of the unpaid household work than do men.[5] This is one of the few social constants—it is true regardless of social class, race, ethnicity, religion, age, geographical location, etc. The nature of the work varies drastically across countries and across classes: There is a great difference between preparing meals in rural Ethiopia, where the girl or woman will have to haul the water over a long distance to her hut, fetch the firewood, and grind the corn by hand, as compared to Canada, where the water comes out of a tap (unless one happens to live in one of the Aboriginal communities that have a dangerously poor quality of drinking water), the fuel is available with the turn of a knob, and the grain comes in the form of flour rather than kernels, typically from a store. What is constant is the fact that women do much more of this work.

That women do a significantly higher amount of household work is often seen as "natural." As one of our respondents said in a focus group after the women had detailed a long list of emotional, managerial, and cognitive work they did, "I think it's something that's natural. We're naturals at it."

It is this notion of the "naturalness" of women doing household work that compels women to engage in this activity and results in men expecting women to do the lionesses' share of it. It is one of the major ways of "doing" gender (West and Zimmerman 1987).

Connell (2002: 61) argues that there are four main structures in the modern system of gender relations: (1) power relations, (2) production relations, (3) emotional relations, and (4) symbolic relations. The whole economic sphere is culturally defined as a men's world (regardless of the presence of women in it), while domestic life is defined as a women's world (regardless of the presence of men in it). Connell argues that this division is the structural basis of the modern Western gender order, and that the social relations that govern work in these two spheres are different. Part of this difference is that the unpaid household work is socially constructed as a "labour of love," profoundly different from work in the money economy. Since love is not seen as work, therefore obviously household work cannot be work.

What Is Household Work?

Feminist scholars have been dealing with housework for a significant period of time. Early works forcefully made the point that housework is work (e.g., Lopata 1971; Oakley 1974; Delphy 1984), although to this day work is, in common parlance, understood as paid work. In an influential article, Benston (1969: 16) argued that women constitute "that group of people who are responsible for the production of simple use-values in those activities associated with the home and family," i.e., housework, while men are responsible for the production of exchange values on the labour market. This put women and men into two distinct sets of relationships to the means of production, and therefore into two different social classes. In the early 1970s, an international campaign for "Wages for Housework" started to raise awareness of the importance and ubiquity of housework with the intent to drastically alter the conditions under which housework is performed (for a summary and critique of the movement, see Eichler 1980: 133–139). In turn, this campaign led to the demand that the state should pay for the socially useful aspects of unpaid housework—that is, the care for people who are unable to care for themselves (small children, chronically ill people, etc.). By contrast, people should be recompensed for those aspects of household work that are privately useful by those who directly benefit from them (Eichler [1983] 1991: 129–133). To a limited degree, this was achieved through a series of reforms of the Divorce Act in Canada, which defined marriage as an economic partnership, regardless of whether both partners were in the labour force or not. There is thus a rich tradition that understands housework as playing important functions at the macro level, through the production and reproduction of the labour force, or as a reserve army of paid labour.

However, when we look at the empirical household literature in mainstream sociological journals, here is the dominant picture that we get: Housework (which we understand to be one aspect of household work, the other being carework) consists of a set of repetitive, relatively low-level tasks that are performed without pay by wives and, to some degree, by husbands (occasionally women and men) in their own homes. It includes child care, but not care of adults.

What is wrong with this picture? Quite a bit, it turns out. The description makes assumptions as to the nature of the work (repetitive, low-level tasks), who is doing it (only wives and husbands, or women and men), under what conditions (no pay) and location (in their own homes only). Any definition or understanding of a phenomenon not only makes statements about what *is* part of it, but also what *is not* part of it. So what is seen as unimportant?

In terms of the nature of the work—since it is understood as repetitive and low-level—it is therefore not seen as complex, difficult, demanding, requiring significant learning, and as constantly evolving, with sometimes dramatic changes, such as when a new member joins a household (a new baby, a spouse, an elderly parent). As to who is doing it—looking at the division of labour between wives and husbands, as much of the literature does, is obviously an important issue—but it does not catch the totality of the work that is being done. Different households are composed differently. Some consist of heterosexual or same-sex couples, with or without children, some of a single person, some of unrelated housemates, some of three generations of a family. If households include people other than a heterosexual couple, are we to assume that none of them do any household work whatsoever? Children, housemates, and older relatives may all contribute work, as may relatives, friends, and neighbours who are *not* part of the same household.

As to the condition—performed without pay—that is undoubtedly true for much household work, but many households do employ people for at least part of the work: housecleaners, nannies, window and eaves-trough cleaners, snow shovellers, repair people, carpet cleaners, and others. Finally, as to the location—yes, much of the household work does take place within one's own household—but is there no cross-household work? Housecleaners and others come into our households and we pay them for their work. Others who come include grandparents who babysit; adult children who go to their parents' homes to help with various aspects of household work; neighbours, friends, siblings, and other relatives who help and support each other without pay. Sometimes people bring their child, their pet, or even their plants into someone else's place to be looked after for a while. Finally, care for adults—adult children, siblings, parents, and friends—may be a very important part of household work.

We concluded that the manner in which household work is usually conceptualized is based on five assumptions. We decided to empirically examine them.

ASSUMPTIONS WITHIN THE HOUSEHOLD LITERATURE[6]

All of the assumptions are implicit rather than explicit. In order to extract them from the literature, we looked for what researchers asked and what they did *not* ask. For instance, a fairly typical question is: "Could you tell me who does the following things in your family? It might be always you, or usually you, both you and your wife about equally, usually your wife, or always your wife" (Twiggs, McQuillan, and Ferree 1999: 716). What is interesting in this formulation is that the only people who can be named as doing household work are a wife and a husband. There is no way to indicate that some of the work was performed by a child, a housecleaner, a grandparent, etc. We applied the same logic, looking for who or what is excluded, to identify each of the five assumptions.

1. Assumption: Housework is performed exclusively by wives and husbands (women and men) within their own homes[7]
We found that many people do receive help from outsiders, many provide help to others, and a person or a household may both receive help in their own household and provide help in someone else's household.

In Phase 1 of our research, we sent out questionnaires to members of women's groups and, in the case of one group, to their male partners (see Appendix 1 for a more detailed description). Of the 254 questionnaires that were returned, 59 percent of the women said that they performed some unpaid household work for someone outside of their own household, 49 percent said they received such unpaid out-of-household help, and 48 percent received some form of paid help with their household work. Putting these various activities together, 76 percent either received and/or provided unpaid help, and if we add paid help into the equation, a total of 86 percent of the women indicated that there was some exchange of household work across households on either a paid or unpaid basis.

People who contributed to unpaid work were close and more distant relatives, neighbours, friends, co-workers, a landlord, and others. Since our data are not representative of any particular population, we cannot generalize these findings, but they do suggest that cross-household exchange of unpaid labour may be significant, and that restricting studies to only within-household labour between husbands and wives may severely limit our understanding of the type and amount of work that is actually performed. For instance, equality between spouses with regard to the amount of household work each does is much easier to achieve if some of the most strenuous and undesirable tasks (one thinks of cleaning the toilets, scrubbing the floors, etc.) are regularly performed by someone else, such as a housecleaner.

An older couple may have a housecleaner, and spend one evening a week in the home of their adult child to babysit. By failing to ask what work exchanges happen between households, the work is presented as if it were performed only within one's own household. By failing to ask who all the people are who contribute to the work involved in maintaining a particular household, the work is presented as if it were performed only by wives and husbands (or women and men within their own household). Contributions of children, other household members, and people from outside of their own household are made invisible.

2. Assumption: Housework consists primarily of a set of repetitive physical tasks

Most empirical studies of housework use a list of activities such as preparing meals, doing laundry, cleaning house, shopping for groceries, and doing dishes. There is nothing intrinsically wrong with using lists of activities. The problem again is not what is included, but what is excluded.

One of the ways in which we explored whether the common assumptions make sense, was to run 11 focus groups, involving 66 participants (57 women, and nine men) in three Canadian cities (Phase 2 of our research). Three groups consisted of White women only, diverse in age and socio-economic status; two groups of Black women; one group of Aboriginal women; one group of White disabled women; one group of mostly disabled women of colour; one group of Chinese women who recently immigrated to Canada; and two groups of men, all of whom were White except for one Chinese man (see Appendix 1 for a more detailed description of the focus groups).

We posed eight questions in the focus groups. The ones most relevant here are the following: we first asked participants to list some of the unpaid household and carework they normally did, and usually received a stereotypical list of predominantly physical tasks such as cleaning, shopping, cooking, etc. In order to go beyond the physical, repetitive tasks, we then asked:

Did you do any of the following tasks?
- provide emotional support to someone (comfort, console, counsel, give advice, listen)
- organize, plan, manage, or arrange matters (e.g., family events or schedules, arrange repair people, tutors, play dates for children
- deal with crises
- maintain contact with family members or friends through telephoning, writing letters, or visiting
- take care of yourself
- resolve conflicts

Without exception, people in each of the groups would agree that this was certainly what they did. One participant exclaimed spontaneously, "This is my life!" while the others in the group nodded and agreed verbally.

Looking just at emotion work, a repeated refrain from the women was that they were the ones who were carrying the emotional burden in their families, and that their husbands were either incapable or unwilling to share the load. "I was always the one who was providing emotional support" was a sentiment that was frequently expressed. One Aboriginal woman stated simply that her husband "doesn't know how to go through the emotions. He doesn't know what it is."

Regarding the men, although most of them stated that they provided emotional support to their wives and occasionally to others, their examples were much less specific, and some indicated that their wives did more of it.

Overall, then, housework is not restricted to only repetitive physical tasks.

3. Assumption: Housework includes child care, but does not include care of adults
When looking critically at the lists researchers use, we also find that child

care is often included, but that care for adults is usually excluded. The many examples of caring for adults we encountered included a Chinese woman whose mother-in-law in China had had a stroke. The respondent—the daughter-in-law—had to arrange help by telephone. An Aboriginal woman had to deal for many months with a brother who behaved bizarrely and was later found to be schizophrenic. A divorced woman, whose ex-husband had died, helped her adult children, one of whom was in B.C. and the other in Ontario, cope with the loss of their father by bringing them together. Her son, however, drove an unsafe vehicle. "So it was, like, very emotionally trying because my son was not being safe with his travel arrangements. And it worried me.… I felt like I was constantly masterminding how to make it so he could be safe, and here he is 21."

At a less dramatic level, there were many examples of people providing practical support to their adult children, their older parents, their friends, and others. Care for adults was an important part of our participants' lives.

4. Assumption: Housework remains largely stable

Like the other assumptions, this assumption is implicit in that it is embedded in the way data are collected, and what questions are and are not asked.

The list of activities that researchers employ is relatively stable, across authors and across time, suggesting that housework itself is relatively stable. This has to do with the fact that there are some ongoing needs: we need relatively clean shelter (although definitions of what that means may vary greatly), we need food, relatively clean clothes to wear, etc., regardless of age or stage in the life cycle. However, there are two ways in which household work may change: circumstances change or the person herself (or himself) changes.

We encountered many examples of changing circumstances, some very dramatic, some mundane. One of the most dramatic changes is acquiring a disability, which often connected to becoming poor. Sometimes more than one family member becomes disabled at the same time, such as the woman in our focus group who had been in a car accident along with her husband.

People talked about caring for an aged parent, and women commented on the changes that take place when their husbands retire. Rosalie recounted:

> My husband was a teacher, so the summer wasn't bad, but we were ready to kill each other by the middle of September, [laughter] which is true. A big, big adjustment to make. You've got this body in the house that you never had before. [laughter] I mean it was just me and my cat before.

Even the same activity may be carried out quite differently due to a change in circumstances. For instance, Rosie, a young Black woman, reported that her cleaning habits had changed drastically after she moved in with her boyfriend, who has a child with asthma. She became much more meticulous. By contrast, Maggie lets her dishes pile up now that she lives on her own and there is no one else to be irritated by them.

Sometimes it is just the people themselves who change. Alberta turned, in her eighties, from a "neat freak" into a relaxed homemaker who looks at the dust on the coffee table and thinks "maybe tomorrow." When we asked, "What changed?" she simply answered, "I changed."

Both types of reasons are important to note: that the household work changes because of some event or circumstance, or because people change. This change is not apparent when we simply ask whether Rosie or Maggie or Alberta clean: they all did so five years ago as well as now. However, the manner in which they perform this specific task varies significantly.

5. Assumption: Housework and carework are two distinct types of work
When we first devised the questionnaire that was sent to the various women's groups, our community partner, MAW (Mothers Are Women—see Appendix 3 for a brief history of MAW and our relationship) insisted that we separate the questions into household work and carework, arguing that people would not list much of their carework if we asked only about household work. They were right. We did find out information about the unpaid work people perform within their households by asking

two questions, but a number of participants had problems with the double-barrelled set of questions. Several called me and asked, "What do you mean by carework?" My standard, quite uninformative answer was "Whatever it means to you is what we are interested in." Fortunately, it seemed to satisfy the questioners.

Others expressed their confusion right on the questionnaire. One commented that she had trouble distinguishing between household work and carework. A number of other people commented that they identified "carework" with care for the sick. One person answered the carework question by referring us back to the answer she had given for the household work question.

In other words, some people were able to make a distinction between household work and carework, others were not, or were unclear about the meaning, or used a highly restrictive interpretation by equating carework with care for the sick.

The real problems for us emerged when we started to code the answers to the open-ended questions in Phase 1 of what household work and what carework people had recently performed. The activities were mostly identical, with the difference that in the case of household work, the activity was simply listed, while in the carework question they listed the person(s) for whom they performed this function.

We came to the conclusion that household work and carework are two sides of the same coin, which form a unity (one coin), as well as showing us different faces. If I want to buy something, a Canadian quarter is a quarter is a quarter. However, if I collect coins, I may wish to see whether there is the head of a moose, the heads of two veterans, a maple leaf, or a B.C. landscape on the tail side.[8]

We solved our methodological dilemma by developing one unitary coding system for household work and carework. We resolved our theoretical dilemma on how to code the activities with a simple decision. If an activity was listed simply as the activity, without indication for whom the work was performed, we coded it under the household work category, no matter for which question the answer was given. If, on the other hand, the respondent had indicated that the work was done *for* someone, we coded it as carework, even if it was in answer to the household work questions. If it was indicated that the work was for oneself—for instance, "took care of myself"—it was coded as carework.[9]

ASSESSMENT OF THE FIVE ASSUMPTIONS AND A NEW DEFINITION OF HOUSEHOLD WORK

We concluded, on the basis of our data, that all five assumptions, which are widespread within the housework literature, are untenable. At this stage we decided to devise our own definition of household work.

We had asked about emotion work and managing a variety of tasks, and found overwhelming evidence that people do significant amounts of this type of work in the regular pursuit of household work, once it was made clear to them that we were interested in the totality of work and not only in those specific tasks that tend to be more physical and routine. Physical, mental, and emotional aspects were dimensions of household work that we had expected to find and, on that basis, asked questions about.

However, another dimension emerged in Phase 2 about which we had originally not thought and hence had not asked specific questions: a spiritual dimension of housework. This exposed one of our own implicit assumptions, namely, that spirituality would be irrelevant in this context. We define "spiritual," with Lois Wilson,[10] as anything that gives meaning to one's life. English (2000: 30) identifies three different aspects of spirituality in informal learning: (1) a strong sense of self; (2) care, concern, and outreach to others; and (3) the continuous construction of meaning and knowledge. We found many examples of all three. (See Chapter 5 for an elaboration upon how these aspects of spirituality emerged in learning through carework.)

In particular, the women who led lives on the margins because of disability, low income, and/or exposure to racism volunteered information about a spiritual aspect of housework. While all three aspects of spirituality were in evidence in all focus groups, five groups in particular brought this forward: the Aboriginal women's group, the two groups of Black women, and the two groups of disabled women. Spiritual activities, which were spontaneously labelled as such, included prayer, meditation, going to church, and participating in healing circles for Aboriginal women. When we asked whether changes in household work had altered the meaning of their lives, many answered affirmatively. Activities that were mentioned as particularly meaningful included spending time in nature, engaging in artistic activities, and cooking.

Because this dimension had emerged so strongly during Phase 2 of our study, we included an explicit question about learning about the meaning of life in Phase 3 (individual interviews with 75 people who had undergone a major life change within the past five years). We will report on our findings on this issue in the next chapter.

In sum, we found that household work includes mental, emotional, physical, and spiritual aspects in a variety of contexts. That is how we arrived at our definition of household work as *the sum of all physical, mental, emotional, and spiritual tasks that are performed for one's own or someone else's household, and that maintain the daily life of those for whom one has responsibility.*

This definition does not make any of the assumptions discussed above. There is no assumption that work is exclusively or primarily performed by husbands and wives. Neighbours, friends, children, as well as paid help, may all perform some or all of the functions. There is no assumption that household work is performed only within one's own home—it may be done in someone else's home. The various dimensions of the work—physical, mental, emotional, and spiritual—are specifically acknowledged. All carework—child care, elder care, self-care, and care of other adults, whether healthy or ill, disabled or not—is included.

The fact that household work changes is implied by stating that the work maintains the daily lives of those for whom one has responsibility. Responsibility is here not meant to be interpreted in a legal sense, but solely in a social sense. For instance, if I invite my grandchildren to an Easter egg hunt, it is my responsibility to create such a hunt. If I acquire a pet, I need to care for it. If I promise to provide a ride to someone, I need to be there to pick up him or her. This is in accord with Thiessen and Looker's (1999) conceptualization of "work as an activity that entails obligation and responsibility."

The people I may have responsibility for, and the type of responsibility, are likely to be constantly in flux. This implies that my work may constantly change, depending on who is part of my life. Even if only the same people are involved, they—and I—get older and develop different needs. The way people interpret their responsibilities may also change, as in the case of Alberta, who decided that dust bunnies are no longer a problem.

Our definition of household work informed the way in which we approached learning about it. We looked for and found the same four dimensions in learning about household work as we found in the work itself. Before turning toward learning (Chapter 2), we need to examine when household work is, and when it is not, experienced as work.

When Is Household Work Understood as Work?

Once we understood the nature of the work in which people were involved, we wondered whether they defined the performance of the various tasks as work or not, and why. In the focus groups, we went through the various activities we had identified in our questions (provision of emotional support, managerial tasks, handling crises, etc.) and for which we had received so many examples, and asked in each case: Do you consider this work? Why? Why not? We made it clear that we were not looking for consensus, but for the varied understandings different people had about what makes certain activities work.

There are a lot of contradictions associated with how people think about work in general. Normally, it is seen as something we have to do in order to live. Yet there are exceptions: being unemployed is generally deplored, but retirement is looked forward to and we are supposed to enjoy it, although we are not engaging in paid work in either case. There is an extensive sociology of work literature in which housework is dealt with only cursorily. The usual nod in the direction of the voluminous research on housework consists of adding a chapter on unpaid household work, using what has been called "the add-women-and-stir approach," although it usually does not even "stir." Even when framing work as being paid and unpaid, the unpaid portion is not followed up on.[11]

One recent book (Pettinger et al. 2005) avoids this problem by taking an integrated approach to work and exploring the interconnections and blurred boundaries between paid and unpaid work. Glucksmann (1995) argues that we need to look at the total social organization of labour, which consists of paid and unpaid work, in order to properly understand both. We agree with this, and add to it an exploration of *what* people define as work or non-work, and on what bases they do so.

People in our study identified four different axes, which they used to decide whether a particular activity constituted work or not:

1. The closer an activity was related to money, the more clearly it was seen as work.
2. The less enjoyable an activity was, the more likely it was seen as work.
3. The more remote an activity was from directly benefiting the self or one's family, the more likely it was to be seen as work.
4. The more energy was expended, the more likely an activity was seen as work.

Underlying all four axes is the assumption that work is a purposeful activity that is oriented toward achieving some goal, which might be getting paid for doing something, raising a well-adjusted healthy child, creating a clean living space, cooking a meal, helping one's brother who is raising his child on his own, preparing a festivity for a special occasion, and much more.

1. RELATIONSHIP TO PAY

Practically everyone in the focus groups agreed with the idea that if an activity is paid, it is work, regardless of the nature of the activity. This is the conventional way of defining work. As one older woman said, "It's the money that makes it work." Being paid for an activity makes it work, regardless of whether it is enjoyable or not, who benefits from it, or how much energy is expended. However, receiving payment is only one way in which an activity may be related to money, albeit the most direct one.

Activities may also be related to pay in an indirect manner. Three of these indirect relations were identified in our focus groups: (1) the third-person criterion; (2) the two-person career; and (3) preparation for a paid job.

The third-person criterion postulates that any activity that could be performed by a third person for pay therefore qualifies as work.[12] Someone else can make my bed, hence making my bed counts as work, but no one can eat my breakfast on my behalf, therefore eating my breakfast is not work.

Papanek (1973) defines the two-person career as one that requires a husband-wife team to perform it, but in which only the husband is paid, while the wife renders supportive and necessary but unpaid assistance.[13] Examples in our focus groups included the wife of a politician who described how she helped her husband when an election came around, or the wife of an ambassador who, along with her husband, had to represent the country.

Finally, some women argued that preparation for a paid job also constituted work. As Dorothy explained:

> If I'm going to work, that's when you feel like you really have to make the effort, and to me, that's work. I mean, just getting up and washing your face and going about your day, that's one thing. But having to go to work, you have to do a little extra.… I'm that much older, and I figure if I start looking sloppy or something, then I'll get dumped.

Although the examples mentioned here represent unpaid work, nevertheless the fundamental reasoning underlying the designation of "work" is that the activity either could be paid or increases someone's pay (the husband's or one's own). We call this definition of work the extended conventional definition.

2. RELATIONSHIP TO ENJOYMENT

A quite different basis on which to distinguish work from non-work is whether or not an activity is enjoyable or not. In this case, activities that are hard, unpleasant, not freely chosen, or drudgery are counted as work, whereas those that are enjoyed are not seen as work. As one woman said, "For me, work is often something that you don't want to do, that you have to do in order to provide for your family. It can be paid, it can be not paid." She cited as examples: "Oh, I just love scrubbing toilets! [laughter] Or killing spiders, yeah, that's right up at the top."

Providing emotional support to others was one of the activities where opinions diverged greatly as to whether this was work or not. Most people either stipulated the conditions under which it would be work and when it would not be: if it was strenuous, difficult, and not convenient at the moment but necessary, it was work. Crystal, for instance, explains, "When I'm taking care of my son and supporting him emotionally, and I feel like I'm making a difference, that doesn't feel like work." She contrasts this with a situation where she feels this turns into work:

> But then, when I have to really dredge it up to, you know, to really do the mental machinations. Okay, how do I tell him what words not to say without saying all those swear words myself? You know, that was work to do that.

Like the provision of emotional support, maintaining contact with family and kin also generated considerable debate as to whether it constitutes work or not. One person summed it up quite succinctly when she stated: "To me, it depends on the quality of the relationship."

In this view, work is not determined by pay or its relation to pay, but by a number of variables that make it unpleasant. Either the activity itself is intrinsically unpleasant (e.g., cleaning toilets) or the activity itself can range from pleasant to unpleasant, and it depends on the circumstances on which part of the continuum the activity falls, e.g., friends whose visit is a pleasure versus demanding, high-maintenance in-laws whose visit constitutes work. The quality of the experience can also be affected by one's own personal situation at any given moment in time: if one is feeling rested and energetic, an activity may not feel like work, but if one feels tired and stressed, the same activity may turn into work. It is definitely experienced as work when the locus of control is external—if it is something that one must do against one's wishes. It can be either paid or unpaid.

The feeling of being compelled may be the result of an external compulsion, for instance, in the case of a woman who is married to an abusive man who insists on a certain level of service. It may be also an internalized standard of a behaviour that, although socially generated, comes with considerable leeway with respect to its implementation. For instance, when entertaining visitors, there are differences in internalized standards as to what degrees of cleanliness and hospitality are necessary. This may affect whether such visits are experienced as work or pleasure. Activities that are enjoyed, then, are seen as non-work by people who subscribe to this definition of work unless, of course, the activity is paid for, in which case it is classified as work regardless of the enjoyment it brings.

3. ON WHOSE BEHALF IS THE ACTIVITY PERFORMED?

In instances in which this dimension was at the forefront, a line separating work from non-work was variously drawn around the self, or the self and the immediate family, and sometimes the family and close friends. Many, but not all, people drew the line narrowly around the self—if something was done for oneself, this was a reason for not counting it as work. People who drew the line this way very clearly considered the work done for their children, spouse, or close friends as work. However, as we will see in Chapter 3, the issues of self-care are considerably more complicated than stated here.

Others drew the line a bit further. If the work was performed for members of one's own family, it did not count as work.

(a) Work on behalf of family members or close friends

The Chinese women, as a group, all agreed that none of the unpaid housework/carework activities under discussion were work. However, all also agreed that these activities felt like work. "In China, women always do the housework, but we don't take it as work. It's really work, but we don't take it as work because there is no pay." Obviously, there is a discrepancy between the cognitive aspect and the emotional experience of activities as simultaneously work and non-work. This was so not only for the Chinese women but also for some of the older White women who had paid jobs at a time before it was common for women to do so.

We asked the Chinese women what providing emotional support, solving crises, etc., are if they are not work. "If you call your parents in China, or if you talk with a friend, is that work, or is it not work? And why, or why not?" One answer was "I think that's my responsibility" and it is definitely not work. The women also maintained that it was enjoyable, and did not admit the possibility that it could ever be anything but a pleasure. This was very different from, for instance, the Black women, who talked freely about the complications of maintaining contact with their parents and relatives in Africa or the Caribbean, and who eloquently expressed both the joys and frustrations of maintaining such relationships.

In the Chinese group, the discussion then turned toward looking after children. Xiaomin said:

> … but as to taking care of the children, sometimes you must supervise him, like, every day…. It's very boring, but I have to, so I just think, I must do that. It's not work, but … it's my duty.

We explored this issue further. Why was supervising your children not work? The answer was provided in very explicit cultural terms, and agreed to by all group participants: "Usually we don't think of some work happening in our family as work. We just feel it as a duty, responsibility. We don't take it as work." Consciousness is the important issue here, as indicated by the parting remarks of some of the Chinese participants. One of the assistant facilitators (Lingqin Feng, a Chinese graduate student) took notes of the comments made by the participants as they left the room, talking among themselves in Mandarin. An excerpt from her notes reads as follows:

> I see everyone still excited from the conversation just held with Margrit…. They are talking in Chinese. One says, "I've learned from Margrit that housework is work." Another says, "Next time, I may argue with my husband and tell him what I have learned here if he would say I do nothing at home. I can even ask for payment for housework I do every day, ha-ha." Someone else agrees, saying, "Now I know housework is work, but I did not realize housework is work before."

Similarly, a recent immigrant from Kenya reported that she used to think of work as happening only outside the house, but that she learned in North America that unpaid housework is work.

(b) Self-care

There was no agreement across groups or within most groups as to which aspects of housework or carework constitute work or not. The one point on which participants differed the most was self-care.

Originally, we included self-care in the list of questions we used in the focus groups because we assumed that people with disabilities would have a different definition of what aspects of household work constituted work, and specifically that they would include self-care when others would not. This did not turn out to be the case in the focus groups, but became very evident in the individual interviews of women with disabilities (see Chapter 3).

While some participants rejected the idea that self-care could ever be work, others made some fine distinctions. They argued that self-care could be work in two situations: when it is preparation for self-care, or when it involves minimal self-maintenance. *Preparation for self-care* is work; enjoying the activity itself is not. For instance, some argued that preparing to take a bath, getting ready to go out for dinner, driving to yoga, or scheduling time for such activities is work, but engaging in the activity is not. As one young woman explains:

> I would say it's work to make it happen. I had to make the decision to not go shopping, I had to come home, and then I had to assert myself with my family and say, "I'm going up to take a bath." And then I had to, you know, set the mood, with the candle and the bubble bath. I mean, that's work, right? But then it wasn't work once I was in there—it was great.

The notion of *minimal self-maintenance* includes all activities that are needed to maintain your health and well-being and that may not be enjoyable or relaxing, but that are necessary. A middle-aged woman recounted:

> I enjoy my yoga class, but all the way there, I'm sort of thinking, I'd rather sit in a coffee shop and read. My feet keep moving, but it's, like, I really want these two hours in the coffee shop to just read, but afterwards I'm always glad I did it. So it is work, but I know … I need it.

Everyone within her group agreed that minimal self-maintenance means different things for different people. It includes looking after one's health, such as getting blood tests done, which no one saw as pleasurable, and it included (for at least one woman) getting a massage, which others, with less muscle tension, saw as an explicit example of non-work.

4. THE ENERGY EXPENDITURE DEFINITION

The energy expenditure definition came up in each and every group, including the group of Chinese women, which was the only group in which there was unanimity that unpaid housework activities do not constitute work. The wording is almost identical among members of the different groups: "I think anything that takes time and energy is work, whether you're paid or not."

This definition jives with that given in various social science dictionaries and encyclopedias. For instance, Reskin (2000: 3261) defines work as "the exertion of effort toward some end" (see also Marshall 1998; Nolan 1993: 715–716). The difference, of course, is that these authors then proceed to ignore the unpaid work, while for us everything centred on this type of work.

For those who used the energy expenditure definition, non-work was whatever restored energy, which again meant different things for different people. Spiritual activities, such as prayer, meditating, going to church, participating in healing circles for the First Nations' women, were all examples of activities that replenished energy, and which were definitely non-work for most (but not all) people.

Household Work Is Invisible Because of the Common Understanding of Work

Understanding why people define certain activities as work or non-work helps us understand the difficulties inherent when dealing with household work. Most basically, since unpaid household work is unpaid, it is defined as non-work by all those who hold to the conventional definition of work, or even the extended conventional definition. Some of the household work may be experienced as pleasurable, for instance, bathing a baby, gardening, or entertaining friends or family. This is a reason for those who define work as an activity that they would prefer not to do to consider the pleasurable aspects as non-work, even though some aspects of paid work may also be experienced as pleasurable, but still counted as work.

Finally, much (but not all) unpaid household work is performed for either the self, the immediate family, or friends, which again results in it being regarded as non-work by people who define work as something done for others who are not part of their immediate social circle.

Given the accumulation of characteristics of unpaid household work— most of it is unpaid, much of it is done for the sake of family, self, and friends, some of it is pleasurable—it becomes clear why many people have trouble seeing unpaid household work as work. Of the four definitions of work, it is only the energy expenditure definition that squarely includes all unpaid household work under the rubric of work. We need to remember that an underlying assumption in all instances was that an activity must be goal-oriented in order to qualify as work.

Household work, then, is invisible not just because it represents work done primarily by women, and because much of it is unpaid and hence seen as valueless, but because the very understanding of what the term "work" means to people challenges our capacity to see it, even if we are the ones who actually do the work.

Why Is Household Work Perceived as Unsatisfying If It Is Complex and Challenging?

We now face a paradox. We have seen that household work is complex, demanding, involving physical, mental, emotional, and spiritual effort, that it is seen as providing meaning for life. Yet there is considerable empirical evidence that demonstrates that full-time homemakers find their work often frustrating, routine, and that doing household work may lead to depression, low self-esteem, etc. Ross and Wright (2001), for instance, conclude on the basis of a large-scale empirical study that:

> Compared to employed persons, full-time homemakers' work is routine: *It does not involve doing a variety of tasks in different ways and it does not involve as much problem solving.* Homemaking is less fulfilling than paid work: *It is not associated with learning new things* and it is not as enjoyable. Homemaking is more isolated, involving less positive social interaction with others than paid work. However, homemaking is more autonomous than paid work: There is more decision-making autonomy and more freedom from close supervision. (Ross and Wright 2001: 257; emphases added)[14]

This quote brings the importance of how we define household work into sharp relief. There are undeniably many routine and boring aspects of household work: few people said they enjoyed cleaning, doing the laundry, paying the bills, etc. Of course, there are many routine and boring aspects in most people's paid work as well. If work is paid, people include the enjoyable aspects of their paid work as work, but if work is unpaid, often the enjoyable aspects are excluded from their understanding of work, hence we end up with work that is perceived as not enjoyable. A similar situation prevails with respect to problem solving. We saw in our research that there is a significant amount of problem solving, sometimes involving life-threatening crises. However, many of those crises involve other people. If carework is excluded from household work, these aspects of the work likewise are excluded.

Finally, most of our respondents were not full-time homemakers, although some were. While we found that the learning often involved a social dimension, undeniably much household work is performed in isolation, or with only small children present, who may or may not be a joy to care for, but who also do not provide the stimulation of adult company.

And, as many others have noted before, the fact that unpaid household work *is* unpaid removes one of the major rewards people get from paid work. The fact that it is undervalued and largely invisible does not help either.

Our argument, clearly, is not that women should give up their paid jobs and rush back into the home because household work is so challenging, rewarding, and leads to great learning. Instead, we argue that women and men should share all of the household work—the routine and boring aspects as well as the challenging and enjoyable ones. In order to maintain independence, it is crucial for most women to have a paying job. However, at present, the social supports to combine paid work with the necessary unpaid work are insufficient, as has often been noted.

Conclusion

This chapter explores how housework is commonly perceived by sociologists and by people in general: as a set of repetitive, relatively low-level tasks that are performed without pay by wives and, to some degree, by husbands (occasionally women and men) in their own homes, that includes child care, but not care of adults. We argue, on the basis of what people told us about their unpaid work, that this image does not represent the work that is actually performed within households, and we devised a broader definition that reflects the many aspects of this work, including its physical, mental, emotional, and spiritual dimensions and its complex and ever-shifting nature.

This led to the question of why so much household work is not defined as work. Participants provided us with varying definitions of work. Only one of them, the energy definition, includes all work. The other definitions, employed frequently, were that work must be paid in order to qualify as work; that, if unpaid, it must at least be unpleasant; and that it should not be performed directly on behalf of oneself, one's family, or one's friends. Given the nature of household work—most which is unpaid and done for the sake of family, oneself, and friends, some of it is pleasurable—it is now clear why many people have trouble seeing unpaid household work as work, even when they themselves perform this work. Part of the invisibility of the elephant in the room is thus explained.

The next chapter will explore the learning that takes place through this mostly invisible work.

Portrait: Munaza

When Munaza came home from her job as a doctor in Pakistan, she would ask her cook to make a cup of tea for her. Living in the house that the government paid for, with her husband and children, her cook and driver, she did very little housework. Her mother and mother-in-law helped look after the children.

It was quite a dramatic change to find herself in Canada, without a job, on welfare, and suddenly single—her husband, who had urged that the family emigrate to Canada, did not follow her. Munaza found out that he had a mistress and no intention of following his wife and children.

So Munaza found herself caring for two children—Ruby, twelve, and Zak, two years of age—on her own, with no servants, no extended family, no job, very little money, coping with harsh weather (they arrived in January), and battling disrespect and suspicion on the part of her landlord and others. "Here," she says, referring to her household work, "I am working like a labourer."

She never dreamt that she would not immediately find relevant paying work, nor was she used to the way household work is conducted in Canada. For instance, in Pakistan, vendors came to their door, while here she had to go to a store, with her small son in tow, and buy the necessary things in small amounts because she did not have enough money to buy them in bulk, which would have been cheaper.

The children were very unhappy, finding it difficult to cope with the altered circumstances. She had to learn to live on an extremely tight budget, to deal with her children on her own, to cook, clean, negotiate the difficult bureaucracy and the equally difficult South Asian community in which she lived, which looks down on divorced women. She needed to learn to plan her life differently.

She felt that through this experience she had gained patience and understanding, and that she would be a much more empathic doctor when she managed to get herself into such a position again. She had dealt with refugees in her previous job, but had never imagined being in a similar situation herself. "But now I know what they would have gone through because now I consider myself in the same position when I am applying for the job or for anything. Now I know how they feel."

And now she no longer undervalues housework either.

Chapter 2
LEARNING THROUGH HOUSEHOLD WORK
Margrit Eichler with Ann Matthews

When I [Margrit] was in high school, one of my teachers posed a challenging question to our class: "What would you do if you had 40 minutes before an important guest arrived for dinner?" In what order, she wanted to know, would we prepare the potatoes, meat, vegetables, dessert, and set the table?

It was a classic example of problem solving that required multi-tasking and time management as well as cooking skills. Obviously, this question must have made an impression on me since I remember it long after I have forgotten almost everything else I was taught in school. Similarly, with prodding, all of our respondents were able to verbalize what they had learned through their household work, although it was usually not the first thing that came to mind.

Introduction

So far, we have looked at unpaid household *work* only, trying to understand its scope and importance. In this chapter, we are looking at the learning that happens in household work (how people learn) and the relationship of that learning to the concept of lifelong learning. Lifelong learning is understood to deal with "learning for life" through one's lifeworld (Collins 1998: 21; Welton 1998; Williamson 1998). Our households—and the work that maintains them—are important parts of our lifeworlds.

We found that the learning involved in unpaid household work was exponentially harder to uncover than the work itself. Respondents typically did not see unpaid household work as a site of learning and when they did identify what they had learned, they still had trouble describing how they had learned it. As one of our participants in a focus group said, "It's that unnamed stuff…. I remember when I was young and I had children [that] there were no words for it." Learning is most often associated with formal education and with learning required for paid work. Specific aspects of household work, particularly those relating to learning, are blacked out by being defined as non-work.

Learning takes place when things change and we need to adapt to new situations. Jarvis (2006b: 16) suggests that change results in a disjuncture between what is known and current reality. "Disjuncture occurs when our biographical repertoire is no longer sufficient to cope automatically with our situation, so that our unthinking harmony with our world is disturbed and we feel at unease. We have a tension with our environment." Disjuncture creates a need for learning. In turn, the learning itself leads to change (Illeris 2002: 17; MacKeracher 2004: 8).

We reasoned that a major life change would lead to changes in the way people perform their household work. If the work itself or the conditions under which it is performed changed, people would have to learn how to do things differently or even learn completely new skills. For Phase 3 of our study, we therefore selected people for individual interviews who had undergone one of the following life changes within the past five years:[1] they had either lost a partner, lost a job, took a new job, integrated a new child into their life, immigrated from China, or were people who self-identified as having a disability. The five-year time frame did not apply to respondents with disabilities. These respondents were a mix of people who either had an impairment from birth or childhood, or who became impaired in adulthood.[2]

Literature on Unpaid Household Work and Lifelong Learning

Given the emphasis in lifelong learning on the lifeworld, of which household work is an inescapable aspect, we expected a substantial literature on lifelong learning and household work. Unfortunately, we were destined to be disappointed. We ran into two problems: First, lifelong learning literature almost completely ignores unpaid household work. Second, lifelong learning rhetoric has been hijacked by neo-liberalism. Some of our colleagues suggested that it might therefore be cautious to abandon this approach altogether. We will consider both problems in sequence.

There have been a number of theoretical calls for studying unpaid household work within the framework of lifelong learning. For instance, Hart (1992: 178) argues that the ultimate purpose of subsistence work, which includes household work, is "to maintain and improve life," and that education needs to focus on issues that are life-enhancing rather than profit-driven. Gouthro (2000) argues that rather than focusing on the marketplace, adult education theory should focus on civil society, and that this concept should be broadened to include the homeplace as a site of work and learning. This, she suggests, may lead us to "find an alternative focus for the development of a global civil society. This would be a type of global civil society built on concerns that cross cultures and nationstates [*sic*]; concerns that impact on each of us in our everyday lives" (Gouthro 2000: 7).

However, when it comes to empirical studies of lifelong learning through household work, we found only four.[3] Hasselkus and Ray (1988) interviewed 15 family caregivers in a Midwestern US community. All of them provided daily personal and/or instrumental care to family members without being paid for it. The care recipients were 60 years of age or older.

The care providers learned through their care about their sense of self, their understanding of managing, of the future, of fear/risk, and of change in customary relationships.

Butler (1993) was interested in what competencies people could acquire through their unpaid work in the home and whether anything they learned would be transferable to the paid labour force. She found that people were "competence-blind" with respect to the skills required to engage in many types of household work. They failed to see the parallels between managing their homes and the management skills required in business until they were specifically made aware of the parallels (Butler 1993: 68).

In order to make people aware of the range of activities in which they engaged in their unpaid work, she conducted a series of workshops. The participants came to the conclusion that the skills required to manage a household included the development and management of systems to meet routine and non-routine needs, the optimization of the acquisition and use of material and financial resources to support and care for adults, the care and supervision of children, and much more.

They concluded that unpaid home work should be seen "as a domain in which the full range of levels [of competence] can be discerned. The level will vary from function to function, from individual to individual, at different points in time, just as it does in paid occupations" (Butler 1993: 77–78).

Livingstone (2005: 983) found, through a large-scale survey involving about 10,000 Canadians, that "(a) over 60% were involved in learning about home renovations and gardening; (b) nearly 60% were learning home cooking; and (c) over half were learning home maintenance." Even more stunning is his conclusion that it appears that "Canadians are now devoting about as much aggregate time to informal learning related to housework as to paid employment" (Livingstone 2001: n.p.).

The latest study comes from the European Union, which organized a research project on the competencies acquired through family work (Gerzer-Sass 2004). The aim was to create individualized profiles of competencies that had been acquired through family work. In order to make people aware of the range of functions they actually perform in their family work, participants were advised to imagine the sudden illness of a child. They then identified which competencies are required in coping with such a situation and how this compares to responsibilities in a corporate setting.

By the end of the exercise, participants had a profile of the competencies that they judged themselves as having acquired through family work. Some of these included: reliable execution and completion of tasks; approaching other people and establishing contacts; contributing one's own interest and strengths to the team; a willingness to compromise in favour of team-friendly solutions; and the ability to cope with various requirements simultaneously (Gerzer-Sass 2004).

Beyond these four studies, we have so far found no other studies that address the issue directly; however, we found, surprisingly, an interesting set of studies in the management literature. The interaction between unpaid family work and paid work has long been of interest to management studies. While early studies focused primarily on family-work conflict, particularly for women, a more recent emphasis is on positive and negative family-work and work-family spillover, which tends to be discussed under the heading of "work-family facilitation." This latter term refers to "the extent to which individuals' participation in one life domain (e.g., work) is made easier by the skills, experiences, and opportunities gained by their participating in another domain (e.g., family)" (Grzywacz and Butler 2005: 97).

The management studies are usually theoretically located in role theory, and are not oriented toward learning or learning theory. Their language is problematic for us: family work is regularly called "non-work" (Kirchmeyer 1992a; e.g., Cohen and Kirchmeyer 1995; Sumer and Knight 2001) and "work" refers to paid work only, nor is "family" synonymous with household work as we have defined it. Nevertheless, these studies are intriguing and suggestive for our topic as they suggest that learning that occurs in the paid work sphere carries over into the unpaid work sphere, and—more important within our context—vice versa.[4]

Claiming Lifelong Learning for Learning through Household Work

Lifelong learning has been called a chameleonic concept (Grace 2004)—a "vague and contested term"—that is used with different meanings over time and that is employed for quite different purposes. In particular, a trenchant critique argues that lifelong learning has become the "handmaiden of the market" (Cruikshank 2002: 151), which makes individual workers the scapegoats for an economy that fails to produce good jobs for people and then suggests that it is their own fault for not having learned enough. Indeed, there is ample evidence that Canada does not have a shortage of skilled workers, but instead a shortage of skilled jobs for workers (Livingstone 2004).

The various incarnations that lifelong learning has taken have been charted in different ways. Cruikshank (2002: 141) suggests that lifelong learning in Canada has historically had "a broad base that included learning in a variety of spheres," but that it is now "tied solely to skill acquisition and is considered to be 'vital to maintaining competitiveness in a global knowledge-based economy" (OECD 2001: 13).

Field (2001:3) traces the history of lifelong learning from a European perspective through lifelong education, arguing that this is merely a "slightly different guise". According to this account, in the 1960s and 1970s lifelong learning was perceived as an essentially humanistic concern that achieved "the 'fulfilment [*sic*] of man' through flexible organization of different stages of education, through widening access to higher levels of education, through recognition of informal and nonformal as well as formal learning" and through new curricular concerns (Field 2001: 6). The sexist language is apropos: housework, although it is certainly a way of "Learning to Be," the title of an influential publication by UNESCO on the subject matter (Faure 1972), was never a focus.

By the late 1970s, lifelong education had been reduced to a nostalgic concern of the professional adult education community, but during the 1990s it made a remarkable comeback. Although there continue to be disparate messages, Field (2001:14) concludes that today "Lifelong learning does not solely serve to reproduce existing hierarchies and inequalities, but may potentially create and legitimate new ones. It therefore poses new and frequently contradictory challenges, both to the policy community and to the increasingly fragmented community of practice that promotes and encourages learning throughout the lifespan."

We share the concern that lifelong learning has been co-opted by neo-liberalism. As currently understood and practised, it uses education to make the labour force more flexible in the name of efficiency. Olssen (2006: 225) asks the question, "How can a model of learning which is not the servant of neoliberal reason, be developed?"

Our project is part of this effort. By focusing on learning that is informal, self-initiated, and often tacit, we aim to reclaim lifelong learning as "learning for life" (Grace 2004: 391). Household work is rich in learning that is accessible to women as well as men, young and old, with and without a paid job, and it continues throughout the lifespan.

Regardless of which account we listen to, most of the approaches to lifelong learning share the following traits:

- They are addressed to the educator, not the learner.
- They deal with paid work, not unpaid work.
- Much of it deals with formal or non-formal education, rather than self-initiated informal learning.
- Lifelong learning is largely understood as consisting of educational opportunities that are created or fostered by the state.
- It is recognized by the state and by corporations as being of prime importance for becoming or remaining competitive in a global market.

In this book, we start from the opposite end:

- We start from the experiences of the learner, not from what educators should do.

- We deal with learning through and for unpaid work, not paid work.[5]
- The learning is self-initiated and usually informal, rather than formal or non-formal.
- Lifelong learning through household work consists of learning opportunities that arise out of people's lives and for which people have to find their own resources.
- It is invisible to the state, corporations, and people in general, including those who engage in the learning.

An important part of the intention of this book is to make unpaid household work and the learning associated with it that is currently invisible, visible, to look at the tensions between the private and the public spheres, and to focus on the learner rather than the teacher.

What Do People Learn through Household Work?

FOUR INTERSECTING DIMENSIONS OF LIFELONG LEARNING[6]
The basic question we asked ourselves, then, was not what *we* (educators of all types) should teach people, but: What do people learn on their own? How do they learn when there is no one else who guides the process? Why do they learn?

We identified four dimensions of household work: the physical, emotional, mental, and spiritual dimensions. We therefore looked for those same four dimensions in the learning that takes place through the performance of household work. However, while it soon became clear that indeed people learn along all four dimensions of housework we identified, in reality people do not experience them as neatly distinct.

As Jarvis (2006a: 206) suggests:

> ... human learning is the combination of processes whereby
> the whole person—body (genetic, physical and biological) and

mind (knowledge, skills, attitudes, values, emotions, beliefs and senses)—experiences a social situation, the perceived content of which is then transformed cognitively, emotively and practically (or through any combination) and integrated into the person's individual biography resulting in a changed (or more experienced) person.

This complex and intertwined process is obvious in our data. Consider the case of Charles. Charles is a professional who, through an accident, was left with, among other things, a severely weakened right arm and very few fine motor skills in his right hand, his dominant hand. The injury was severe enough to be classified as an amputation, and he is in constant pain. He talked about some of the physical things he had to relearn: how to tie his shoelaces, clean himself with his non-dominant hand, how to chop tomatoes.

Among other things, he trained his family "through many hours of gentle discussion, sometimes not so gentle, that when they park the car, they turn the steering wheel so the large open part is on the right-hand side."

If we look at this statement within its context, we can see that even this one act involved all four dimensions of learning. First, Charles had to mentally figure out that he would still be able to start and then drive a car if the steering wheel is turned a particular way. He had to accept emotionally that his hand and arm will not improve, even with constant exercise to keep them from deteriorating. He had to work with his family members to get them to change their ways in order to accommodate his impairment, which involved both cognitive and emotional work. He had to train himself physically to use his left hand to do things he did not previously use that hand to perform and, of course, it required spiritual work to be able to continue to live positively and productively.

We think of this as the stew pot model of lifelong learning. In a stew, various ingredients simmer together for a hopefully savoury result. When the stew is finished, we can still recognize the various ingredients that make it up. We can identify the meat, potatoes, carrots, and onions in the finished stew, but they are intermingled, and each gives its flavour to the other.

In spite of recognizing the actual intermingling of the four dimensions of learning, we find it helpful to separate them analytically, in order to examine the nature of learning that may occur within each dimension.

Learning to do physical tasks differently: Learning in an embodied manner

Learning is an act of doing that involves the use of the physical body to learn about and perform various tasks. Most people stated that they had learned some physical tasks, such as cooking (which has, of course, many non-physical aspects as well—see Chapter 4). When people acquire disabilities, they need to adapt the way they do their housework. Marie, an older woman, twice widowed, was no longer able to bend down. "If I get down on my knees, I have to have somebody to help me up." Rather than scrubbing the floor on her hands and knees, she now uses a sponge mop. She does not like to cook, but learned to use the microwave for heating food. She finds it hard to learn to use new technology—she was in the process of learning to use her son's cordless telephone when we interviewed her. On the other hand, she is extremely savvy when it comes to taking medicine, checking up on side effects, monitoring her reactions, and arguing with her doctor about what to take and how to take it.

Marie was listening to her physical body, an act of self-care through which she learned what her body needed and the best way to take care of those needs (see Chapter 3). This method of learning was also mentioned by a number of other respondents. Ardea, for instance, said:

> I learned to listen to my body, so when I know I'm getting sick, I can feel it right away. I start taking more vitamins, eating differently, or resting, or I'll take a day off. I definitely take off a day every month—mental health, for my mental well-being—because if I don't, in my job [as a teacher] I would go insane.

Similarly, Gabriella said:

> You get to learn your own physiological responses to stress in everyday life and then you say "Yep, throat's getting a little tight, time to go for a walk" or whatever. For me, that's what it is.

People who acquired an impairment had to learn to adapt to it in multiple ways. The degree to which we depend on our bodies becomes dramatically obvious when disabled people are included in the research. Normativity is disrupted, and what is often unseen becomes visible. As Shilling (2003) suggests, the body is an "absent presence" of which we become aware consciously either through a process of reflexivity or because the normativity of a healthy two-handed, two-legged, etc., body is disrupted. As we grow older, most of us who are "temporarily able-bodied" will experience this.

Changes in the physical aspects of household work may, of course, be necessary for other reasons, such as the loss of a partner. Some men who lost their partner had to deal with their own household work for the first time. In such cases, we are not only dealing with an adaptation, but with the acquisition of brand-new skills. Similarly, some women had to learn aspects of household work that their husbands had previously done. For instance, Sondra, who had lost her partner, talks about having to find tools to open jars and adds:

> I remember buying these things from Canadian Tire that you put under pieces of furniture that you can move, which I would never have needed previously because there were two people to move things, but when there's just one, so yeah, … you become more innovative, you learn more to attune to TV ads or something, or radio ads, that tell you about products that you think oh, hey, … I could use that.

Learning is therefore intertwined with the body in multiple ways: all learning is mediated through the body, and changes within the body itself (such as getting older) may require us to discard old ways and learn new ways of doing them. As Shilling (2003: 20) notes, we both *have* and *are* a body, meaning that we are capable of reflecting on what happens within our bodies at the same time as it happens.

Learning new mental skills

Learning also involves the act of thinking. Cognitive processes have been the most prominent focus in studies of adult learning to date. Our respondents reported that they had learned a multitude of mental skills: for instance, those who experienced a loss of income learned to budget more carefully and systematically. This may have become necessary because they acquired an impairment, went back to university, lost a job, or for other reasons.

Others talked about organizing themselves and their family routines differently when the need for it arose. For instance, when Helen tore two ligaments in her foot, she was unable to do the grocery shopping for several weeks, or even move around the house, so she prepared a "master list of everything that can be bought for the house, including toothpicks." Every Saturday, she printed out the list and had her children go around the house and check. If there was less than half of the appropriate amount of something, they had to tick it on the list. She also wrote down what quantities were needed and how much each item should cost. When she was able to walk again, she realized that the children were quite capable of doing the shopping and maintained this routine:

> So I found that very, very useful because before, I was always … struggling. I had to go home and make sure that I've done groceries for everybody, and make sure they have what they need. But I realize I don't need to do that. I think what I need is just to plan to make sure that the money's there for them to use it, so that was helpful.

Others learned to plan by using a calendar, having immigrated from a culture where this is not the usual practice. Many said that they had learned to prioritize better when their life became more complicated for various reasons.

Ardea, whose husband has a progressive muscular disability, describes how she learned to organize for a bit of spontaneity. Given that her family's life is circumscribed by her husband's disability and her job as a teacher, she always has everything prepared to leave at a moment's notice:

> We're actually pretty impulsive, so what I do is when we go some-place, I have a bag packed with extra clothes or diapers, lots of diapers, or a bib, or if we want to go out to dinner or if we want to go shopping and then go out somewhere, I'm always prepared.

Like other activities, learning is also gendered. Women, in particular, learned how to plan and organize. Given that women carry the major responsibility for administering the household, this is not surprising. Multi-tasking emerged as a particularly strong skill among women. As Mithreal (a house husband, discussed in more detail in Chapter 5) said about himself: "I think it's a guy thing, having trouble dealing with six things at the same time."

Learning to deal with emotions differently

Learning also involves *feeling* (emotion). The study of emotions (affective processes) is a more recent focus in the study of learning. MacKeracher (2004: 15) states that learning is affected by "emotions from three sources: those we bring to the learning process, those that are generated during the learning process, and those we feel when we receive feedback about whether we have succeeded or failed in our learning endeavours." Beyond the presence of emotions, there is also what has been called emotion work. Sociologists have defined this in different ways:[7]

- managing one's emotions for the sake of a job or other people
- providing emotional support to others
- carrying emotional baggage on behalf of others
- managing one's emotions for oneself

We will look at each type of emotion work in turn.

(a) Managing one's emotions for the sake of a job or other people

This was Hochschild's (1983) original use of the term "emotion work." We found examples of it in terms of how women (it was only women, no men, who talked about this) managed their own emotions for the sake of family members, for instance, a mother or nanny who suppresses her own feelings of irritation and impatience for the sake of her child, or a wife who says, "One thing I will say that I have the hardest time with is not being able to express how I really feel. It always has to be reinvented to be presentable to him [her husband]." She adds: "I keep a lot inside and that causes a lot of turmoil, animosity."

(b) Providing emotional support to others

The amount of emotional support that people provided for others ranged from modest to simply astounding. It included lending "an ear to chew on" as one husband did for his wife, to daily phone calls and emails to friends and family members who were undergoing a stressful situation, such as coping with cancer or job loss, etc. Sandra has a brother with dementia. She provides some care for him, and particularly for her niece:

> It is very emotional because I feel sorry for her because it's her dad and there's no communication between him and her anymore, and there used to be, you know. So things like that, you need another shoulder to cry on, and that's [why] I feel like I'm there for her at any time.

Most respondents claimed that they had learned to provide emotional support differently—better—especially if they themselves had undergone some traumatic experience. Even some people who did not undergo dramatic changes told us that they had learned to provide emotional support better.

For instance, John is a young man who within the past five years broke up with his girlfriend, moved away from his parents, was accepted into dentistry school, and now lives with roommates. When asked whether he now provides emotional support in a different way, he said, "I used to be terrible at it." He used to think that he had to "say something or fill the silence." Since that time, he learned that "you don't have to say anything … or you don't have to say much," and instead let people know that you hear and "understand to some degree what they're going through." He learned this through the change in his own life circumstances, and now finds that he applies this new skill to his dentistry patients.

Fang, one of our Chinese immigrants, describes how she has learned to express her concern for her husband differently. She says:

> In my family, in the past, we were not used to say[ing] anything like 'You must have had a hard day,' warm words like this. We thought we didn't need to say that as we are an old couple. Now I learned to show my concern for him. I would say 'Drive carefully' when he was to drive, and 'How was your day today?' when he comes back. Remind him to go to bed earlier as he likes to stay on the Internet late. Anyway, I show more concern for him now than before.

(c) Carrying emotional baggage on behalf of others

Many women talked about carrying emotional baggage on behalf of others. Rachel recounts that if anything happens in her family, "my mother calls me, so she kind of unloads on me, then she doesn't have to worry so much, 'cause she's got someone else to worry for her now." Melanie says that "the emotional stuff, I carry a lot of that crap too in my family." By contrast, Doris says about herself that she "used to be the referee through everything," especially when her brother and sister were fighting. This became so demanding that she burned out. And so, she says, "I started delegating even emotional baggage."

(d) Managing one's emotions for oneself

Women talked about the need to control their emotions for their own sake and how hard this was for them. One woman talked about the fact that her husband was emotionally unavailable to her, always had been, and that she either had to accept this or get out: "And I'm taking it."

Sylvia, whose husband cannot emotionally handle the possibility that they might split up—she describes him as "a caring asshole"—learned how to control her own emotions. She says, "I learn a lot from Rachel" (another woman in the focus group), to which Rachel responds, "Numb! Comfortably numb!"

Another woman reports that her child would call her from the West Coast with endless recriminations. It was so exhausting that she was almost shaking when she hung up. And even though she would not let this child go for anything, she eventually told her that she wants to talk with her, but "it's got to be more positive." After that, "things changed." Even though this last case might be identified as managing someone else's emotions, we also consider it as managing one's emotions for oneself because this mother had to get herself emotionally to the stage where she was able to change her daughter's behaviour. This is an effort that many women have to undertake.

Learning about the meaning of life

Learning involves *meaning-making* in a central way. It is the process we use "to understand our feelings, to weave ideas into meaningful patterns, and to really understand something" (Flannery 2000: 112). We interpret meaning-making as spiritual work when it involves reflecting on the meaning of one's life. In many ways, this is another "absent presence."[8]

In Phase 3 of our study we asked people explicitly whether the learning they had achieved and that had been triggered through a life change also changed the way they thought about themselves and the meaning of their own lives. Notwithstanding the advice of some of our colleagues, who suggested that it was meaningless to ask about the meaning of life, we received thoughtful answers from almost all of our respondents. Only a very few stated that there had been no change or that there must be a meaning, but they did not know what it was. Even more interesting, the issue of spirituality was mentioned by some respondents when we did *not* specifically ask about it. This happened when we asked what challenges they experienced in their household work because of the life event they had identified and how they overcame these challenges.

Most of the respondents indicated that they had learned something through their past experiences about the meaning of their life. Women and men who had become parents, for instance, generally said about themselves that they had become more responsible, less selfish, more caring, and more invested in the future of their children than in their own personal lives.

For instance, Garfield, a 50-year-old man from Jamaica, and his wife adopted a daughter: this was an event that transformed his life. He learned to do a lot of housework and carework he had never done before, and his life is "much more fulfilled." It now revolves around his daughter. "She is my life!" He adds, "I think of myself as much more responsible, so much more caring, and she brings out the best things in me.… It's not about anything else anymore. My entire life is her life now and you sometimes sit back and think about that and you tell yourself *whoosh!* This is incredible."

Others, including some who had lost a partner or else had witnessed the death of some other person significant to them, said that they had learned to enjoy life more, to live day by day.

A number of people talked about materialistic values versus other values. In particular, the Chinese immigrants, who all held professional jobs and were relatively well-to-do in China, experienced significant downward social mobility in Canada. None of them held jobs at their previous professional level and most of them had to cope, among other things, with restricted financial resources. Zhong described the changeover as follows: "While in China, I am adult, middle-aged, quite well-educated, but here I am nothing. You know—the PhD—that's a joke. PhD means Pizza Hut Delivery. That's nothing." Spiritual meaning-making often becomes necessary when people have to adjust to adverse circumstances.

Instead of seeking meaning through social status and excellent performance in their jobs, family relationships took on a greater importance for many. Ling, for instance, told us that with the birth of her son, the meaning of her life changed from being focused on herself to seeing herself as an influence on her son's life. Xiaomin noted that in China she strove after money and fame, but in Canada she found that enjoying life is more important. Wei learned to place more importance on diverse experiences rather than stability. "I now have a more philosophical view of money. I don't think it's very good if you have money or very bad if you don't have any. It all depends.… I value more of what I have experienced now."

Spiritual learning, then, was explicitly present for most of the people we interviewed. From a lifelong learning perspective, this is, of course, in no way surprising. Meaning-making (Rager 2004) or sense-making (Taylor 2000) are front and centre in lifelong learning, although this is usually not identified as a spiritual dimension. An exception would be Stehlik (2003: 376), who sees parenting as a spiritual task and, interestingly, this is an observation that also comes from a study on unpaid household work, since parenting is—for parents—an important aspect of this type of work. In terms of its epistemological position, "knowledge is seen as cumulative and as emerging from experiencing the social world. Knowledge emerges from the interplay of body, mind, and soul" (Dei 2002: 126).

WAYS OF LEARNING

We can now take it for granted that people do learn through their unpaid housework, and that what they learn is important for their lives, even if they are not normally aware of this.

When we asked people about *how* they learned, they experienced some difficulties in answering the question. Many authors have noted that learning is both a product and a process. We first focused on the product—what is learned—as this aspect of learning was more identifiable, and then on "how" this knowledge was learned—the process. The intermingling of process with product makes it difficult for respondents to identify learning outside of formal learning situations.

In the context of unpaid household work, learning is largely *informal* and starts with an *experience*; it happens usually after an experience of disjuncture in the person's environment—something has changed. The learning process is *self-initiated* and most often *self-directed*. Respondents used a variety of resources when learning. These were both internal and external to the self. The former involves the use of *explicit* as well as *tacit knowledge* that has been generated throughout the individual's life course. But, while it is the individual who learns, learning always happens in a social context and is socially constructed within the normative demands and values of different cultures (Jarvis 1987). We interact with other people and with the material world when we learn. In some instances learning is a *necessity*, but it may also be a *choice* of what and how to learn or even *not to learn*.

(a)"I didn't take a course for anything": Informal learning
Theorists of learning usually distinguish between three different types of learning: formal, non-formal, and informal. "Formal learning takes place in educational institutions and often leads to degrees or credit of some sort. Nonformal learning refers to organized activities outside educational institutions, such as those found in learning networks, churches, and voluntary associations. Informal learning refers to the experiences of everyday living from which we learn something" (Merriam and Caffarella 1999: 21).

In general, there is more emphasis on formal and non-formal learning than on informal learning[9] in adult education, and this misses a large chunk of life. Learning through household work is, by definition, informal.[10] Livingstone (2004: 7) identifies two types of informal learning. The first is "informal education or training," social learning, which may be spontaneous or planned, involving mentors who instruct without referring to a pre-established curriculum. The second is "non-taught, self-directed or collective informal learning." He suggests that for adults, informal learning of either kind "continues to represent our most important learning for coping with our changing environment."

While some participants mentioned non-formal ways of learning, e.g., by taking classes, most modes of learning were informal. People discussed the issues they wanted to learn about with others, primarily friends (rather than parents). Many read about the issue, watched TV (e.g., cooking shows), listened to radio, used trial and error, and other methods to facilitate their learning.

(b)"It's just through experience": Experiential learning

Experience is central to the learning process as we learn both from and through experience. Respondents talked about four ways in which they use experience when learning.

First, all learning begins with an experience (Jarvis 2006b). For instance, Sondra said she received a "heart healthy" cookbook from her friend after her friend's husband had a heart attack. Because of her "exposure to their experience," Sondra changed what and how she cooked.

Second, people bring their past experiences into the learning situation. Carol-Ann, when asked how she learned to think of herself differently, said, "I think maybe it's just from past experiences, from other people, maybe the roads that I took in life and the people that I met in life."

Third, we initiate experiences through which we learn.[11] Here, the learner is directly involved in the experience. This type of experience is obvious when respondents talk of "doing" as being an important part of their learning processes. When asked how she learned new technology, Ardea replied, "by using, by just, you know, diving in, trying it." Morgan responds to how she changed her time budgeting with "I just sort of fly by the seat of my pants! For better or worse, I tend to learn by doing."

In the fourth instance we bring the experiences of others into our learning process. Respondents did this by having discussions with other people and using various information sources when learning.[12] These are the content of the narratives and discourses we engage in that are "the interpreted experiences of others" (Jarvis 2006b: 85).

Trial and error is a method often used in informal learning. Here the learner is directly involved in an act of doing. Such learning is frequently referred to as experiential learning in the literature. Sondra, for instance, experienced some weekends "where I didn't have anything planned and got very bored and annoyed with myself that I hadn't arranged things." She has the experience of boredom and reflects on it: "If you don't take charge of your own calendar, nothing's going to happen; you're going to be sitting, twiddling your thumbs." She conceptualizes this experience as a failure to "take charge of your own calendar," and through active experimentation—"it was … a trial and error kind of thing"—she learns how to avoid weekends during which she twiddles her thumbs, which is "not something I like to do!"[13]

As Fenwick (2003: 128) suggests, "Experience focuses on the messy problems and tedious practices of everyday life, which continue to run counter to the logic, language and disciplines of the academy, particularly those privileging the rational and, increasingly, the linguistic and discursive." When we move our gaze from the educator to the learner, as we have done in this study, Fenwick's observation is frequently played out in the everyday learning that takes place in unpaid household work.

(c) "I learned because I was very frustrated": Self-directed learning

Learning about unpaid household work was most frequently a self-directed process in which learners took conscious and primary responsibility for their learning. [14] Jane, for instance, learned about home repair and maintenance by deliberately asking for advice: "You know, what do you do if blah blah, blah …? How do you deal with x, y, z?"

Notions of the autonomous learner and individual agency have been an integral part of the literature on self-directed learning (Burstow 1994). "In terms of learning, it is the ability or willingness of individuals to take control that determines any potential for self-direction. This means that learners have choices about the directions they pursue" (Hiemstra 1994: n.p). Hiemstra's notion of agency, taken literally, implies that learners have the freedom to choose what they need to learn and how they would learn it. But, in the real lives of our respondents, necessity rather than choice often motivated learning. When Christina, who has MS and is now in a power wheelchair, was asked how she learned, she replied, "Necessity, … by having to…. [By] being put in a situation where I was forced to…." Choice was further limited by the person's knowledge of and access to resources. Dorica, who spent many years recovering from a serious concussion, said:

> I learned because I was very frustrated because of how limited I was and how limited the resources were to help me…. It has taken so long for people to recognize that when somebody's in trouble, we need to bring things in place to help them, … we need to do that sooner, we need to do it quicker…. We need to be able to take people … and give them the help that they need.

Choice might also involve choosing not to learn. We will see this in the case of Teddy (below) who chose *not* to learn how to do his laundry and other household tasks after his wife died.

(d) "I just know it": Tacit learning

People find it hard to explain how they have adjusted to change. They just go about doing what they need or want to do, often without recognizing that they are engaging in learning activities. In other words, the learning process itself may be explicit, in that we consciously go about learning something, or tacit, in that we may unconsciously engage in learning. A phrase frequently used by respondents when they were asked how they learned was "I just did it." This, along with the phrase "I just know," alludes to the tacit dimension of both the learning process and the knowledge resulting from that process, which, because it is tacit, is also invisible.

We use both explicit and tacit knowledge when we learn. Explicit knowledge, which can be transferred from one person to another, is valued more highly than tacit knowledge because it is recognizable and visible, whereas tacit knowledge is not. Polanyi ([1966] 1983) identifies tacit knowledge as knowledge that we cannot describe or explain. Thus, we go about learning and doing without necessarily being conscious of the prior knowledge that guides our actions. As Marie says, "It's automatic for me. It's very hard for me to explain." She adds, "It all came natural to me … except for cooking, you know, that never came natural to me."

The explicit knowledge we acquire from our learning may over time be internalized and become tacit. Such knowledge is exhibited in our taken-for-granted ways of doing things. When we asked people how they learned to do things, they had to cast back in their memories for it. For instance, Christina, who had been diagnosed with multiple sclerosis at the age of 28, had learned many tricks to conserve her energy, tricks that she simply takes for granted now. She says, "Some of it I don't even realize anymore, it's just so natural. It's like if I take a pot off [the stove], sliding it along the counter. It's just the way I do it now."

Not only do we bring prior knowledge of what we had previously learned to our learning experiences, we also bring knowledge of the ways in which we might go about the process of learning. These too may be explicit or tacit.

(e) "I didn't give up": Using multiple methods

It is interesting to notice the many ways in which people said they learned: using trial and error, gaining experience in doing it, discussing the issue with others (friends, family, group members, colleagues, neighbours, as well as professionals), reading, watching/listening to TV and radio, and using the Internet. Some took non-formal classes; some mentioned that therapy had been helpful to them. Some learned by teaching others.

The vast majority of people employed a multiplicity of methods when trying to learn something. For instance, Jackie describes how she learned to deal with her son's ADHD:

> I just kept going. I didn't give up. I did a lot of research on the Internet, reading, I bought books, I spoke to people. Every time I wanted to give up, my husband would tell me, "We can't give up," and then when he'd give up, I'd tell him he couldn't give up, and we just loved him so much.

The differences between the sexes in how people learn were not large in our study. Women were slightly more likely to discuss things with people, and men to take informal classes, or to use tapes or videos, but for all of them, learning from and through primary and secondary experiences is the most important mode, and the differences are small rather than large. It was not always possible to determine whether people are more likely to learn from females or males since they often only indicated that they learned from friends or colleagues, sex unspecified. What was clear, however, is that friends are the ones from whom people learn most often, edging out family members as sources of learning. People most often referred to professionals as the ones they learn from about budgeting and health issues, "someone more knowledgeable than myself" for learning about technologies, for example.

In other words, the sources of learning are very diverse, and vary by the subject about which a person is learning something. The same person is likely to utilize multiple sources to learn about a particular issue if this issue is important to the person, as learning about ADHD is for Jackie. Some of the learning is individualistic—e.g., reading, searching the Internet—but much of it involves other people, and the boundary between the two is blurred. Jackie reads and uses the Internet, but discusses what she finds with different people, including her husband.

Learning through unpaid household work is—or can be, if we exclude those unwilling to learn—a lifelong process. It is learning in a holistic sense as it involves the physical body, the mind, emotions, and the spirit. The difficulties some people had in identifying what and how they learned suggests that it is, for them, a form of tacit learning that they must become conscious of in order to appreciate it. Sometimes this happens because someone asks them questions about it, as we did in our research, and sometimes it happens because people experience a major shift in their life circumstances.

For instance, Nzanzi, a young man from sub-Saharan Africa, recounts the effect of breaking up with his girlfriend of three years. While they lived together, she took care of most of the housekeeping tasks, although he would help occasionally. "I wasn't really aware of how things work around the house because she was pretty much a tidy person," he says. So, when she left, he continued, "I discovered that it's not as easy as I used to think." He had to start doing everything himself, and says "that was also an eye-opener for me."

Being a young man in his early thirties, he coped with it, although it took him a considerable amount of time, and greatly changed his appreciation of how much work is involved and how much time it takes. "It's difficult to live on your own once you've been living with someone," Nzanzi said. This simple statement is based on a deeply gendered view of life, an assumption that the female partner will look after the household work, and that the male partner will profit from her work. He does note that "she'd make sure that everything was fine," but "I didn't value it that much." It is only after his girlfriend left that he became aware of the amount of work involved in running a household, and the skill and time required to perform it. Having gone through this process, he had no problem identifying what he learned, as was the case for others.

"I HATE THAT SORT OF STUFF": REFUSING TO LEARN

Just as people choose to learn certain things, for whatever reasons, they may also refuse to learn things that would be advantageous for them to learn. One of the reasons why we included loss of a partner as a base from which to select respondents was the assumption that this would be especially important for men. Given that men's household work tends to decrease while women's tends to increase after they marry or move in together (Gupta 1999), we reasoned that the loss of a partner would create a need for learning, particularly on the part of men. As the case of Nzanzi demonstrates, this was indeed the case. However, occasionally, someone would refuse to learn. Teddy was such a tragic case.

He lost his wife of 53 years unexpectedly, and never learned to cope with it. His marriage was obviously a very traditional one, in which his wife did all or most of the interior household work and looked after Teddy's needs. After his wife's death, his neighbours, as well as his adult children, helped. They brought him food from time to time, and he also got Meals on Wheels through the Red Cross, but he desperately missed his wife.

Teddy never learned some of the things he needed in order to survive comfortably, for instance, cooking, nor was he willing to learn them. "I'm not a cook. I never was, I never will [be]. I *hate* doing that sort of stuff," he says. "I get heck from my family that I don't do more cooking, but … I just can't get into it. It's just one of those things that I can't do." He then goes on to say: "I don't want to do it. Maybe that's it."

With regard to grocery shopping, he is constantly surprised by the cost of things, and he has obviously not learned how to check which items he needs to buy. One of his daughters has to remind him when he should shop for non-routine items. "My daughter might say, 'Well, we need something,' you know, we maybe should have something that I've run out, or am about to run out of, particularly laundry detergent and Fleecy and all that sort of stuff. She lets me know when that's out or getting down, so I pick those up when I'm out."

His daughter comes and does his laundry, which is another thing he never learned to do for himself. Lately, his daughter was sick and was not able to come over. When the interviewer asks him whether doing laundry is "something you feel you could do if you had to," Teddy answers, "Oh yeah, I guess it's just a matter of knowing which cycles you put what on, you know. I guess I could get my neighbour over to show me. She's terrific."

However, characteristically, although he assumes it is easy, he did not ask his neighbour—or, for that matter, his daughter—to show him how to do the laundry himself. This unwillingness to learn or to reach out for help is most tragically played out in terms of his health. He needs "a cataract operation, but, to be honest with you, I'm quite concerned [about] how I'm going to put the drops in because I'm not sure that I can do that, so I've put that off for this year, and hopefully it won't get so bad that it can't be done next year sometime."

Teddy sounded depressed because of his wife's death, and we learned that he had died when we tried to invite him to a report-back session we held with our respondents some months later.

Teddy's case is important because it brings to the forefront the implicit fact that unless people are willing to learn, they will not learn. There is little in the lifelong learning literature that we found about the failure to learn. The focus on how and what people learn is implicitly oriented toward success. Yet it may be equally important to investigate when people fail to learn.

Relevance of Learning through Household Work for Paid Work

It is now clear that people do learn through performing unpaid household work. However, is what they learn relevant for paid work? Unless they have a job that requires some of the specific skills involved in household work, is the unpaid work that people do at home relevant to their paid work?

We approached this question in two different ways. First, we appended a sheet to the questionnaire that was sent to Mothers Are Women (MAW) members in which we asked respondents: "In what way do the skills you use in your unpaid family work transfer to your paid work?" Second, in Phase 3 we asked them which of the skills they developed in their unpaid housework were useful in their paid work. We will disregard the responses of people who held jobs that included housekeeping functions and who noted that they transferred knowledge from the unpaid sphere to the paid sphere on that basis. Instead, we will look at the answers of people who held jobs that were not obviously related to household work.

Of the MAW women, 59 filled out the supplementary sheet in Phase 1. Of these, 48 held a job and 11 were not working for pay but expected to be back in the labour market at some point. In answer to this question, the majority simply listed the skills they have acquired, for instance:

> I feel that my "motherwork" has made a huge contribution to my skills and competencies: time management, organization, patience, perspective, conflict resolution, organizational behaviour, budget and financial management, leadership, and, best of all, humour.

With one exception ("price comparing"), all of the skills that were mentioned can be summarized under the heading of management skills (e.g., organizational skills, multi-tasking, time-management skills), human relations skills (e.g., communication skills, people skills, teaching skills), and management of self/work ethic skills (e.g., patience, adaptability, assertiveness, coping with stress). These skills are not task-specific; they are general and transferable from one set of circumstances or type of work to another.[15]

In Phase 3, we asked what skills people developed in their unpaid housework and carework that were useful in paid work. Again, people found it difficult to answer this question even though it came at the end of an interview that had asked about what they had learned through household work. Thirty-four percent expressed some difficulty in answering this question—a consequence of the fact that much of the learning is tacit—and that they still had difficulties in recognizing its value.

Fox, for example, exclaimed spontaneously, "Where do these obscure questions come from! Oh. My immediate reaction is one of impatience and absolutely not." But as he goes on musing about the question, without any interruption from the interviewer, he recounts that, from time to time, he relieved his wife in taking care of his mother-in-law:

> … and I guess that I learned patience, which I thought I had a lot of and I think is really, really important in dealing with others, in every way, whether you are giving care to them or not. But having patience and understanding are things that are key in almost every walk of life and so those two things, I guess, were heightened in my awareness over the past five months. And, yes, I would use those—you know, patience and understanding—to a greater degree in my next consulting job than I would have in my last one.

"Learning patience" is a theme that cropped up repeatedly in this study. Munaza, for instance, also saw patience as one of the major things she had learned through taking care of her children, and people in Phase 1 mentioned it frequently, as did the nannies (see Chapter 6).

Regardless of the difficulties that a minority of respondents had in answering this question, the majority provided a clear answer that they had learned skills through their unpaid household work that were useful for their paid work. For instance, a woman who worked in the hospitality industry replied:

> Holy cow! Skills! I think just being able to prioritize. Ah, being able to recognize what needs to be done, seeing the big picture, timeliness, and being organized well enough, or just sticking to a schedule, that sort of thing, so prioritizing, time frames, and being realistic about time frames. Doing things well—that comes from personal pride of mine to do well. Ah [long pause] resourcefulness. I think that is a skill that people already have, that they can develop even greater. Resourcefulness and creativity.

Looking at all the responses we obtained, it is apparent that learning through household work may be directly beneficial for one's paid work. Of course, the same may be said for the reverse: people can transfer skills from the paid work sphere to the unpaid work sphere as well, although this may not always happen (see Chapter 5, the case of Mithreal), and problems may, of course, also be transferred between spheres. We are well acquainted with this type of transfer, which is usually dealt with under the heading of family-work conflict. This terminology is problematic for us because it implicitly restricts "work" to paid work, and because "family" is not synonymous with unpaid household work, as we have seen. Here we are simply making the point that beside negative spillover, there may also be positive spillover in terms of what is learned through household work.

What People Should *Not* Have to Learn

So far, we have been looking at learning as a positive outcome. People learn skills that enrich their lives, which are sometimes useful for their paid jobs, which make their home lives run more smoothly, and which expand the scope and nature of their relationships. This type of analysis is very much in line with lifelong learning theory, which stresses the acquisition of skills that are useful for paid work.

However, we can take the analysis a step further and consider critically the circumstances that force people to learn new things. Whenever learning is the result of encounters with a social hierarchy (such as those based on sex/gender, age, race, ability, etc.) and whenever the learning is a form of adjustment to living within such hierarchy, we need to go beyond the learning aspect and critically assess the hierarchy itself (Burke and Eichler 2006).

We had a number of examples where people learned to adjust to things that, in a fair and equitable society, no one should have to adjust to. So, for instance, Marie learned that "when you get older, people don't give a damn." Munaza learned to pretend that her husband (from whom she was divorced) would follow her from Pakistan to Canada, so that her landlord would not give her such a hard time: "He was keeping at me all the time. Looking at me, what I am doing, where I am going." Susan said, "I learned not to call Telehealth" because their service was so inferior. Many of the women with disabilities learned to adjust to severe poverty. People with disabilities also learned to cope with Wheel-Trans, a transportation system that is unreliable, often not on time, and requires the users to allow for much extra travel time if they wish to arrive somewhere at a given time.

All the Chinese immigrants in our study learned to adjust to downward social mobility because none of them were able to find jobs at their previous professional level. Although many managed to derive some positive aspects from this experience, e.g., by intensifying positive relations within their family, nevertheless, we need to remain critical of an immigration system that lures highly qualified immigrants with expectations of professional jobs and then defaults on delivering them. While nannies realize what type of job they are recruited for, nevertheless, they are often disappointed with the conditions they have to face.

It is thus important to consider not just the learning that people achieve but also to reflect critically on the social context within which it occurs. For this reason, each of the following chapters has a section on what people should not have to learn.

Conclusion

By including learning through household work as a central aspect of life-long learning, we can approach the promise of understanding learning as life-wide and lifelong. Given the location of household work at the point of tension between the private and public realms (see chapters 5 and 6), we can counter the prevailing notion, which Cruikshank (2002: 147) describes as follows:

> Lifelong learning (read "human resource development") is used to increase the skills of a small number of core workers in the high wage and high knowledge tier. At the same time, lifelong learning (read "learnfare") forces welfare recipients into dead-end training programmes, which keep them trapped in poverty. Thus lifelong learning, which should be used to enhance the lives of Canadians, instead has been used as a tool to advance and support the creation of two very distinct classes of workers.

Does the inclusion of learning through household work in lifelong learning theory bring us closer to the ideal of democratizing society, which is posed as the desired outcome by people writing in the humanistic tradition? Gouthro (2005: 16) suggests that:

> By broadening the lens through which lifelong learning experiences are assessed to consider the homeplace as an important learning site, the underlying values reflected in our society and in our educational system will be challenged.… Learning that does not focus primarily on profit, on bottom-line accountability and on corporate needs can be considered.… [T]he traditional parameters of what constitutes important lifelong learning experiences will be opened up to create new avenues for discourse, reflection and investigation.

Considering learning through household work validates this important work, which is primarily performed by women, and demonstrates that it can be beneficial for men to participate more actively in it in terms of the learning that occurs.

Nevertheless, for as long as much of the knowledge that is acquired through this work remains tacit, for as long as the people who perform and/or benefit from it see it is as natural, as private, as being of value only to themselves and their immediate household or family members, the effect of including it in lifelong learning will be muted.

Asking people about what they had learned through unpaid household work made those who struggled to explain to us—and to themselves— aware of tacit knowledge. Asking what defined work for them challenged people to reflect on the perceived "naturalness" of the division of labour— which is of course deeply social!—and the undervaluation of the work women do. Looking at some of the work that is both performed for pay and without pay, as in the case of nannies, makes it clear that the public-private divide is significantly more blurred and overlapped than is often acknowledged. Exploring self-care by people with disabilities demonstrates the tenuous and unclear boundaries between control, dependence, and independence. Researching what learning to cook in a Canadian context means for Chinese immigrants makes the complex socio-cultural aspects of a seemingly mundane set of tasks visible.

Starting with learning through unpaid household work seems like a good way to explore lifelong learning that is shared by all. Avoseh (2001: 482) has argued that in traditional African societies, education "was a life-long process that could not be separated from the rest of life's activities." All of us do some household work, even though how much and how it is performed varies greatly by sex, by place of residence, by type of ability, by age, household composition, and many other factors, and, as we have shown, people learn from it. It seems like an appropriate starting point for understanding lifelong learning.

Portrait: Dorica

*I never expected not to work until I was sixty-five.... I didn't have any
intention of not doing that. So to have this thrown in my face was
pretty dramatic because it totally stopped me.*

It was Christmas and Dorica was ice skating with a friend. Then it happened.
She tripped and fell. At that moment, her life changed forever. Dorica's concussion was so severe that she had to relearn how to do many of the tasks
we regularly perform every day. Debilitating pain made movement so difficult
that the activities of daily life had to be negotiated differently as Dorica slowly
regained the ability to care for herself. She refers to this as a very difficult
journey, "a real painful growing experience" that appears to have no end.
Pain is a constant in her life. "I'm still taking physio [physiotherapy] to this
day for it, because I can't get rid of it.... It goes all the way down into my right
shoulder blade.... [I get] terrible headaches."

One of the most frustrating parts of Dorica's impairment was its invisibility.
She said, "I encountered rudeness from people because it was something
that you couldn't see. If I broke a leg, or I became [visibly] disabled in any
way at all, people can see that and they relate to that, but as soon as it
becomes something that's in your head, nobody sees it, nobody understands
it because you look normal.... It was such a strange period to have so many
people look at you and not believe you." Self-nurturance and self-affirmation
must be cultivated when other people fail to provide adequate support. For
Dorica it meant going "through that whole trauma of always trying to give
myself credit and validity for what was happening to me. I wasn't getting it
from nobody."

Yet Dorica found ways to relearn old skills and to learn new ones. She
did so by learning "slowly and with detail," taking everything one frustrating
day at a time. Dorica lives alone, and is very much responsible for her own
care. Her husband died of cancer at a young age and the two sons she had
raised on her own no longer live at home. Drawing inspiration from a mindfulness course and therapy, Dorica recreated her life. With much patience
she learned once again to read, write, and comprehend. She relearned how
to do the tasks involved in household work. And she learned new ways of

balancing her life. So now she nurtures her mind, body, and spirit by practising and teaching yoga, by practising Reiki, and by taking time for meditation.

When she started her journey, Dorica focused on how to heal herself. But now she uses her newly found skills to nurture others. She says I am "doing things I never dreamed I would be doing. And because I'm a person, honorable, I don't like to take something [referring to her insurance money] and not give it back." She does this by helping with cancer patients and by getting involved with the wellness initiative at her church. Dorica is on a journey she never expected to be on. It is a journey that happens within her, but also a journey where she experiences new relationships with those around her and her social world. She hopes, most of all, that this journey will "end up with dignity and grace. That is my wish—to have both of those in place."

Chapter 3
ENCOUNTERS WITH THE SELF:
DISABILITY AND THE MANY DIMENSIONS OF SELF-CARE
Ann Matthews

I [Ann] could not twist a cap off a bottle. I had trouble holding anything marginally heavy (a pan, a teapot) with my right hand, my dominant hand. I could not tie my shoelaces. I had difficulty brushing my teeth and drying my hair. Shaking hands was painful. Computer work became difficult. The medical diagnosis was trigger finger, a condition where the ring finger on my right hand locked in a bent position. It would not release until I opened it with my other hand. The pain in my hand was constant. I tried to hide my problem by learning how to perform the many acts associated with daily living differently. But I also had to learn not to do certain tasks and reluctantly came to depend on others to do them for me. I became frustrated, annoyed, and at times angry at the inconvenience this pain was causing in my life. Fortunately, medical intervention returned my right hand to normal, meaning full use of my hand, like it was before. Life is much easier when the body functions "normally."

Introduction

My short narrative reveals that, even with a minor impairment, I had to learn to do things differently in my daily life when confronted with a physical change in my body. The learning that was necessitated by this change was, in part, focused on acts of self-care. How could I protect my hand and yet function as normally as possible? How could I function in a world designed for hands that did not have my problem? How would I take care of my body? How could I feel okay in my world when my relationship to that world had changed? The challenges I was having with my hand required me to think about the ways in which I took care of and used my body. As certain acts of self-care became difficult for me, I had to learn how to do things differently.

We typically think of carework as the care we give to others, not the care we provide for ourselves. Shilling comments that:

> Body work is rarely called work, but in cleaning our teeth, washing our bodies, cutting our nails, making-up, or shaving our legs or faces, we are all working on our bodies. Sociologists have talked of the work that carers do for others and, implicitly at least, the bodies of others, but have yet to look at the work the cared for do on their own bodies. (Shilling 2003: 104)

Shilling (2003) is speaking of self-care with respect to our physical bodies. The following discussion will show that self-care is this and more; it is also the care and nurturing of the emotional and spiritual self with and through the corporeal body and the mind. Thus, self-care involves the four dimensions of work and learning that have been identified in this research: the physical, mental, emotional, and spiritual.

In this discussion I am using data from those who self-identified as having a disability in Phase 2 (two focus groups with a total of 11 women, and one online focus group of 20 women) and Phase 3 (individual interviews with 10 women and five men). It became evident that for these respondents carework had two explicit dimensions. These included care-work for others and carework for the self. While carework for others is not the focus of this chapter, it should be noted that respondents with disabilities engaged in a great deal of carework for others in their daily lives.

For the disabled respondents in this study, attention to self-care became a necessity, not something that could be ignored when other things got in the way. Aspects of self-care, which are seldom recognized until some event in the life course forces us to acknowledge them, are made visible. The work and learning involved in self-care, while seeming to be based in the individual, are actually framed within and influenced by the material and social world. When the individual interacts with the social, tensions and contradictions exist between dominant societal beliefs and expectations about such things as independence, dependence, and control and the ways in which disabled people contest the taken-for-granted social meanings, which are attached to these words. For respondents with impairments, interactions with the social world also make visible the ways in which the material world is constructed for the able body. Furthermore, making the invisible aspects of self-care visible makes it possible to challenge domi-nant perceptions of disability.

Self-Care

In the academic literature, discussions of self-care are most frequently found in the medical literature. Within this field, occupational therapy is closely related to housework as it is concerned with the rehabilitation of people who are learning to manage their daily lives as they experi-ence changes in their functional abilities. Medical personnel believe that self-care involves adherence to medically prescribed treatment regimens. Adherence is perceived to be the primary way that people with an impair-ment can become independent, adapt to societal conditions, and have quality of life. Researchers explore issues of adherence and non-adherence to treatment regimens in a variety of different impairments, seeking to understand why some people follow the prescribed treatments and others do not (Ingadottir and Halldorsdottir 2008; O'Connor, Jardine, and Millar 2008). They hope that this understanding will help practitioners create programs that are more effective in encouraging patient self-care.

Different authors, studying a diversity of impairments, have identified a variety of factors that affect self-care practices. These include "self-care, self-care agency, and basic conditioning factors" (Baker and Denyes 2008: 38); "confidence in one's self-care abilities, perceived control, and knowledge on self-care behaviors" (Heo et al. 2008: 1807); group interaction (Viklund, Rudberg, and Wikblad 2007); personality and personal characteristics (Ingadottir and Halldorsdottir 2008); and systemic barriers, financial needs, limited self-knowledge, and self-efficacy (Schmuttte et al. 2009). Heo et al. (2008: 1814) note that there are gender differences in the factors that affect self-care behaviours. Ingadottir and Halldorsdottir (2008) comment on the different meanings health care providers and the participants in their study give to the concepts of adherence, balance, and control. Health care providers viewed "nonadherence … as a matter of knowledge deficit" and as "irrational and irresponsible behavior" (Ingadottir and Halldorsdottir 2008: 615), whereas the study participants saw adherence, balance, and control as individual choices "to modify the regimen or be selectively compliant" (Ingadottir and Halldorsdottir 2008: 616).

Other academic literature related to carework focuses on the work and role of the caregiver rather than on self-care. Thomas (1993: 667) claims that the concept of care has been inconsistently defined in the literature because "care means different things to different researchers." She develops a unified concept of care that takes into account the gender of the carer, the care recipients who may be able-bodied or dependent adults and children, the work activities (paid or unpaid) and feeling states involved in the carework, the location of carework as being private/domestic or public, and the nature of care as both formal and informal. The research on unpaid household work confirms these assumptions about the carer and the cared for (Eichler and Albanese 2007). However, Thomas (1993) does not adequately account for self-care in her unified concept of care.

Further literature on self-care can be found in bookstores, which display a variety of self-help books that provide information on medical, psychological, nutritional, and lifestyle issues. Such books did become part of the informal, self-initiated learning efforts of some disabled respondents. However, medical advice, rehabilitation, and self-help books are most often written from the perspective of the professional and the author as teacher. In this study we took a different viewpoint by looking at self-care from the perspective of the learner.

The research on unpaid household work on self-care differs from the approaches taken in the academic literature. First and most noticeable is that the data on self-care are not related to any specific impairment and were collected outside of a medical context. Second, the medical literature is focused on formal and non-formal learning through programs planned by medical personnel; in other words, teaching rather than learning. This research, unlike a lot of the literature on self-care, is written from the perspective of the learner and focuses on informal learning. It does not comment on the treatment regimens set up by medical personnel, but rather, on individually planned and executed efforts to engage in self-care that happen within the constraints of social and institutional structures and practices that are based on the able body. Self-care from this perspective is a story about learning to cope and adapt. It is based on individual motivations and individually perceived needs. Third, this study, unlike the medical literature, establishes that effective self-care requires attention to a balance between the physical, mental, emotional, and spiritual dimensions of the body. What this research shares with and builds upon in the current self-care literature is an emphasis on the body, control, knowledge, group interactions, systemic barriers, finances, and gender difference.

To reiterate, while self-care as a concept has widespread relevance to many people, the actual practice of self-care varies from person to person. Self-care is an individual act that is influenced by both individual and social factors. These not only include such things as individual abilities, biographies, and personal characteristics, but also social attitudes, social and structural supports, and cultural ideologies.

Disability

Statistics Canada, when reporting on the Participation and Activity Survey (PALS), 2001, stated, "About 3.4 million adults aged 15 and over or 15% of the adult population have a disability" varying in severity from mild to very severe. This accounts for one in seven adults at the time of the survey.[1] Disability rates get higher as people age, and the percentage of older people in Canada is increasing as the baby boomer population approaches retirement. Given this outlook, understanding impairment and disability, its social construction, and the consequences of this in a society designed for the able body becomes increasingly important to the well-being of many Canadians.

The medical model of disability is the dominant base from which disability is understood and from which perceptions about disability are constructed in Western thought. The focus of this model is on the abnormalities of the biological body, which are perceived to require medical intervention. Such intervention is intended to cure and rehabilitate so that people with disabilities can adapt to and function in the world as it is currently structured. The medical model positions disability as an individual problem, concentrating on what the person is not able to do, rather than what a person can do. It is the "basis for a 'personal tragedy' approach, where the individual is seen as someone who is in need of 'care and attention' and dependent on others …" (Barnes, Mercer, and Shakespeare 1999: 21).

Unfortunately, the notion of dependency is often essentialized, thus masking differences in the need for care. Furthermore, in the binary construct of independent/dependent, where independence is valued over dependence, those who are dependent are considered "less than." Thus, the abilities of people with impairments are not only masked, they are considered not worthwhile. Yet, as the following discussion shows, the disabled person's need for care from others is very much dependent on the nature of the impairment and the life circumstances of the individual. Furthermore, for those who have impairments, independence may not mean being able to do something for themselves, but rather having control over how it is done and by whom.

In recent years, disability activists have developed a different model of disability, the "social model," which challenges concepts embedded in the medical model. The social model "rests on the distinction between disability, which is socially created, and impairment, which is referred to as a physical attribute of the body" (Corker and French 1999: 2). It is society that is the problem, not the individual. The intent of this model is to identify the physical, social, and attitudinal barriers that prevent the participation of persons with impairment in society. Barriers include such things as access to paid work opportunities; inaccessible homes, buildings, and transportation; and prejudice. The social model has been very important in stimulating advocacy for disability rights, and political and economic change. However, its singular focus on political, economic, and social barriers that prevent people with impairments from participating in society has been criticized by some feminist authors (Budgeon 2003; Morris 1998; Thomas 2007; Titchkosky 2003; Wendell 1996, 2001). They suggest that the impaired body cannot be separated from, but rather is an integral part of societal practices that disable.

When we talk about learning, it is difficult to separate the concepts of impairment and disability as the body is "a fundamental element in the person" who learns (Jarvis 2004: 68) and learning happens in a social milieu that disables. The work and learning required in self-care involve care of the body by the body, physically, mentally, emotionally, and spiritually. Thus, the body, together with societal structures and social norms and expectations, has a noticeable influence on what has to be learned, how it is learned, and why it is learned. A focus on the functioning abilities of the body, as well as the disabling aspects of society, makes visible the normative conditions of unpaid household work and self-care activities. When we can no longer do something, the taken-for-granted relationships to that activity become visible. There is a perceptible rupture between the knowledge that people acquire throughout their lifetime and the current realities of their lives. Learning happens because the relationship of the body to an activity and to societal constructs and expectations changes.

Respondent Impairments

In this study, a few respondents had their impairments from birth or early childhood, but most acquired them in adulthood. Some impairments are temporary, some a constant for life, and others will get progressively worse over time. The impairments experienced by our respondents were both visible and invisible. They included such things as chronic pain; fibromyalgia; arthritis; functioning issues with the back, the legs, knees, arms, hands, and feet (not all in one person); hearing difficulties and deafness; low vision and blindness; epilepsy; progressive multiple sclerosis (MS); depression; brain injuries; diabetes; cognitive impairment; learning disabilities; and others. Several people had multiple impairments. In sharing their experiences with our team, respondents with disabilities highlight a world that many of us will enter in our lifetime. In a conversation with one respondent, she referred to me as a TAB. I learned that this stands for temporarily able-bodied. We often ignore and marginalize those who are impaired because we would prefer not to acknowledge the potential of impairment in our own future. We choose to think of ourselves "as is" rather than face the realities of what might be. In this discussion I look at what our respondents learned. At the same time, we who are able-bodied should look at what we can learn from their experiences.

Self-Care: Caregiving for the Self by the Self

> I take care of myself. I dress myself, do for myself in all areas (ablutions, cooking, cleaning, etc.), but I make sure that I take my naps when I need them, pamper myself with bubble baths and massages [on my feet]. (Wendy*)

For some of our respondents, tasks that required physical use of the body

---

* Wendy has invisible disabilities which include severe obstructive sleep apnoea and fibromyalgia.

became difficult as the functional physicality of the body changed. To meet such challenges in unpaid household work, most respondents were, in Narcissa's* words, "doing the same things differently." Differently may mean doing the same task in different ways or having someone else do the work. In some cases, respondents learned new skills, but most of the time they had to relearn how to do various household tasks. Respondents talked about learning to adapt, adjust, modify, and cope with daily living as they listened to and attended to their bodies. The physical body, geographic space, technological aids, institutional structures, and social attitudes that comprise the normative world became obstacles rather than supports as respondents learned to function in a world that was constructed for the able body. Respondents learned to pace and nurture themselves, to conserve energy, to let go, and to forgive themselves for not getting things done. They learned to pay attention to their well-being by creating a balance in the four dimensions of work and learning identified in Chapter 2: the physical, mental, emotional, and spiritual. Respondents were learning to live with their homeplace and the social world in ways that accommodated their abilities.

LEARNING TO COPE WITH PHYSICAL CHALLENGES

> I can't still do what I used to be able to do. Some days it's better, some days worse. As you can see, I'm drinking from a cup with a straw because lifting a cup is hard. I have a long reacher. When I can't reach something, you squeeze the handle and it picks up if I drop something on the floor. I slide the pot across the counter as opposed to lifting it.... You learn to eat differently; you learn to feed yourself differently. I have utensils that are better for people who don't grip well, and so, yeah, you learn to modify things to make it work. (Christina†)

---

* Narcissa has progressive deteriorating vision and hearing.

† Christina has MS. She uses a power wheelchair as she can no longer walk. The tremors in her hands and double vision make it difficult to perform manual tasks. An actor by trade, Christina acts in community productions when the opportunity arises.

Respondents not only learned to work within the parameters prescribed by the physical abilities of the body, but also to create a healthy environment within the body. Prompted by the need to address personal health concerns, Christina and others learned about nutrition and learned to cook using different techniques. Some respondents talked about using food processors instead of knives to chop vegetables, and Charles* said it was easier to barbecue and eat precut meat when you were doing it with one hand. Safety became an issue for some respondents. Sally† said that she has "trouble holding pots and pans…. I think I'm scared now. I'm scared that if I pull something out of the oven and I lose my grip, I'm going to burn myself."

Care for the body was a challenge for many. Bathing was difficult for Christina, so caregivers performed this task. Christina also needed a caregiver to get her into bed every night and out of bed in the morning. Charles, who lost the use of his right hand, talked of going to classes to learn how to take care of himself by using his non-dominant (left) hand. He said:

> It taught me how to dress with my left hand, so there's a lot of personal care things that you learn how to do with your non-dominant hand as opposed to your dominant hand. There are things that become a little bit more difficult if you think about bathing. It's difficult to get to certain parts of your body with only one hand. And you adapt. I'll use a mitt as opposed to just my hand.

Self-care tasks that could or could not be performed varied from respondent to respondent. When they learned that there were tasks they could

---

* Charles, because of nerve damage, after an accident, lost the use of his right arm and hand. He is in constant pain.

† Sally has multiple impairments, some short term and some chronic. Mobility is affected by arthritis in her hands, loss of discs in her back, and fractures to both ankles. She has had breast cancer, and currently has diabetes, high blood pressure, and high cholesterol.

no longer do, respondents learned to do things differently, to do less, to avoid certain tasks, to delegate, and to prioritize. Sally talked about this when she said:

> I learned that there are things that I'm doing that really I should never have done, like shovelling the snow when it is -20 didn't help my arthritis and my shoulders. So that's basically what it is. It's the things you can't do. There's things you have to cut down on. You change your way of doing things.

For Claire[*], learning not to do some things and learning to do less had a positive effect on her life. She wrote: "My health physically and mentally is better than it was five years ago because I've had excellent support and therapy. My back and legs seem to ache less, although that's partly because I've reduced the amount of carrying and cleaning I do and I'm more gentle with myself."

LEARNING TO ADJUST TO THE PHYSICAL ENVIRONMENT

Difficulties that disabled people face in their homes and in their external environment highlight the ways in which public and private space is constructed for an able-bodied world. In her online response, Cindy[†] wrote:

> I do laundry, [and] have a stacking washer and dryer in the kitchen, so I don't have to go downstairs. I have stair chairs installed to my second floor, but chose to have smaller appliances (the washer, dryer, and a small freezer) installed on the main floor when I moved to this house three years ago, rather than pay for a second set of stair chairs to the basement.

---

[*] Claire has mental health issues and suffers from physical pain and stiffness.

[†] Cindy uses a wheelchair because of foot problems she has had since her childhood. She has a list of impairments that include degenerative disc disease in the low back and neck, fibromyalgia, and deteriorating vision.

The typical physical design of houses and other buildings does not work for some people with disabilities. Adjustments are made by moving to more convenient locations when possible and/or rearranging existing living space. Sally, with the help of her son, had her kitchen cabinets altered so she could reach them and divested herself of anything too heavy for her to lift. Cynthia* ripped up all the carpets in her apartment because they posed a health problem for her and she could not keep them clean by herself.

In some cases it is not the physical ability of people that prevents them from performing a task, it is the ways in which appliances and tools are constructed for the able body. Technological advances are not always a benefit for all people. Debbie,† who is blind, could not operate the oven in her rented apartment because it had a digital dial. Christina is not able to do her own laundry as she cannot reach the controls on the machines in her apartment building from her wheelchair. When Charles lost the use of his right hand, he quickly found out that the world is structured for people with two hands. He said:

> The home repair things—I still do some, but a lot of them do require two hands to work properly. I've adapted to using more things like power screwdrivers, using tools to twist things, like using a pair of pliers to twist a key because you don't have the strength to turn. And then, you know, there's certain things where you just have to say I can't do this and I'm going to have to get someone to do it for me.

Accessibility to resources such as grocery and retail stores, and medical personnel is an important consideration for many respondents. Cindy

---

* Cynthia has rheumatoid arthritis with constant stiffness and pain in her joints.

† Debbie is blind and deaf in one ear from a car accident in her late teens. She completed a PhD but is unable to find work. Interestingly, her expertise is valued in a non-paying capacity.

comments on finding ways to be independent in her daily activities. "I use an electric scooter to do my shopping, have a lift in my (old) van, so I can be independent, as long as it all works. I also make a point of shopping at Loblaws, Sobeys and Walmart, as they provide scooters with large shopping baskets. All do carry-out to my vehicle as well."

For those who have mobility issues, Wheel-Trans (as it is called in Toronto) provides affordable transportation for going shopping and attending appointments, meetings, paid and unpaid work, and classes. While grateful that the service exists, Christina and others commented on the challenges of using it. They were frequently late for appointments and Debbie, who is blind, was once dropped off and left at the wrong location. Other forms of transportation are too costly for the limited budgets of many people with impairments. Andrea* comments on her inadequate financial support. "My biggest challenge in life is a lack of money and finding myself, through no fault of my own, in the poverty trap…. I haven't had a vacation in 15 years and I can tell you it's not a priority for me. I can barely afford to buy feminine hygiene products every month—that's how bad it is."

LEARNING TO DEAL WITH THE TENSION BETWEEN INDEPENDENCE AND DEPENDENCE

> And once again you have to accept that you have to ask for help.
> You have to accept the assistance that might be offered to you.
> You have to be comfortable, you have to learn to have to ask those
> questions. (Christina)

As Christina's reflection indicates, asking for and accepting help from other people becomes a necessity when the ability to do certain tasks is lost. In her online response, Cindy wrote, "It's harder to deal with everything on my own. For example, I need help with taking out the garbage,

---

* Andrea has Hodgkin's disease and was diagnosed with MS when she was 34 years old. She is unable to engage in paid work.

housework, shopping, etc." Family and close friends provide much of the carework required. Sally said, "I count on my kids a lot more." Because of Sally's physical limitations in the kitchen, her daughter regularly cooks meals for Sally and her husband. Help also comes from paid caregivers. Alicia* commented, "I used to cook for myself before I had this treacherous disease. Now Ethel does all my cooking for me." Ethel, Alicia's paid caregiver, also does the dusting, vacuums and mops the floors, and cleans the bathroom.

Asking for help means knowing what help to ask for and where to get it. Dorica† suggests that it is sometimes difficult for people who need help and support to find it. The problem for many people with impairments is twofold. First, they have to find out what resources are available so that they can help themselves in terms of their physical, mental, emotional, and spiritual well-being. Second, because many people with disabilities have relatively low incomes, they do not always have the money to pay for resources not funded by the government.

In a society that values independence and the ability to overcome what would be described as personal impediments, asking for help can negatively affect a person's self-esteem. Christina comments: "I think you have to swallow a lot of pride, especially in the beginning." Charles said that having to ask someone else (sometimes strangers) to do up the zipper on his coat was very embarrassing but necessary. Any movement from independence to dependence comes with deep feelings of loss of control over one's life.

LEARNING TO MAINTAIN AND RELINQUISH CONTROL

An important question that people with disabilities must ask themselves is, How will I get on with my life? Issues of contingency and control

---

* Alicia is in advanced stages of MS. She cannot walk, dress herself, fix meals, or do housework in her apartment as she has problems with mobility and the use of her hands.

† Dorica has been making slow recovery from a severe concussion. She has had to work hard to move beyond debilitating pain to regain mobility and the ability to read, comprehend, and write. Pain is still a constant in her life.

feature highly in decisions that are made (Frank 1995). Life is repeatedly contingent on how the person feels that day and on commitments to and responsibilities for the self and others. Inability to do certain things and reliance on caregivers means that a certain amount of control over one's life is lost. In addition, control of a person's body is often taken over by the medical profession. Thus, the critical question for disabled people is: What areas of my life can I control and how do I do it?

Planning and organizing time around contingencies and commitments is an important aspect of maintaining control. Self-care, for many respondents, became a matter of choices and setting priorities. Charles commented on his approach to life with an impairment:

> I could sit in a corner and cry, or I could get on with it. That's the sort of attitude that I've taken with the everyday situations I run into. Do I get frustrated and cry about it, or do I move on? [I] do what I can, and, if it's important to me, [I] find a way of adapting to it. Getting something that will work. Or, if it's not that important, can I just say, you know, I really don't care.

Respondents learned to "get on" with life in the best way possible. For some there was a willingness to let things go and do only those things that are essential. Adele* wrote about this. "I couldn't keep up with everything, so sometimes I just try to do the bare necessities, and sometimes [often] supper is just canned soup and grilled cheese." Christina cared for herself and maintained independence and control by directing her caregivers when they tended to her physical needs. She comments that self-directing without being offensive is "a big one for the disabled." Christina attempts to lessen the tension over who should control what, which often exists between the caregiver and the person being cared for. She does this by having, what are for her, difficult and stressful conversations with her caregivers.

---

* Adele has mild hearing loss and cares for her husband who is in a wheelchair.

LEARNING TO MAKE DIFFERENT CHOICES

Time and energy expenditure are critical factors for many people with disabilities. The necessity of making choices in terms of what one is able to do and accomplish is often based on what that choice means in terms of energy depletion. Christina said that "a big thing that's taught when you're first diagnosed with MS is energy conservation…. Sometimes someone's in a wheelchair not because they're paralyzed, but because every little ounce of energy goes into walking." For Cindy, the task of changing her bed is so painful that she loses "the next couple of hours to rest and recovery time." Difficulties in performing tasks also means that it takes more time and energy to do them. Thus, self-care becomes a choice among the many tasks that need doing. It is often a no-win situation for people with disabilities. "I need to take better care of myself, but I don't have the energy to do it."

Energy depletion means that people with impairments need to find ways of conserving and replenishing energy. Christina comments: "I remember in rehab that was something they talked about, conserving your energy and planning the best time of day to do things." If energy was not conserved, respondents had less capacity to engage in self-care. Most respondents made sure that they found time for energy rejuvenation. This might be relaxation, doing something enjoyable, and/or limiting what is done in a day.

Claire described one of her Saturdays:

> Today (Saturday) I got up and read all day (like 10:00 a.m. to 7:30 p.m.) on a novel because I felt like I could not move. I did move occasionally to change chairs or stretch out on the couch and to make a cup of tea, etc. I use reading as my main way of "getting away from it all" without having to exert too much energy.

Respondents listed a variety of ways in which they replenish their energy. These included reading a good book, listening to music, going to the movies, walking the dog, walking around the mall, and getting some form of exercise. Sally said that "about every 10 days I just shut down, like I did yesterday. I came home from work, went up and had a shower, sat and watched TV. Didn't do laundry. Didn't do nothing really." Narcissa likes to think and reflect. Christina naps, meditates, and listens to soft music to calm down. Others used various forms of meditation to replenish energy and find a balance in their emotional and spiritual worlds. Dorica said, "I meditate, and lots of times my energy comes from yoga. Yoga is very good for the body and the mind. What it does is it puts the balance back in place. It teaches you control again, and it helps with the self-value and all of that."

The intermingling of the four dimensions of unpaid household work is evident in these responses. Reference is made to the performance of physical tasks, to energy expenditure, and to mentally planning, organizing, and managing time. Mental activity is involved in making choices and setting priorities. Spiritual activities such as meditation help achieve mental, physical, and emotional balance. The need to change and adapt requires emotion work to reduce the frustration entailed in the process.

LEARNING ABOUT EMOTIONS

Emotions are an integral part of our being, our feelings, our thoughts, and our actions (Ahmed 2004; Goleman 1995). They directly influence our well-being. We may or may not be conscious of the ways in which emotions affect our actions. And at times, we engage in emotion work, which is "the act of trying to change in degree or quality an emotion or feeling…. the act of evoking or shaping, as well as suppressing, feeling in oneself" (Hochschild 1979: 561). I see emotions and emotion work as aspects of self-care, as both affect the well-being of the person. Goleman (1995) suggests that achieving emotional balance, some level of emotional well-being, is important to the corporeal body and mind.

There was frequent mention of emotions in the data. Christina talked of hoping for a cure for MS, yet worrying that it will not happen in her lifetime. Charles commented that "basically, it's the little things that are frustrating. The big things, not only I, but other people seem to be able to learn ways … to adapt to them…. Those little things [are] what eats at you…. They're the things that tear you apart." Respondents who became impaired in adulthood talk about being in denial, being angry, and being frightened. Some found it emotionally exhausting trying to cope with the physical implications of impairment in daily living and self-care activities. Emotions are also evoked when dealing with institutions and societal attitudes. Dorica talks about her concussion and the treatment she received from insurance companies.

> I'm happy that I can now talk about it, whereas before, all I did was cry all the time. Now I just get tears once in [a] while. It was such a strange period to have so many people look at you and not believe you. And the harassment I received from work was unbelievable! From the insurance companies. Every one of those people should be shot for what they did. They would phone me on a daily basis and tell me to come in, drive out to work. I said, 'I can't drive, I can't drive!'

Respondents engaged in emotion work when they sought to create emotional well-being for themselves. Cynthia identified this notion when she said, "Your emotions, if you let your emotions control you, you've lost the battle. You've just got to put a hold and say you take over." Reducing stress and subsequently the emotions involved was a way of taking care of the self. Sally commented, "I let things go more. I don't worry." Maria* said, "You know, there's no point in stress because it doesn't help…. So I'm not going to make my health any worse than it already is by stressing myself out."

---

* Maria is in remission from Hodgkin's disease. Her legs became temporarily paralyzed when her son was born. She has vasculitis and Sjogren's syndrome which has caused permanent nerve damage in her feet and legs. She always has severe pain in her feet and experiences weaknesses in other parts of her body. The government considers her disability permanent, her insurance company does not.

LEARNING TO NURTURE THE SPIRITUAL

For many respondents with disabilities, nurturing the spiritual aspects of their lives was an important act of self-care. It meant asking questions such as: What does my life mean to me? How do I make my life meaningful? Frequently, particularly for those who acquired impairment in adulthood, it meant seeing life and the self differently. In her online response, Doreen* wrote about her feelings about living with an impairment.

> I find now I have less zest for life, and what dreams I did have of doing things in and with my life have now just turned into faded fantasies. To be able to do the simplest things are now *major* feats for me. I think it is partially due to my physical situation and a lot to do with financial (what finances)????? ... My world has changed drastically in the past five or so years and I personally have changed as well. A lot of the time, I do not like my situation and can see why many feel that they just want to give up. But somewhere, deep down inside, there is still a part of me that wants to and hopes that one day I can seize the day and live it with full zest, vigour, and pain-free as when I used to in earlier years. My mind isn't trashed, just my body!

Life definitely had its ups and downs as respondents tried to deal with the tensions between what they were and what they are now. Charles commented, "Some days I'm quite happy with myself, and happy with what I've done and where I am, and everything. And other days, I get really blue and tired, and think why me? I've learned a lot about myself and what life means."

Honouring the spiritual is, as one focus group respondent described it, "[a] lifetime trip. It's become the path of understanding who I really am, what my needs are...." Respondents worked at creating meaning in their lives in many different ways. Another focus group participant said that in

---

* Doreen has lower spinal injuries, chronic Epstein-Barr syndrome, fibromyalgia, and allergies. Her mobility is affected and she is in constant pain.

order to cope, she learned to "stop seeking approval from elsewhere, and learn to appreciate and value my gifts and skills, and do whatever it was that brought me satisfaction." She went on to say: "I've managed to keep my household together, despite all our deficits, and I periodically stop to give myself a pat on the back, 'cause nobody else does that, so I do that for myself." Self-affirmation is a way of feeling good about yourself.

Facing the realities of life is often cause for reflection and for looking deep within oneself. A number of respondents talked of seeking peace and balance through such activities as meditation, Tai Chi, yoga, and communing with nature. Charles said for him, meditation is "concentrating on my breathing, and relaxing, and trying to get to a calmer place." A respondent in a disability focus group talked of nurturing the spiritual by following a "spiritual path of quietude. Creativity … art, reading, drawing, writing, living in the present, and making the most of the moment." Dorica sums up her spiritual journey as she seeks new meaning in her life in the following:

> It's been a difficult road to re-teach and to relearn all the positive things that there is in life, and to recognize that I was still of value. I think we get lost when we get into stuff like this because when you start running around in the medical field and in this whole illness thing, it's a whole animal that runs just the same way as the corporate world. Everybody wants their little piece. [There is a need] to back away, and sort of keep your dignity and to try and build that again. So what I want to hope for in the future is that I end up with dignity and grace. That is my wish.

How Respondents Learned

Respondents with disabilities told us a great deal about what they learned about self-care and unpaid household work. We then asked them how they learned and although we did not ask them directly, they did, in their conversations with us, sometimes indicate why they learned. An analysis of these responses gives us a glimpse into the learning processes used to acquire skills and knowledge. For people with disabilities, learning in unpaid household work is often learning to adapt to a world that is constructed for the able body. The learning process is a complex path that is helped and hindered by such things as knowledge of and access to resources, the abilities of the body and mind, and emotions. There are many reasons why people engage in learning. One that surfaced regularly in conversations with respondents was "necessity." Respondents initiated learning because they needed to live in their environments differently. They talked about accepting themselves and recognizing that they had to learn to adapt and cope with their life situation. When Maria was asked how she learned to plan and organize differently because of the paralysis in her legs, she responded, "I had to. I just had to do it. Nobody taught me how to do that. I just taught myself."

Jarvis (2006b) points out that it is the person who learns, but that this learning happens in a social context. Many respondents were proud of the fact that they learned by themselves, but often they initiated learning processes that were accomplished through a combination of individual and social resources. Each respondent brought to the learning process his or her own personal knowledge and abilities, which were used in conjunction with various material and social resources both inside and outside the home. Respondents talked with family and friends, with people more knowledgeable than themselves, and with professionals. In addition, a wide variety of visual sources, technology, and non-formal courses were used while learning. For those for whom mobility was an issue, the Internet became an important source of information, and a means of keeping connected with friends and the world. Many used reading, television, and the radio to learn about the world, the environment, and health issues. Dorica found courses on mindfulness, yoga, and Reiki very helpful in coming to terms with her changed life situation as she recovered from her concussion. Narcissa and Debbie found courses at the Canadian National Institute for the Blind useful. Christina learned a lot from professionals when she was in rehabilitation and commented on learning by having access to a community of like people. Reza* said that he learned by watching what is happening in the world around him. "I learn from the environment … from the place that … you live in."

Respondents learned from past experiences and through the experience of the learning process itself. Frequently, this process was one of trial and error. Christina said she learned by "attempting to do things, and failing, and getting frustrated." Narcissa remarks, "If you tackle something and it doesn't work out that way, you just put something else into motion and say, well, this didn't work [so] I have to try something else." Charles commented that the learning process also required imagination and creativity. "There's also a lot of things that you do unconventionally where you would use things in a way that normal people would not use things. And some of it is just using your imagination to adapt things."

Several authors talk about the naturalness of learning in all aspects of life (Jarvis 1992; MacKeracher 2004; Tough 1999). While the process of learning and the knowledge acquired may appear natural, it is, in actuality, a product of the ways in which life is socially constructed within a particular culture. As skills, knowledge, and such things as personal and gendered attributes are embodied, they become part of a person's being, a repertoire of acts that are performed without thinking about them. They have, in effect, become taken-for-granted knowledge that takes on a tacit dimension.

Both tacit and explicit knowledge is used in the learning process. The former refers to knowledge and skills that we use without realizing that we are doing so. Billet[2] suggests that the brain, in order to cope with the large amounts of knowledge that we store, uses compiling procedures to remove certain learning processes and learned knowledge from the conscious memory. This is a process of internalization "where explicit knowledge is re-embodied into tacit knowledge like individual skills, competencies, and mental models" (Kostiainen 2002: 619). Billet[3] proposes that with thought and reflection, tacit knowledge can sometimes be "uncompiled."

---

* Reza had a back operation that still leaves him in severe pain when sitting or standing.

For instance, riding a bicycle becomes an automatic task, but when we have to teach someone else how to ride a bicycle, we need to uncompile the steps that we used in the learning process. Kostiainen (2002: 619) refers to this as externalization. He describes this as "a process of articulating tacit knowledge into explicit concepts." Respondents revealed the taken-for-granted ways in which they performed various tasks and re-evaluated them in light of the physical and social challenges they faced.

What People with Disabilities Should Not Have to Learn

As people go about living life and about learning things that they consciously plan to learn, they also learn things that they should not have to learn. For persons with disabilities, this learning is often associated with dominant cultural ideologies related to disability: the social constructions and attitudes that unnecessarily marginalize and disable people with impairments.

When individuals have or acquire impairments, they learn that they can no longer meet society's normative expectations of the able body. They learn that they are no longer part of mainstream society but part of a marginalized group of people who face barriers to participation in various aspects of daily social and economic life. They learn that their needs are often not met or at times even considered in government policies, and business and medical practices. They also learn that there are differences between what society sees or believes disabled people can do and what they actually do.

CHALLENGING SOCIAL BELIEFS ABOUT DISABILITY

Social ideologies have much to say about how we think about and treat those who are impaired. Yet, many of the generalized assumptions we make about disability are beliefs that stereotype people with disabilities and do not take into account differences in terms of the nature and severity of the impairment, the abilities of the person, and the social conditions of his or her life. This research refutes two such beliefs. First, there is "a presumption that disabled people do not work, either for a wage or on an unpaid basis in the home." (Thomas 2007: 88). Contrary to this assumption, the disabled respondents in this research, whether they engaged in paid work or not, did a great deal of unpaid work in the home. They shouldered many responsibilities to do with themselves, family, and other people. These activities are hidden from view and get little recognition in terms of their ability to do things.

Another belief challenged by this research is the way in which "[o]ur culture attributes 'neediness' and 'dependency'—devalued, sometimes stigmatised, states of being—to the person with impairment ..." (Thomas 2007: 88). Respondents had varying degrees of dependence on others, but also provided varying levels of support and care for others and for themselves. Contradictory societal expectations and beliefs create a tension between independence and dependence. On the one hand, the medical establishment promotes rehabilitation that will enable the disabled person to become independent, and society valorizes the independent heroic figure, the person who overcomes the setbacks he or she has because of impairments. On the other hand, as Thomas indicates above, people with impairments are commonly perceived as needy and dependent. But when disabled respondents talked about self-care, they demonstrated that they are both independent and dependent, and these two states vary from person to person, depending on abilities and life positioning.

POLICY, ECONOMICS, AND THE LOSS OF SELF-ESTEEM

Potentially devastating to self-esteem are prevailing societal attitudes that marginalize disabled people and government and business practices that fail to help people with impairments to live more independently. Francine,[*] from the online focus group, expressed her feelings in the following:

---

* Francine was diagnosed with retinitis pigmentosa when she was 24 years old. She is now in her early 50s. This is a genetic disease of the retina that through time causes blindness. Francine has approximately 3% of her vision left and uses a white cane. She is no longer able to find paid work so lives on government subsidies.

The systems that govern us all are very generic and adversarial. They do not take into consideration the consistent and continual differences in people, and their situations and needs. Economic derailment is responsible for loss of dignity and self-esteem. The combination of these two factors, when assistance and guidance is absent, in my opinion, negates a person's ability to rise above the mire into which these economic situations throw them…. Changes, when made, often are critically dependent on dollars and cents. Monetary sustenance is not the same as monetary freedom…. My experience has been that women with disability are at the lowest end of the spectrum. Because of this, control over our lives and the directions they should take, are almost non-existent without some form of outside help.

Lack of access to resources, financial constraints, and a medical community that too often disregards personal feelings and personal knowledge batter self-esteem and feelings of personhood. While medical and social systems worked well for some, for many the bureaucracies in government and other institutions were sources of frustration and, at the least appropriate times, inaction. Maria, who felt she knew her own body best, found that doctors, while helpful for diagnosis and medication, could not truly understand how she feels and the ways her abilities differ from day to day. Such instances abound in a society that has negative attitudes toward impairment and sees it as an inconvenience rather than as another way of living.

THE LACK OF FINANCIAL RESOURCES

Many who have impairments find that their paid work potential disappears and that government subsidies will not support an adequate quality of life. Some respondents stated that they would still like to contribute to society in a paid work capacity. They would like to feel useful. However, this was not a choice if paid work opportunities were not available, and if this work could not provide an income sufficient to live on. Qualification for support from insurance companies and the government is based on the inability physically and/or mentally to work. Those who are on government disability support are limited in what they can earn to supplement this income. One such case is Andrea, who in her online posting, said, "I'm only allowed to make up to $150 a month and any earnings above that are deducted dollar for dollar" from her disability support payments. In terms of earnings, many women learn that gender makes a difference. Women with disabilities are less likely to be employed, have lower incomes (often at the poverty level), and receive a larger share of their income from government transfer payments than their male counterparts (Fournier-Savard 2006: 294–297).

WHEN GENDER MATTERS

Gender matters in many ways, and women with disabilities learned that it mattered even more when they became impaired. Several women described their status in society as the lowest of the low. Disabled women should not have to learn this. Societal structures are such that women with disabilities, more so than disabled men, and significantly more than women without disabilities, have difficulty finding employment, and if they do, difficulty in earning a livable wage (Fournier-Savard 2006). Statistics Canada, in the 2001 PALS survey, reports, "Employment rates for women with both mild and moderate disabilities were around 10 percentage points below those of their respective male counterparts" (Fournier-Savard 2006: 294). Furthermore, "in 2000, women aged 15 and over with disabilities had an average income of $17,200, versus $26,999 for men in this age range with disabilities" (Fournier-Savard 2006: 296). Women with disabilities are disproportionately poor. For them, living in poverty is an outcome of our inequitable social systems. While physical and functional limitations are a factor in the lack of employment opportunities, the larger issue is the way in which society is constructed to accommodate the fully functioning body and mind rather than bodies and minds with different functional abilities.

The medical model of disability, which influences common perceptions of disability, focuses on what people cannot do rather than on what they can do. When we turn this thinking around and look at what people can do, we get a different picture. Regardless of whether they are able to engage in paid work or not, women with disabilities contribute to society in many socially important and productive ways, but these ways are not valued and counted. This is evident in discussions of carework, where women with disabilities are not only instrumental in their own care, but also initiate and participate in carework for others.

There was an implicit gendered component in respondent attitudes toward unpaid household work. In this research, most of the women with disabilities assumed roles, typically associated with women, such as those of caregiver for children and/or adults, household manager, planner, and organizer, and caretaker of many household chores. Though the sample of men was not large, the roles they assumed in unpaid household work were described differently, affirming that women and men with disabilities display the same gendered patterns in their unpaid household work as do women and men without disabilities. Those men who were living on their own talked of having to learn how to do the many unpaid household tasks that had previously been performed by the women in their lives. Charles, who lives with his wife, commented that he had conveniently forgotten how to do a lot of household work when he got married. And, although Van,* one of our young respondents, was living on his own for the first time, his grandmother still prepared meals for him. With respect to caregiving, female respondents were far more aware of and more vocal about their role in caring for others and for themselves, and they took a greater responsibility for this work than the men. The role of caregiver, as it is assumed by women, is the product of societal constructs that cast them in the role of nurturer. Over time, this belief has been internalized to the extent that many men and women see it as "natural," and thus buy in to societal expectations in terms of gendered behaviour.

———————————

* Van has a learning disability – dyslexia.

Conclusion: What This Tells Us about Learning and Disability

This chapter offers a perspective on self-care not currently found in the academic literature. I talk about self-care from the perspective of the individual learner rather than that of the teacher or "expert," and focus on a context where a great deal of learning about and activities of self-care take place: unpaid household work. I reveal the largely unacknowledged work and learning in this context by looking at self-care through the perspectives of persons with disabilities. By looking at the ways in which disability necessitates a change in how self-care is performed and in how life is understood, it is possible to shed light on the largely invisible learning that happens in unpaid household work in respect to *what* is learned, *how* it is learned, and *why* it is learned.

Learning about self-care was most often informal, although a few respondents did participate in some formal and non-formal educational activities. Learning was self-initiated and self-monitored. Respondents learned through their experiences, through trial and error, and by accessing their personal knowledge, both tacit and explicit. They also learned by using a myriad of other resources either through personal contact (professionals, family, friends, etc.) and the Internet, or through media resources such as books, magazines, television, and the radio. Thus, learning was an intermix of the individual and the social.

At the centre of the work and learning of self-care was the need to achieve physical, mental, emotional, and spiritual balance and well-being. Well-being was sometimes enhanced, but more often hindered by societal constructions and ideological attitudes that marginalized the impaired body and created dependence. The intermix of the individual with the social brought up tensions and contradictions between different perceptions of independence and dependence. And the stereotypical view of disabled people as dependent and not able to work was challenged by the self-care activities of the respondents in this research.

We all know we should take care of ourselves, but even though disability heightened the necessity for self-care, our respondents did not become paragons of virtue in this respect. Some said they did not give it enough attention, some said that other needs and interests competed for their time, and some said that care for others often took priority. Sometimes self-care was a necessity and sometimes a matter of choice. Do I do something for me or something for someone else? Do I honour my commitments to work (unpaid and/or paid) and/or society, or do I listen to my body? Regardless of the choices made, the disabled respondents in this study had a heightened awareness of the needs of their body, mind, and spirit as the body demanded attention by sending out messages, sometimes with annoying frequency, that enough was enough. This meant that respondents with disabilities learned to listen to their bodies as the consequences of not doing so could have a significant impact not only on their lives, but also on the lives of others. Cassie* was very aware of this when she wrote: "I ensure I rest when my body tells me to. I can't afford to push myself because I am of no use to anyone if I go beyond my daily capacity at all."

---

* Cassie has clinical depression caused by sexual harassment and the abuse of authority by her employer.

Portrait: Fang

"Immigration has changed my life completely," said Fang, a woman in her late fifties. "I used to be a college professor in China, [but] now I've become a housewife." Before she eventually joined her husband in Canada in 2001, Fang waited 10 years in China, supporting her two young daughters on her own. As a new immigrant without knowing much English, Fang felt like "an illiterate" and "isolated," not able to find a job, or make any new friends, not even with the Chinese in her neighbourhood, most of whom are Cantonese-speaking while Fang spoke only Mandarin. As a result, Fang took up all the housework in her family: cooking, cleaning, laundry, managing the household, and doing the grocery shopping.

Fang began her new life as a housewife by learning to adapt her cooking to accommodate the different design of Canadian kitchens, such as the absence of a powerful fan to eliminate the smoke. Fang made a number of changes to her cooking to avoid smoke produced by traditional Chinese stir-frying. Steaming, boiling, and baking are among some of her newly acquired skills to help reduce smoke and promote a healthy diet. Eating less fried food, avoiding heating food in a microwave oven, and eating more raw vegetables (salads) are among the new things Fang did for herself and her family. While her husband was struggling with two part-time jobs, Fang was working hard to manage the household: budgeting bills, carefully planning meals, and shopping for bargains at different stores.

As a new immigrant woman, Fang also learned something she did not expect to learn: her newly acquired identity as a housewife, a reversion to traditional gender roles, and a deterioration of her position in the family. "Before, I was economically independent. I felt good using my own money, but since I came here, I don't have a say in money matters, and in decision-making as to what to buy, except for the purchase of food. I felt so embarrassed around activities that need money in the community centre. It is a big blow to my self-esteem." Yet, Fang's loss of status and power in the family gives her a new perspective about the work she does. "I think housework is work, although there is no pay. It is important for a family. I do housework so that when my husband comes home, he can relax and get refreshed. My daughter is also busy, so I cook good food for her. That's also my support to her and her studies."

Chapter 4
"HAVE YOU HAD YOUR MEAL YET?": CHINESE IMMIGRANTS, FOOD-RELATED HOUSEHOLD WORK, AND INFORMAL LEARNING
Lichun Willa Liu

> To people, food is heaven.
> —An old Chinese saying

It was Saturday morning. A friend of mine came to ask me a favour, and brought with her two big buns of steamed bread, a staple Chinese food that I have not been able to make well since I came to Canada. At first I was not impressed by the look of the buns. While waiting for the water to boil to make my morning coffee, I took a tiny piece and put it into my mouth. It tasted good! So I grabbed another piece, then another.... Just then, my daughter walked in. She laughed when she saw me standing there, taking bites of a bun. "Are you having your breakfast like this?" she asked curiously, grabbing a little piece and putting it into her mouth. "Umm, it tastes quite authentic," she said. "I know what you are going to do next. Ask her for the recipe, right?"

She was absolutely right. Over the years, my daughter has seen me collecting recipes for making steamed bread, and has also enjoyed steamed buns of different sizes, shapes, and even colours—the outcome of my experiments with various kinds of yeast, baking soda, or baking powder. Indeed, I would feel very proud when I heard my daughter say, "Mom, your buns look much better now. You can show them off to your friends!" The sense of accomplishment I got from the food I cooked and from my daughter's subsequent compliments was no less than the joy I felt the moment I heard that my chapter was accepted for publication!

Introduction

Since the 1990s, there has been a new wave of Chinese immigrants arriving in Canada. According to the 2006 Census, there were over 1.3 million Chinese in Canada, making it the largest visible minority group in the country (Statistics Canada 2008b). Compared to their predecessors, who were mostly from south China (Canton) and Hong Kong, the majority of recent Chinese immigrants came from different parts of the mainland, and have distinct food styles due to their geographical locations and climates.

So far, research on food work is largely embedded in discussions of housework. Only a few scholars have given their focus exclusively to feeding work (Charles and Kerr 1988; DeVault 1991). Literature on immigrant food focuses on food security (Koc, MacRae, Mougeot, and Welsh 1999), food identity (Koc and Welsh 2002; Lessa, Rocha, and Fields 2007; Vallianatos and Raine 2008), and food habits and food acculturation (Lv and Cason 2004; Pan et al. 1999; Satia 1999).

Based on in-depth interviews with 20 new Chinese immigrants in the Toronto area, this chapter explores the impact of cross-cultural migration on food-related household work and related informal learning by focusing on the changes in the way people plan, shop for, prepare, and cook food, and what they have to learn to adjust to those changes. This chapter will pay special attention to the gender division of food work, the informal learning involved in this work, and its impact on the Chinese immigrants' food choices and practices, as well as their gender and cultural identities.

A Brief Look at the Pertinent Literatures

FOOD AND EATING IN CHINESE CULTURE

Food and eating are an important part of Chinese culture and central to the Chinese way of life. Marked by its variety and distinctive regional styles of cooking, Chinese food, nevertheless, is primarily made up of two parts: *fan* and *ts'ai*. *Fan* includes grains and other starchy foods, such as rice, noodles, and steamed buns, and *ts'ai* usually includes stir-fried vegetable and meat dishes. Greatly influenced by the *yin-yang* principle, Chinese food emphasizes a balance of both *fan* and *ts'ai* (Chang 1977), and has relatively few or no food taboos compared to many other cultures in the world (Wu and Cheung 2002: xvi). The great preoccupation with food in the Chinese culture is also reflected in the Chinese language. For instance, the most popular Chinese greeting is "Have you had your meal yet?" which is equivalent to "How are you?" in English. Many common sayings and phrases used in daily conversations are also related to food, such as *min yi shi wei tian* ("to people, food is heaven") and *duan tien fanwan* ("holding an iron bowl," meaning having a stable or permanent job). A person who does not engage in paid work is called *chi xianfan* (someone who gets food without working for it). These expressions clearly demonstrate how important food is to the Chinese way of life, especially in relation to paid work. In contrast, this chapter will shift the focus onto unpaid (food-related) work, a much neglected aspect in research on Chinese food culture.

FOOD, IDENTITY, AND IMMIGRANT EXPERIENCE

Research on immigration and food identity indicates that food choices and practices, in terms of eating and cooking, are an essential component of culture and identity, which can be carried over during migration from the country of origin to the country of destination. Influenced by individual, cultural, historical, and social and economic conditions, our food choices and practices also reflect the way we present ourselves, shape our identities, and differentiate ourselves from others (Koc and Welsh 2002: 46–47).

Furthermore, changes in our food choices and practices are often used to measure how well we adapt to the new culture and integrate into the host society.

In their study of immigrant women and food identity, Lessa, Rocha, and Fields (2007) argue that food is an important practice of performing home, and that food plays a crucial role in mediating settlement experiences of immigrant women and the changes in their roles, responsibilities, and identities. They found that food has an enormous symbolic connection with immigration, and that changes in food habits and practices also bring about changes in women's food perceptions, food identities, and food relations.

Research on Chinese and other Asian immigrants' food practices suggests that while certain traditional dietary practices remain intact, some foods from other cultures are incorporated, usually through substitution, addition, or modification (Pan et al. 1999: 54). Dietary changes are often related to age, gender, length of residence, fluency in the new language, and social contact with people of the new culture (Lv and Cason 2004; Pan et al. 1999; Satia 1999). Younger people and male immigrants were more likely to change their food habits than older immigrants and women, who had more experience preparing traditional cuisines (Pan et al. 1999: 54). Longer exposure to the new culture and more frequent social contact with the local people, as well as good language skills, also contribute significantly to food acculturation and dietary changes (Lv and Cason 2004).

FOOD WORK AS "WOMEN'S WORK"

Studies on contemporary women's roles in the kitchen and family indicate that cooking at home, along with housework in general, is considered women's work, and that variations in time and place do little to disturb this gendered pattern (Charles and Kerr 1988; DeVault 1991). Furthermore, women from different social, cultural, and economic backgrounds (across country and race) also view cooking as their responsibility, whether they like it or not, or whether they do it in practice (Mennell, Murcott, and Van Otterloo 1992: 95). It is also well documented that all aspects of food work, whether it is food preparation, cooking, serving, storing, and procuring, are intimately related to women's roles and responsibilities (Van Esterik 1999), and how they see themselves in the family and community (Lessa, Rocha, and Fields 2007).

Many scholars argue that women's responsibilities for food work and feeding the family, as well as their food practices, result in gender asymmetry, contribute to the reproduction of patriarchy, and reinforce women's subordination in both the family and society (Charles and Kerr 1988; DeVault 1991; Furst 1997; Luxton 1980; Murcott 1984). As food providers, women usually design and organize their meals with their husbands' and children's preferences in mind (Charles and Kerr 1988; Counihan 1999; DeVault 1991; Vallianatos and Raine 2008). However, this does not necessarily mean that women have the power to control the flow of food into the family (McIntosh and Zey 1989: 318). Charles and Kerr (1988) highlight the power relations in food work. "Women cook to please men, they decide what to buy in the light of men's preference, they carry the burden of shopping for food …" (Charles and Kerr 1988: 40), but it is men who have the power and control of the food that their family eats.

In her book *Feeding the Family* (1991), DeVault argues that this gendered nature of cooking and food preparation, although central to the construction of family, has consequently led to the invisibility of such activities as work. Food work is ignored and undervalued not only by those who enjoy the fruits of this work, but also by the women who perform it, as well as by sociologists who study work and family. The reasons are, as DeVault notes, partly due to the devaluation of women's work, and partly due to the invisible and hard-to-measure nature of some of the work, for example, planning, organizing, and coordinating, which are largely mental work, and often combined with other activities (DeVault 1991: 55).

HOUSEHOLD WORK: A LONG NEGLECTED SITE OF LIFELONG LEARNING

In recent years, lifelong learning has become a popular concept in adult education because it is seen as covering a whole range of learning activities: formal, informal, and non-formal, and because it is believed to have the potential to promote economic development, democracy, and social justice (Leathwood 2006: 41). However, so far research on lifelong learning has focused mainly on formal training for paid work in the labour market. Informal learning, although most widespread among Canadian adults (Livingstone and Scholtz 2006), has remained largely the submerged portion of "an iceberg" (Livingstone 1999), undervalued and unexplored.

Feminist scholars have criticized the dominant discourse of lifelong learning for ignoring the gendered pattern in lifelong learning participation in formal education and job training (Leathwood and Francis 2006), and more relevant to this research, for bypassing the homeplace as a learning site (Gouthro 2005). Yet, unpaid household work is a means to gain knowledge and skills that are useful for both paid and unpaid work (Eichler 2005). Contrary to past beliefs that the home is a location of few opportunities for learning, and that skills in housework and child care are intuitive and natural rather than learned (Hayes and Flannery 2000), Gouthro (2005) argues that, as a core aspect of the lifeworld, the homeplace is the first site for individual learning experiences, a place where values, beliefs, morals, as well as gender roles and identities, are learned and negotiated. In my own research on lifelong learning through household work among new Chinese immigrants in Canada, I find that lifelong learning through housework is gendered, with more women reporting learning about food, cooking, cleaning, and child care, and more men reporting learning about their children's education and home repair/renovations (Liu 2007). Thus, I argue here that learning for the new immigrants is lifelong, as well as lifewide, and is influenced by gender, race, ethnicity, and class with regard to what and how they learn.

In the following sections, I will explore some of the changes, as well as the learning involved in food-related work, including food preparation, cooking, and grocery shopping among newcomers from mainland China. I use the term "household work" and the new definition of household work (see Chapter 1) to guide my research and a gender lens in my analysis. The goal of this chapter is to make visible the different dimensions of food work, as well as the invisible learning involved in food-related household work, which has not received due attention in the literatures on housework and lifelong learning (Liu 2008b).

Chinese Immigrants, Food Work, and Informal Learning

Like many other recent immigrants to Canada, the new Chinese immigrants I interviewed,[1] who are mostly women and were professionals before immigration, reported a sudden increase in their housework and child-care responsibilities upon arriving in Canada. They experienced a dramatic downward social and economic mobility due to the obstacles that new immigrants face in accessing the Canadian labour market (Li 1998; Wang and Lo 2005), and the absence of social support networks that they used to rely on for housework and child care in their home country. As we will see in the following sections, much of the increased work is related to meal preparation and cooking, especially of staple foods.

"I DO ALL THE COOKING BECAUSE THAT'S A GOOD WAY TO SAVE MONEY"

Many of the new Chinese immigrants, especially the women, reported spending more time on cooking in order to save money, especially in the initial stage after immigration. Yun, a woman in her mid-forties and an engineer who used to work at a large research institute in China, is now a daycare assistant in Canada, and talked about her added housework in making steamed bread, a staple Chinese food:

In China, I used to buy steamed buns and many other dishes (*ts'ai*) in our cafeteria. They are very cheap: five big buns for just 1 yuan.[2] So why bother making them yourself? For sure there's more housework here because I want to save money. I have to cook with the very basic ingredients, like flour and vegetables. To make the steamed bread, I have to mix the flour, wait for it to rise, knead the dough…. It is a long process, and takes a lot of time.[3]

Apart from cutting down food expenses, preparing the right kind of ethnic food constitutes another, and perhaps the most important reason for the new household routines among the Chinese newcomers. Ying, a woman in her mid-forties and a medical doctor before immigration, explained why she had to spend more time preparing her food every day. "Cook[ing] Chinese dishes is not easy. It is very time-consuming, but the problem is that I am not used to Canadian food. I must do cooking by myself. I must cook Chinese food, otherwise I will lose weight." Mei, a woman close to 50 and who rarely did any cooking in China, became solely responsible for all the housework in her family after immigration. She expressed a strong dislike of having to cook every day. "Cooking is the biggest challenge for me here in Canada. I hate cooking, the mess, the smell … but I have to learn to do it, otherwise I will starve."

To many of the women, doing more cooking is a strategy they learned in order to cope with the declining social and economic situations in the host country: to save money, to stay healthy, to have their own ethnic food, as well as to adapt to new living and workplace arrangements. Jie was a married woman with a three-year-old son. However, at the time of interview, Jie was living alone with her son in Canada as her husband returned to China after he failed to get a job in Canada. In addition to a demanding job with an IT company, Jie had to spend most of her spare time cooking and taking care of her son. "I don't do much housework, although I do a lot more than before," said Jie. Besides saving money, Jie finds she has to do more cooking because of changes in her working conditions. "In China, the company provides lunch, but here we have to prepare lunch. We have to bring lunch every day. That's a challenge." Yet Jie refused to see her increased food work as work: "I really enjoy cooking, so I don't think it's work." Lisha, another lone mother in my interviews who claimed not to see differences in her housework before and after immigration, admitted that she had to cook not only each meal, but also more food each time as she had to pack lunches for herself and her son.

According to these women, the dramatic increase in food preparation and cooking affected their way of life in a number of ways. For example, Lisha complained that her life is getting harder as she juggles her increased food-related tasks, her sole child-care responsibilities, and her paid job in a factory. "I don't have time for anything else, just cooking, going to work, and doing housework. There is no entertainment, nothing else." Juan, another single mother who used to be a college professor before immigration, shared a similar sentiment about her life after immigration:

> When we were in China, we used to go out on weekends. If we didn't want to cook, we could go out to eat, but here we have to cook because that's a good way to save money. Now we always stay home. Before, we always went out, to different places to play. Now we have to stay home, so sometimes I feel life is so boring.

Although they are married, Juan, Lisha, and Jie were living with only their young children in Canada at the time of interview while their husbands had returned to China. The three women experienced the hardships that most new immigrants encountered, including doing manual labour in a factory or service jobs in a supermarket in order to support themselves and their children. In addition, they had to shoulder the challenges and difficulties facing single parents: taking sole responsibility for all housework and raising their children on their own. For them, the impact of the double burden is quite obvious when they say that there is "no time for anything else."

However, things do not always change for the worse for everyone. Contrary to the many reports of increased housework, Hua, a middle-aged woman who used to be a college teacher and who now works as a building superintendent in Canada, talked about doing less and lighter housework after immigration:

> Housework is much less here in Canada. In China, we had a big
> family, mostly my brothers and sisters. They all lived close by. If
> they didn't feel like cooking, they all came to my house. I had to
> cook for them, even during weekdays. Later my parents-in-law
> came to live with us. Although we hired a helper (*baomu*), I still
> had to do everything. It's very tiring, cooking and washing. Here
> in Canada, there is nobody bothering us, just the three of us. I feel
> housework is a lot easier than before.

Clearly, Hua's decreased housework after immigration was related to the
absence of her extended family in Canada. Compared with the heavy
burden of cooking for her siblings and in-laws before immigration, Hua
found cooking for her own small family a pleasure. When asked if there
was any change in the types of housework she did, Hua replied, "No, not
much change. [As there are] only three of us here, no friends, relatives, it
is easy." But when I asked her if she learned any new food and new cooking, Hua told me in vivid detail about her various experiments in making
steamed bread, and gave me good advice on how to make it myself. When
asked about the reason for her learning to cook steamed bread and many
other foods, Hua simply answered, "to save money."

"I LEARNED TO EAT RAW SALADS AND TO MAKE SANDWICHES"

As a new immigrant woman myself, I have observed many changes in
my own food choices and practices in the past few years. I continue to
cook rice and noodles, and enjoy Chinese dishes (*ts'ai*) like bok choy, bean
sprouts, and tofu, but I also learned to cook a variety of other ethnic foods
like lasagne, pizza, sushi, and dips. I have tried to make different types of
cookies and cakes, and I now enjoy eating cheese and raw salads, and have
developed a liking for food from other countries like Korean, Indian, and
Thai foods. I learned to drink coffee or tea instead of milk at breakfast. I
learned to check the labels for ingredients on food items before they find
their way into my kitchen. I also learned to use a scale and measuring
cups when I cook. Indeed, the longer I stay here, the more varied my diet

has become. I am also more aware of healthy foods and healthier ways of preparing them.

Similar changes in food habits and practices were also reported by many of the women in my interviews. For instance, many new immigrants talked about incorporating Western-style or other ethnic foods, such as pizza, sandwiches, and sushi, in their diet. Yun reported learning to make pizza and sushi from her friends and classmates in her LINC class.[4] Jie mentioned learning to make sandwiches for lunch as they are easy to make and do not need heating. Jie also learned to make Western-style cookies and cakes from cookbooks and the Internet. Fang reported learning to eat raw vegetable salads because they are easy to prepare and healthy. Ping talked about learning a variety of other ethnic foods from the community centre in her neighbourhood. Mei learned to cook shrimps because they were easy to prepare.

Ying, a middle-aged woman and a medical doctor before immigration, showed a keen interest in learning new foods, and revealed to me some of the changes in her diet. "I am not used to Canadian food, but I am eager to learn," said Ying. "Now sometimes on my table, we prepare some Canadian food, like salads. They are very easy and healthy. I didn't like to eat potatoes before. Here, I like to cook and eat potatoes." Ying also revealed another reason for some of her changes: to save time "because there is a lot of housework, such as cooking, and Chinese food takes a lot of time. I'd like to have a change, to learn to cook some Canadian food."

Despite learning foods from other cultures, many of the interviewees also talked about learning new Chinese foods. This is especially the case with the few male respondents, who reported doing little or no cooking at all before immigration. For example, Guang, a young man who was alone here in Canada, began cooking his own meals only after his arrival. "When I first cooked rice, I didn't know how much water it needs, so I tried and tried, and eventually I succeeded." Zhong, a married man in his early forties, talked about learning from his wife to make noodles, his favourite food, because she was doing a physically demanding job in a factory. Liang, a young man who claimed to do 90 percent of the cooking for his family because his wife was pregnant and working full-time, talked about cooking different Chinese regional cuisines and baking some traditional Chinese cookies, his favourite desserts. "[M]y wife enjoys making some Western cookies and cakes, but I don't do that. My favourite is Chinese dishes (*ts'ai*) and the Chinese snacks and cakes or sometimes Korean or Japanese [food]."

Hua talked about relearning to prepare some staple foods, like steamed bread, by experimenting separately with yeast, baking powder, and baking soda as the traditional way of making steamed bread does not work well here. Hong, a young mother with a one-year-old son, learned to cook healthy food for her son, but simple, fast food for herself and the other adult members of her family as she had to juggle her household responsibilities and her busy school studies. However, as a young mother without much English, Hong said that the foods she learned to cook are all Chinese.

"I LEARNED TO BAKE BECAUSE STIR-FRYING PRODUCES TOO MUCH SMOKE"

When asked if there are any changes in the ways they cook and prepare their food, several respondents replied immediately, "In China, we use gas; here we use electricity." "Here they don't have the big fans in the kitchen to pump out the smoke," and "we don't use the oven to bake things in China." For some of the new immigrants, accommodating those changes in a Canadian kitchen made up an important part of their cooking and learning experiences in the host country. While Liang, a man who reported doing most of the cooking in his family, found these differences "no big trouble for cooking," Ying, a middle-aged woman, complained about the flat electric stoves not being powerful enough for Chinese-style stir-frying and their inability to accommodate traditional Chinese cooking pots. Lisha, another female respondent, gave a more detailed account on the adjustments she had to make in cooking:

When I came here, I bought a shallow, flat-bottom pan to replace the steep, round, scooped pan that we normally use in China as the stoves here are flat and are different from the gas stoves we use in China. When I was living in the basement, I tried to reduce smoke by lowering the temperature of the oil when I cooked as they don't have the powerful fans in the kitchen to pump out the smoke, so I have to put the vegetables in when the oil is lukewarm to avoid the ringing of the smoke alarm.

Similar to Lisha, Fang, the woman in the opening portrait and a housewife who did all the cooking in her home, also made a number of changes in her way of cooking: steaming and boiling some of her food in the absence of a powerful fan to avoid the smoke produced by traditional Chinese stir-frying.

To the new Chinese immigrants in my research, learning to bake and roast their food in the oven is a totally new experience as the oven is not a common appliance in a Chinese household. Fang reported experimenting with the oven in cooking different kinds of food: making cakes, baking bread, roasting chicken and yams, and for reheating food. "We just bought a new small oven because we learned that microwaved food is harmful for health, so we stopped using it and bought a small oven as the large one uses too much electricity," explained Fang. Similarly, Jie said she learned to use the oven to bake cakes. Xinyan, a live-in caregiver at the time of interview, talked about learning new ways of marinating chicken and beef before putting them in the oven.

"WE HAVE TO LEARN TO BE A SMART SHOPPER"

Grocery shopping is an important part of food work. All the participants in my study who were doing housework reported changes in grocery shopping. "In China, I did grocery shopping every day because it [the food] was more fresh. Now I do grocery shopping once a week or every two weeks." Juan added, "In China, I did my shopping by walking or by riding the bicycle. It was very easy, just five minutes." All the women who do grocery shopping said that they do it less frequently in Canada, yet it requires more careful planning as to what to buy for the whole week, when and where to shop, and how to get to the supermarkets as most of the new immigrants do not have their own cars. Juan, a sales clerk at a large supermarket, talked about how she managed to do her weekly groceries, usually in more than one place:

> I buy some of the food in my own store [where she works]. It is cheap, too, but I usually go shopping on my day off. I have two best friends. When I am off and they are off, they drive me to the Chinese stores to buy a lot of Chinese stuffs. The vegetables and meat are cheaper in the Chinese stores, and some special food, like bean jam and sweet dumplings, are only available in the Chinese stores. Sometimes I go by bus to a Chinese store if I need something special.

Many of the women I interviewed shared similar experiences in grocery shopping. In their home country, many used to live close to their workplace, usually in apartments subsidized by their work units. Therefore, they could do their grocery shopping in the open markets or nearby grocery stores every day on their way home from work. Grocery shopping was easy and convenient. Upon arriving in Canada, however, this was typically no longer possible. Instead of shopping for the day, they have to shop for the week, usually in supermarkets far away, instead of open markets around the corner. For many of the women, grocery shopping became a time-consuming and physically challenging task, especially in the winter. Here Ying compares her shopping experience before and after immigration:

> In China, I worked in a hospital and lived next to it. There was a market nearby, so every day after work, I went to the market and did grocery shopping on my way home. But here I must go to Chinatown for grocery shopping. I cannot do it every day, but

[only] once a week. It is not far, though, but there is still a distance. I always walk to Chinatown to buy something. It wastes a lot of time, walk, walk, walk. But in China, I didn't need to do that.

Several women said that lack of adequate transportation to the food stores is their biggest challenge in grocery shopping. For example, Lisha, a single mother with a pre-teen son, made her weekly trip on foot and pulled her groceries home in a cart. Jie talked about the difficulty in pulling her grocery cart home in the slush and cold. My interviews indicate that people who reported challenges in grocery shopping and who compared grocery shopping before and after immigration were mostly those who did not have easy access to a supermarket either because there was no Chinese supermarket nearby or because they did not have a car.

To cope with the new situation in shopping, some respondents learned to use a carpool with friends, neighbours, or landlords, while others bought small carts to pull their groceries home. Several women talked about learning to make plans for their weekly shopping: making a shopping list for the whole week, and writing down immediately the food items they need while they cook. For example, Lisha learned to plan the meals ahead of time, like what to have for breakfast, what to have for dinner, and what vegetables and fruits she will have and how much she needs to buy, so that they will last for the week. "I have to shop for a whole week and put them in the fridge as the fridge is quite large here." Living alone here in Canada with her three-year-old son and working a full-time job, Jie finds that her weekends seem to become shorter, with lengthier grocery shopping. She has to plan her weekends more carefully so that she can schedule activities with her son.

As many respondents reported financial declines after immigration because of difficulties in getting professional jobs, much of their reported learning around food work is economically driven. Fang, a former college teacher and now a housewife in Canada, explained what she did to reduce the living expenses:

As we are not a well-off family, just my husband working, ... we are frugal. We never buy furniture. We brought almost all our clothes from China. We just buy food and groceries. Now I have learned to read flyers. I couldn't do that before. I also learned the Western way of shopping, usually once a week, and buy cheap things according to the flyers. That's different. In China, grocery shopping is very convenient. There is a store next to my house [apartment]. I could shop anytime.

Zhong reported a similar strategy in cutting down monthly expenses in his family: bringing their clothes from China, cooking everything they eat, and shopping at different stores or supermarkets. "Except for the essential stuffs for life, we almost buy nothing else." Zhong said. "We seldom buy bread or get food from a restaurant. We always cook by ourselves, and make everything from scratch." For Zhong, weekly grocery shopping often involves two or more trips:

> Most of the time we buy from the Chinese food market, like *Dazhonghua*, because everything is fresh, and the prices are reasonable, but we also buy food from Food Basics. We buy rice and flour from Food Basics, and we buy some meat and flour and milk from No Frills. We have to learn to be a smarter buyer, smart shopper. Take milk, for example. We drink milk every day, and the same product, the same quality, the price is different in different places, so we have to be smart shoppers.

While Zhong talked about learning from his neighbours and co-workers where to shop for cheap groceries, Xinyan, a young woman who was working as a live-in caregiver at the time of interview, called her shopping activities "learning from experience." "At first, I didn't know the places well, and just shopped at the store nearby. Now I know every place, and by reading their flyers, I learned to compare the prices and shop at the place where it's the cheapest, where something is better [of good quality]. This is all learned from experience."

Although all of the respondents reported various degrees of reduced financial resources and a greater need for economizing after immigration, food prices are not the only reason for shopping at different stores. For many of the Chinese immigrants, as Wang and Lo (2007: 685) note, shopping for ethnic food is "both a culturally embedded economic activity and an economically shaded cultural experience." Although there are many large Chinese supermarkets in the Toronto area, and getting Chinese food is not a big problem, getting to the Chinese supermarkets, which are often located in Chinatown or in the suburbs, presents a challenge for some of the new immigrants due to a lack of transportation. Contrary to Wang and Lo's (2007: 290) research, which found that Chinese immigrants saw grocery shopping as "a pleasurable activity for family members" or "a family trip with a considerable leisure component" because most of the Chinese immigrants in their study have access to a car, the immigrants I interviewed found grocery shopping a real chore as most of them did not have a car.

"FOOD IS MY CIGARETTE, THE MEDIUM TO COMMUNICATE WITH MY CO-WORKERS"

In Chapter 1, household work is defined as "physical, mental, emotional, and spiritual tasks." This is also true of food work. Cooking, food preparation, and grocery shopping not only require physical engagement, they also involve a lot of mental work such as planning, organizing, coordinating, and budgeting. Furthermore, feeding the family involves emotional work (DeVault 1999: 229) as food and cooking have long been understood as highly emotion-laden tasks in which the preferences, the likes and dislikes, the health and nutritional needs of family members, especially children and spouses, are taken into consideration when making decisions on what and how to cook. As she explained in the opening portrait, Fang did all the food work in her family so that when her husband came home, he could have the meal right away and have more time for relaxation. Fang also talked about strengthening the emotional tie with her daughters, who live elsewhere, by either inviting them home for a big dinner on weekends or by visiting them and bringing along their favourite foods. Liang talked about cooking the right kinds of food for his pregnant wife as a way of showing he cared for her. Zhong talked about taking up most of the cooking as an emotional support for his wife, who often came home exhausted after work and as a way to promote emotional connections between family members. "When I cook, I always talk with my daughter and my wife about their study and work," Zhong said. "In that way, I feel like two persons." Zhong added, "Cooking time is also family time ... the happiest time of the day." In addition, Zhong also revealed how he used food as a way to communicate with his co-workers:

> I found that in the workplace, it is easier for the smokers to make new friends than for the non-smokers. I think Chinese food is my cigarette. Although I don't smoke cigarettes, I "smoke" Chinese food. We exchange food with co-workers from Europe, from Africa. Food is a medium. Food is not only something to fill your stomach with. It carries a lot of information, your passion, your love, your respect for your co-workers. It [food exchange] gives me more knowledge about food, more topics, and more channels to communicate with my co-workers. It helps me to get along with my co-workers.

"I PERFORM FOOD RITUALS TO CONNECT WITH MY ELDERS"

Food is also reported as an important way to express one's good wishes, to promote spiritual well-being, and to connect with kin, both living and dead, through food offerings. Adopting the Chinese traditional ritual of ancestor worship, Hua, a woman in her forties, set up a shrine in her house. She put food offerings and burned incense sticks in front of the shrine as a way of commemorating her dead father and father-in-law, as well as a way of expressing good wishes for her surviving mother and mother-in-law in China. Being physically away and unable to visit them in person, Hua will instead perform rituals on special occasions (e.g., the Chinese New Year's Eve, Chinese Memorial Day, the dates of their birth and death, or when she learned that they were not feeling well). "I never did this in China," Hua said. "Now, as I live far away, by performing those rituals, I feel as if they could see me, or hear me [my prayers], as if they could understand what I am saying, and eat the food I have prepared for them, so that they will recover sooner." In doing so, Hua felt herself connected both emotionally and spiritually with her elders in China.

"YOU DON'T HAVE TO LEARN IT. YOU JUST DO IT!"

Apart from what people learned, I also explored how they learned. Many people talked about using various ways of getting information about food. For example, Jie and Ying learned to cook new foods from cookbooks. Ping learned to make fast food and other ethnic food (e.g., sandwiches, pizza, sushi, etc.) from workshops at a local community centre. Mei, Hong, and Zhong said that they learned cooking by observing and/or asking friends, family members, and colleagues. Fang said she collected recipes at potluck parties or other gatherings. Yong, a man in his early forties who works in a government agency, was the only male in my interviews who talked about learning to make new Canadian food, such as roasted turkey for Thanksgiving and making sandwiches of different types because his son likes them. He also tried out new Canadian foods at home after having it at a friend's place or after eating out with colleagues.

Nearly everyone in the interviews talked about learning new foods through watching TV programs and/or from cookbooks, newspapers, or magazines. Most of the respondents reported the Internet as their most important source of information, including food-related information, such as obtaining recipes, and information on nutrition and healthy eating.

Compared to *what* they learned, which is fairly easy to identify, many respondents seemed to have greater difficulty in recognizing *how* they learned, especially learning involved in some of the less visible tasks, such as meal planning, time management, and food work organization. Many simply said, "It happened naturally. You don't have to learn. You just do it!" A few respondents rejected the idea of learning. Here is

Lisha's response to my "How did you learn?" question: "I don't think that's what you learn to do, but what you must do. Time doesn't permit you to do it the way you did back at home [in China]. You don't have to learn, you must arrange things like that. Time limits you and forces you to do it that way."

In another case, when asked about how she learned to organize and plan her housework differently, Hong, a young mother with a one-year-old son and a student at an adult high school, told me *why* rather than *how* she did it: "Housework is endless. There is always so much to do. If you don't manage it properly, you won't be able to complete all the work. You won't have time for school."

The form of learning varied with people and activities. Most of the learning was self-directed and self-initiated and was achieved in diverse ways: informal, experiential, and incidental.[5] While most respondents reported learning intentionally, what they have learned is sometimes incidental. For example, Ying reported learning about Canadian culture through cookbooks, while Jie said she learned English by reading online recipes. Through food exchanges at picnics and potlucks or by eating at friends' homes or dining out with colleagues, many of the new Chinese immigrants also learned about Canadian society, its customs and traditions, as well as its food practices.

Food, Identity, and Gender Division of Labour

FOOD CHOICES AND PRACTICES AFTER IMMIGRATION

Like previous studies on Chinese immigrants' dietary changes and acculturation (Chau et al. 1990), my interviews reveal that these new Chinese immigrants retain a predominantly traditional Chinese diet (especially for their staple foods, such as rice, steamed bread, and noodles), but have incorporated a number of other ethnic foods (e.g., salads, sandwiches, pizza, and sushi), while rejecting others (e.g., cheese) in their diet. Nearly all respondents who reported doing housework also reported diversifying their ways of cooking, such as baking, boiling, and steaming instead of stir-frying in order to reduce smoke. Fang said she stopped using the microwave oven after she learned that it is not healthy.

Contrary to some studies, which indicate that younger immigrants generally tend to change their food habits more readily than older immigrants (Pan et al. 1999: 54), my research suggests that age and length of residence in Canada do not seem to influence food habits as much as exposure to the new cultural environment and fluency in the new language. While the older women in the interviews seemed more concerned with healthy eating, those who had more contact with people outside the Chinese community, or had better English language skills or worked in an English-speaking environment, seem to make more dietary changes and incorporate other ethnic foods than those who were less exposed to the local culture. However, an interesting phenomenon not reported in previous studies on food acculturation is that, for those (mostly men) who never or rarely cooked before immigration, their learning about cooking often starts with staple Chinese food (for example, rice, noodles, steamed bread, etc.) and the food that they were more familiar with (e.g., Chinese or other Asian foods). For people (all women) who did most of the cooking for their families before immigration, their learning seems to go beyond the staple foods to include new dishes, either Chinese or Canadian. This gendered pattern of learning contradicts previous research on food habits among the Chinese in the United States (Pan et al. 1999), which suggests that men are more likely to change their food habits because they do less cooking and are thus less familiar with ethnic cuisines than women who have more experience preparing traditional food.

GENDER, IDENTITY, AND DIVISION OF FOOD WORK

Despite the changes in their social and economic status, as well as in their food choices and practices, immigration does little to change the gendered pattern of food-related housework. Although most of the newcomers in my interviews reported doing more cooking after immigration because they could no longer afford to eat out as often as they used to, both women and men continue to believe that food work is primarily women's responsibility, regardless of their employment status. For instance, Fang said that she had to do all the household work in her family because she could not find a paid job. "My husband did not do any housework because he thought he was supporting me." Unlike Fang, Mei was working for pay during the day and attended ESL classes in the evening, but she was still responsible for all the household work in her family. This was confirmed in a separate interview with her husband, who was doing a PhD at the time of the interview. Although extremely unhappy with their housework arrangements, Mei did not seem able to change the situation as her husband "refused" to learn to do any housework. "He's been like this for years. He won't learn. Then why bother teaching him again and again?" said Mei. On the other hand, Hong, a young mother with an infant son, does not see doing more household work as problematic. "I think housework for a housewife is primarily cooking," she said. "I do most of the cooking because my husband won't cook, so I ask him to play with the child while I am cooking." When asked if there was anything she used to do but no longer does, Hong said, "No, I don't think so. There is only more to do. How can there be less?"

My study also reveals a gendered pattern in grocery shopping. In most cases, women took sole responsibility for grocery shopping: they made shopping lists, planned for meals ahead of time, and did the actual shopping. Only two men, Zhong and Guang, talked about grocery shopping. The other four men did not mention it at all, suggesting that they were rarely engaged in such an activity. Two women talked about shopping with their husbands, who in most cases acted as the chauffeur, driving them to and from the supermarkets, and helping with carrying the groceries back to the car and home. The women were responsible for the rest of the tasks.

Unlike some time-based quantitative studies on housework, which suggest that both men and women tend to overestimate their own contributions (Coltrane 2000; Juster and Stafford 1991; Kiger and Riley 1996; Marini and Shelton 1993; Press and Townsley 1998), my interviews indicate that when men are involved in some of the routine tasks, like cooking and cleaning, which are often labelled as "female" activities, they often tend to overestimate their share of household work, while women, who perform such tasks on a daily basis all year around, tend to underestimate what they have been doing. For instance, Liang, whose wife was pregnant at the time of interview, and Zhong, whose wife was doing shift work in a factory, reported doing 90 percent and 70 percent respectively of all the household work in their families. As it turned out, what they actually did is mostly the cooking, which they rarely did in China. Furthermore, when men are doing the cooking, their wives often seem to be around, preparing the ingredients. This is quite clear in Zhong's claim that cooking is the best time of his day because his wife and his daughter are around preparing vegetables and meat, and doing the cleanup after the meals. In contrast, Yun, who spent much time during the weekdays and on weekends preparing food for her family, such as making steamed bread and other time-consuming foods, emphasizes her husband's contribution. "When we are both at home, we often cook together. I will cut the vegetables, and he will cook. He is also fast in cooking. I always do wheat products (*fan*). He is good at cooking dishes (*ts'ai*)." However, Yun also revealed that her husband's involvement in cooking was mainly because of his interest in food. "My husband enjoys cooking because he enjoys eating. He thinks cooking is refreshing, a means of relaxation." Thus, it is quite evident that men's involvement in cooking is often related to their preference for food and their preferred ways of getting it done. I have noticed in the interviews that when a woman takes major responsibility for cooking, there is hardly a mention of her husband in the kitchen with her. But when a man is cooking, it is very likely that his wife is around, preparing the ingredients, and cutting meat and vegetables. Furthermore, women usually end up doing the most routine and time-consuming tasks, such as making staple foods like steamed bread and other wheat products, or some of the less visible and less rewarding work, such as cutting vegetables and meat. Often it is the man, the chef, who simply combines all the ingredients, adds seasoning, puts them in the pan, and then collects all the credit.

This is consistent with DeVault's (1991: 104) finding that men seem to have considerable power to define their own contributions to housework, to limit sharply the nature and extent of their participation, or even refuse to participate in family work, while women do not seem to have much choice. For instance, Fang takes full responsibility for the household work, mainly because her husband is the sole breadwinner in her family who expects his wife to serve him when he comes home. Mei, who used to be responsible only for managing and supervising hired helpers in her household in China, is now doing all the household work herself as her husband refuses to learn to perform any of the household tasks. In addition to planning and organizing their meals according to their husbands' and children's preferences, what they learn about food, cooking, and grocery shopping also has much to do with their husbands' and/or children's food preferences, or what they consider to be good for them and their health. In contrast, men rarely make such comments except for occasional consideration of their children's food preference. (Liang was the only male in the interviews who talked about cooking food that is good for his pregnant wife and her fetus, but not the food his wife enjoys).

Consistent with many other studies on the gendered division of feeding work (see Charles and Kerr 1988; DeVault 1991), my interviews show that food-related household work for men is limited and exceptional, and that men "pitched in" or "helped out" only when their wives were less available. For example, Ming admitted that he never did any housework during his 10-year marriage prior to immigration, but had to help with the cooking and the laundry after his wife gave birth to their son in Canada and later when she went out to work as he had no extended family around and he could no longer afford paid help for those household tasks. Liang took up more of the household work mainly because his wife was pregnant and working full-time while he was not holding a paid job at the time of the interview. Zhong reported increased housework since they came to Canada as a way of showing consideration for his wife because she was doing manual labour in a factory. "Every day seeing my wife coming home exhausted, I feel quite guilty. I cannot let her do all the housework."

By doing more housework, many of the male immigrants realized that it is not an easy task. For example, Zhong said that he felt stupid and was laughed at when he first started cooking. While learning to improve his cooking skills, Zhong also learned time management in order to increase his efficiency, trying to finish everything in two hours: cooking, making meal plans for the following day, and balancing the budget with their meagre wages so that he still has time for his job search and for helping his daughter with her schoolwork in the evenings. Guang, the only single male in my interviews, learned to cook his own meals and shop for his own food only after immigration simply because he could no longer depend on his mother, who used to cook for him. Not knowing how to cook or what and where to buy familiar foodstuffs, Guang reported getting little variety in his diet, and became thinner in the first year in Canada due to a lack of nutrition. Thus, it is apparent that men's increased responsibility in household work, especially cooking, was not always only a result of reduced family income or personal preferences, but in some cases it was more driven by the fact that they could no longer depend on women, either their mothers or their wives, to cook for them.

However, it is important to note that for men, housework is often optional, whereas it is always obligatory for women. If a woman wants a more equitable division of labour in the household, she often has to negotiate with her husband or even push for a more equal division of labour in the household. This was the case with Hua:

When we were in China, I did all the cooking, he [her husband] was responsible for the cleaning and washing in the beginning. Later, he worked far away from home, [so] I had to do everything, cooking, cleaning, and shopping. When we came to Canada, he is still in his former habit, not doing anything…. Sometimes, when I don't feel like doing it, I refuse to cook. He has to do it himself when he's hungry. Sometimes I have to tell him, "You must do the cooking today, as you cook it [*ts'ai*] better.' He cooks occasionally,

> once in a while. Sometimes I just force him to do more. "I've done
> the cooking, [so] you have to do the cleaning." He would do the
> cleaning as he is a clean person, and likes to keep things tidy. But
> my problem is I am so used to cooking that I often, without know-
> ing it, start to cook in the kitchen even if I told him that I am not
> going to cook [laugh].

The need for Hua to negotiate constantly or even push for her husband's involvement in household work clearly demonstrates the power relations between women and men in food work, suggesting that there is still a long way to go before an equal division of work can be achieved between women and men in the private home.

Feminist scholars believe that the gendered division of food work is not only an expression of female subjugation in a patriarchal society, it also reflects the way in which women construct their femininity (Charles and Kerr 1988; Furst 1997). As we can see from the interviews, many women are not happy with the unequal division of labour in food work, yet few of them see this gendered work as unfair. Instead, nearly all of the women accept this division of labour with little objection. This is especially true among those who were not or only occasionally involved in paid employment as they felt that the kitchen is the only domain where they can have some control. As Furst (1997: 442) argues, femininity seems to be so deeply involved in the cooking and giving of food that women may hesitate to give up this aspect of their identity. Thus, doing household work for women is doing gender (West and Zimmerman 1987), and the work of cooking and feeding the family plays a vital part in the construction of a woman's roles as wife and mother (DeVault 1991), as well as in the confirmation of feminine gender identity.

THERE ARE THINGS THEY SHOULD NOT HAVE TO LEARN

It is quite evident from the interviews that much of the food-related learning that these new Chinese immigrants undertook is closely associated with their declining economic situation after immigration. Although most of them were engineers, medical doctors, university or college teachers, or administrators before immigration, very few of the new immigrants, women and men, were able to find jobs in their profession. Many ended up doing manual labour in factories or minimum-wage jobs in the service sector; a few were unemployed. About a quarter of the interviewees were returning to school for training in programs unrelated to their previous professions. The sudden increase in household work and carework, much of it food-related, added to the challenges and hardship of life in their new country, at least in the initial stage of their immigration. In addition to learning to navigate the Canadian labour market (Ng, Man, Shan, and Liu 2007), these new immigrants also have to learn to do unpaid work differently, in order to adjust to their changed social and economic situations in the host country.

Some of this learning, clearly, should not be necessary. For example, if their foreign credentials were recognized, many of these new immigrants would not have to go back to school to be retrained in order to get a better-paying job that would enable them to maintain a decent standard of living, including the ability to afford to buy prepared foods or to eat out in restaurants. If they did not have to spend so much time on cooking staple foods, they might be able to explore and learn more about Canadian foods and adopt more "Canadian" food behaviours or practices like shopping by car (which most respondents could not afford), and shopping for healthy foods. Without having to worry about making ends meet on meagre wages, these new immigrants, especially women, would feel less pressured to economize. If they did not have to cook everything from scratch, new immigrants would have more time for themselves and their children to learn English, and to become more familiar with Canadian culture and society. They would be able to pursue more leisure activities, such as travelling, camping, skating, and skiing, which are part of the Canadian dream for many of the immigrants who come to Canada.

If new immigrants were given equal job opportunities, there would be fewer lone mothers, whose husbands have to leave Canada to look for jobs elsewhere. These lone mothers would not have to raise their children on their own or buy the cheapest groceries available, which might not be healthy for their children and themselves. Finally, some of the professional women who sacrificed their careers to come with their husbands to Canada would not have learned to revert to traditional gender roles as housewives, or to accept an unequal division of domestic labour as "natural," mainly because of their loss of status and power in the family (as in the case of Fang and Mei).

Conclusion

This chapter has shown that, upon arriving in Canada, most of the new Chinese immigrants in my interviews found that they faced a sudden increase in cooking and food preparation due to a dramatic decline in family income and the absence of extra household help. They also had to make adjustments in their ways of doing grocery shopping. To cope with the different design of a Canadian kitchen, many respondents learned new ways of cooking, such as baking, steaming, or boiling, so as to reduce the smoke produced by stir-frying, a traditional Chinese way of cooking. More significant and extensive learning was reported in cooking new food. Many women reported learning to cook Chinese food such as steamed bread and dumplings because they could no longer afford to buy them. Many women also learned to make popular Canadian food, including sandwiches, pizza, sushi, salads, and cookies. In learning the physical tasks of cooking and food preparation, many new immigrants made a number of adjustments in planning and organizing food-related housework, such as making shopping lists, planning meals, and arranging rides for shopping trips to the supermarkets. Many also learned to cut down their food expenses through careful budgeting and by comparing food prices by reading flyers and shopping at different stores. Food and cooking have also been used to connect with friends, neighbours, and colleagues, as well as with other family members, near and far, emotionally and/or spiritually. What we see here, through food-related household work, is that, while for analytical purposes, the boundaries of the four dimensions of work and learning are treated as separate, they in fact overlap. Furthermore, given the fact that cooking itself is often thought of as a physical activity done by individuals, what is cooked, how it is cooked, and for whom involves mental, emotional, and spiritual efforts and has significant social, cultural, and economic implications.

Like previous research on household work in general and feeding work in particular, my research on Chinese immigrants continues to show the gendered nature of food-related work. Women continue to do more food preparation, cooking, after-meal cleanup, as well as budgeting, meal planning, and grocery shopping. Although men also cook and share grocery shopping, their involvement is often optional, selective, and minimal. For men, doing housework means showing consideration and care for their wives, and they do it, for the most part, only when their wives are not available or unable to do it (e.g., when she is pregnant or working at a physically exhausting job). For women, food work is routine, obligatory, and a seemingly "natural" expression and fulfillment of their "womanly" role. While some of the women in my interviews seemed to accept the unequal division of labour, others had to negotiate or push for a more equal division of the feeding tasks.

I conclude that food work and food practices are important processes in which the new Chinese immigrants, especially women, learn to create new knowledge, skills, and strategies on food choices and practices, to reconstruct their new gender and ethnic identities, as well as new gender relations, largely due to changes in various aspects of their life: the downward mobility in their social and economic status due to the non-recognition of their foreign credentials and paid work experience, the absence of a social support network in Canada, their emphasis on women's gender roles as mothers and wives, their relocation to a Canadian city with a large Chinese community, availability of ethnic food but uneven accessibility to Chinese food stores. This chapter highlights the shared realities and common experiences of Chinese immigrants in food work. However, this by no means suggests that the experiences of the Chinese immigrants are uniform. The differences between individuals, between women and men, and between Chinese and other immigrant communities should be given equal attention in research on immigrant settlement experiences and in government policies regarding the common issues among immigrants of diverse backgrounds.

Portrait: Mithreal

Several years ago, Mithreal attended the funeral of a friend's father. The deceased man had been very successful in his career, and at the funeral, one of his former colleagues gave a long speech about all of his professional accomplishments. Then his daughter spoke, much more briefly, about what a wonderful father he had been. As Mithreal listened to these speeches and reflected on his own life, something resonated, and he later remarked to his wife, Anne, that at his funeral, he wants his children to say what a great dad he was, and that he doesn't care one bit about whether anyone says anything about his career.

Mithreal's priorities in life have changed since he first entered the paid workforce as a human resources consultant, right out of graduate school. This can be attributed mostly to becoming a parent 10 years ago when his daughter Sadie was born. After some discussion about how to organize their child care and family life, Anne and Mithreal decided that he would leave his full-time job outside the home to work part-time as a home-based consultant and become, as Mithreal puts it, "the house husband." Several years later, Jordie and William, twin boys, were born and Mithreal has been trying to find a sense of balance within family life ever since.

For Mithreal, it often feels like balance evades him—whether it is between the care given to each of his three children, his paid and unpaid work, or family and other social relationships—and much of his learning is in pursuit of this balance. One of the children, Jordie, has Asperger's syndrome, so Mithreal has learned about resources for disabled children, as well as ways of communicating, scheduling, resolving conflicts, cooking, and organizing family life so that Jordie's way of being in the world is valued and acknowledged. At the same time, Mithreal works hard to be equally attentive to his other children, and care for them in ways that also meet their particular needs. Often life is so hectic that there is little time to pause and reflect upon the different issues that come with caring for three young, active children. To help with this, Mithreal and Anne go to workshops together, and sometimes get a babysitter so that they can go out and debrief, strategize, and discuss ways to support one another and their children better.

Learning is a constant part of Mithreal's everyday life, especially through the day-to-day carework that he performs. As his children grow older, and their needs and interests change, Mithreal reads, researches, and talks with other parents so that he can continue to parent effectively. Sometimes Mithreal learns from his children in ways that clearly enrich his own life. They try out new recipes together after watching cooking shows on television and research environmental issues when the children come home from school, excited about climate change, recycling, etc.

Taking time for himself or spending time with his wife and friends has become a bit of a luxury for Mithreal, although this is something he is working on prioritizing again as the children grow older. Many of his social relationships have fallen away as family life became child-centred and busy, and making new friends has been difficult because, as a house husband, he finds himself mostly among women and he is cautious about initiating social opportunities in case his intentions are misunderstood. Ultimately, though, Mithreal loves spending time with his children and does not regret prioritizing his unpaid care-work over his professional career. In his own words:

> Balancing is rewarding and difficult.... It's tough, it's hard, and it demands a lot of you to be a house husband with a career, but it's got a whole whack of rewards that you don't get anywhere else!

Chapter 5
CHOREOGRAPHING CARE:
LEARNING THROUGH UNPAID CAREWORK
Susan Ferguson and Margrit Eichler

Visiting my mother recently, I [Susan] came across an old school project chronicling our family history. Inside was a newspaper clipping featuring a photo of my mother, leaning into a polling booth and smiling; my sister was in a Snugli on her chest, and I was standing beside her. The caption reads: "Like hundreds of other housewives, Mary Ferguson took her children Boubalina,[1] three, and Clara, three weeks, along with her to the polling place at False Creek Elementary School."

I smiled as I looked at the photo, recalling the many ways my mother's work as a "housewife" (though I have never heard her refer to herself that way) caring for three young children took us out of the home and into the community. We went on peace marches, complete with homemade child-sized signs bearing the slogan "No Nukes," visited my father on the picket line when he was locked out, took snacks to our teachers when they were on strike, and delivered flyers door to door during the Operation Solidarity movement in British Columbia in the 1980s, motivated by the promise of Slurpees when we were finished!

All these activities, and more, were woven into everyday family life, taking place amid meal preparation and homework help. Later, another school project that my sister brought home served as a catalyst for my mother's more formal involvement in the environmental movement. This project involved spreading the week's garbage out and sorting it into compost, recyclable materials, and waste. Seeing so much garbage on the kitchen floor was a consciousness-raising moment for my mother, and it ultimately inspired her career as an environmental educator. Whereas 25 years ago, my mother sat on the kitchen floor with her children, sorting through our household waste, today she works with other people's children in schools throughout British Columbia, teaching them about energy conservation and encouraging them to conserve resources in their schools and homes.

Reflecting on these stories from my childhood, I have realized that not only my mother learned a great deal from her carework; I have learned something important as well—from both my parents—about the sheer breadth of activities involved in caring for children and the value of community involvement and political education.

Introduction

The reciprocity characterizing both carework and the learning associated with it was not only present in the stories above, it was also notable throughout the reflections shared by participants in our study, particularly those with children. Indeed, as we have emphasized throughout this book, dominant notions of household work that make it appear private, unidirectional, and unskilled are largely ideological. This chapter explores the learning associated with unpaid carework, highlighting both the significance of this learning and the breadth of activities and relationships involved.

We opened this chapter with the story of Mithreal, even though most carework is performed by women, not by men (e.g., Zukewich 2003). Mithreal is the exception in a number of ways. He is the primary caregiver for his children, he has three children at a time when the average number of children per family is 1.5,[2] and two of them are twins, one of whom has Asperger's syndrome.[3] We highlighted Mithreal's narrative to demonstrate that there are some men who do contribute significantly to household work, even though women generally do much more of it. We also noticed that men seemed to report more learning about household work, and particularly carework, than women, which stands to reason: if you have less experience because you do less, you have to learn more.

In Chapter 1 we reported that our research participants had some difficulty understanding what exactly is meant by the term "carework." This is paralleled by the problem scholars have with defining carework. Thomas (1993) carefully examined the concept of care and how it is employed within sociology, and concluded that it is problematic for two reasons: its boundaries are unclear and vary from author to author, and it is sometimes treated as a theoretical category rather than an empirical one. In order to systematize the discussion, she proposes a "unified concept of care" that "describes the totality of society's people-centred work" as a baseline:

> Care is both the paid and unpaid provision of support involving work activities and feeling states. It is provided mainly, but not exclusively, by women to both able-bodied and dependent adults and children in either the public or domestic spheres, and in a variety of institutional settings. (Thomas 1993: 665)

Our definition of household work (the sum of all physical, mental, emotional, and spiritual tasks that are performed for one's own or someone else's household, and that maintain the daily life of those for whom one has responsibility) includes carework and overlaps with Thomas's definition, except that we exclude paid carework in institutional settings.[4] If the emphasis is on the activities that are performed, we call these activities housework. If the emphasis is on the social relationships underlying the work, the fact that it is performed *for* someone, even if for oneself, we call it carework. Taken together, we refer to the combination of housework and carework activities as household work. Our definition of carework includes both unpaid and paid work as long as it is performed within or between individual households. In this chapter, we will deal only with unpaid carework. The next chapter looks at paid carework by considering the case of nannies.

We tend to think of carework in terms of a dichotomy: there are those who provide care and those who receive care. However, our data demonstrate that this dichotomy is in no way as clear-cut as it is often treated. Most people both provide and receive care. This is particularly evident in the case of people with disabilities, who are often considered only as care recipients rather than also as care providers. In fact, people with disabilities are partners, mothers, fathers, sons and daughters, friends, neighbours, colleagues, employers, and employees. In all of these roles, they may and do provide care and support to others.

One of our respondents, Linda, offers a good example of the reciprocity that can characterize caring relationships. Linda, a woman in her eighties who is now blind, recounts that she has a caregiver, a young woman from another country, who provides for her family through her paid carework. Linda says, "She tells me all her troubles and I listen to her." Although Linda is the care recipient, she reciprocates by lending a sympathetic ear to her care provider. As Jenny Morris has pointed out, "a situation in which one party to a relationship has a clear identity as a carer while the other is clearly cared for can only represent one type of caring relationship—and may, in fact, not be the most common" (1991: 38). Following Morris, we disrupt this dichotomy between care provider and care recipient by focusing upon caring as a social activity that encompasses a broad range of tasks and relationships.

This chapter explores the learning that takes place through the performance of unpaid carework. After a brief overview of the social and economic value of unpaid carework in Canadian society, we describe the ways in which notions of caring reflect deeply gendered social ideologies that, in turn, shape the practice of carework in everyday life. Indeed, normative notions of care as involving only the care of dependants, especially children, so strongly shaped most respondents' perceptions that people often struggled to talk about their carework. In the following sections, we expand this limited understanding of carework and paint a picture of what it actually entails: it is learned, not natural; it involves a wide variety of people, activities, skills, and knowledge; it extends across familial, social, geographical, and pedagogical boundaries; and it is mediated by the social contexts of people's lives and their social locations in terms of disability, race, ethnicity, status, class, gender, age, and sexuality. We conclude with a consideration of those uneven and, at times, deeply problematic aspects of learning, which reproduce social inequalities and marginalization, and suggest that Canada needs alternative ways of organizing care that are grounded in principles of collective responsibility, social justice, and reciprocity.

Caring is a social activity, and despite commonsensical notions regarding the "naturalness" of care, people in fact learn a great deal through their carework, in order to be able to *do* that carework. Using one respondent's characterization of the dynamic interplay between learning and caring, we employ the metaphor of choreography to highlight the pedagogical dimensions of carework. Consistent with our findings regarding learning and household work in general, learning emerged, once again, as most often informal, experiential, and self-directed. Learning through carework does, however, highlight the relational and process-oriented qualities of this learning.

Valuing Unpaid Carework

Unpaid carework is valuable both socially and economically. Even using a very restrictive definition of unpaid carework,[5] Statistics Canada put its value at $50.9 billion in 1998.[6] Additionally, unpaid carework reproduces the paid labour force insofar as individual participation in paid work rests upon the considerable amount of caring labour that takes place primarily without pay and primarily within the sphere of private households. Paid work is therefore very much dependent on unpaid carework.

Canada has a mostly residual approach[7] to social welfare—that is, families are supposed to be the first level at which support is provided to those who need it, and only when families are unable to do so will the state provide help. Under current neo-liberal policies, many programs that used to help people have been cut or curtailed. The assumption underlying these cuts is that family will spring into the breach and supply the care needed. However, there is a great irony here: the less formal support there is, the less family or others are able to help each other because most often, those providing care within families also experience diminished access to resources and their capacity for caring is undermined in the process (Noce 2005).

This may launch a vicious circle as Luxton illustrates in her study of informal caregiving among people who experienced an unexpected medical emergency that incapacitated them for two weeks or more. She found that: "In general, the more support patients had, the more additional people were prepared to join in and the more involved caregivers were prepared to be" (Luxton 2006: 280–201). Unpaid, informal carework performed by families and other individuals thus cannot replace formal support systems. Nevertheless, informal care provision remains an important aspect of social reproduction.

Negotiating Gendered Ideologies of Carework

The unpaid carework we are considering here is provided by individuals to other individuals within private households, but that does not mean that it is not decisively influenced by societal structures and norms. Luxton (2006) has looked at how class, race, and gender, as well as formal support structures, mediate the nature of carework. These factors and others always influence to whom, by whom, and how care is provided, whether or not people are aware of how their behaviour is shaped by societal norms and priorities.

Feminists have analyzed how deeply gendered dominant social understandings of caring are, as well as the ways in which ideological constructs shape the social organization of carework, in both the paid and unpaid spheres (e.g. DeVault 1991; Poole and Isaacs 1997).[8] Much of this scholarship has demonstrated that the naturalization of caring as an inherently feminine quality and aptitude typically results in the devaluing of this work, whether through limited social recognition of unpaid carework or low economic compensation of paid carework in areas such as child care provision, nursing, and domestic labour. Although women are perceived to embody a "natural" capacity for caring, ironically, the notion of "naturalness" is itself a social construct. Caring—and the work that flows from it—is, in fact, a social practice that is subject to gendered processes of learning and relearning throughout the life course.

The "naturalness" of carework as women's work is closely related to another social ideology that shapes both policies and practices related to carework—familial ideology. As we mentioned above, in Canada, families are typically expected to provide the support individuals require, whether related to health care, child or elder care, care of people with disabilities, or carework required in response to crises of various kinds. This is one way that familial ideology is reflected within social policy. However, what constitutes a family, and its significance, is also a social construct.

Motherhood, in particular, is profoundly shaped by societal notions of the "naturalness" of mothers caring for their children. However, motherhood and the qualities and ideals associated with it are not static. As Fox (2006) has argued, contemporary Western ideals of motherhood must be understood in the context of their emergence in the 19th century. At that time, the social and economic (re)organization of life under capitalism led to the creation of middle class motherhood as the means by which children would be cared for, socialized, and ultimately ensured a successful adult life through entry into the paid labour force (for males) and work within the home (for females).

Many women with children in our study described the complex negotiations involved in navigating often contradictory social norms and expectations regarding mothering, as exemplified by the stories of Gabriella and Jean. Gabriella returned to her paid employment after a year of maternity leave, and struggled with comments from other people, as well as with her own internalized notions of motherhood:

> It's interesting trying not to let other people's opinions colour how you feel about it. I'm not going to lie and say that I'm doing it just because we need the income. I like the adult interaction. It doesn't mean that I don't feel guilty about having someone else care for my son because most of his waking hours during the week are spent with somebody else! I just keep reminding myself [that] this is what I've chosen to do and for me, I believe it's the right thing.

Jean, on the other hand, experiences normative ideologies of motherhood quite differently. Jean has chosen to leave her first career as a television producer for what she calls her "second career" as the stay-at-home parent and full-time caregiver of her two sons. Many former colleagues and acquaintances have "dropped" Jean, and she has found herself excluded from some social circles. Jean remarks, "You know, people treat you differently. I guess they have you pigeonholed and [they] don't think that you're so interesting to know anymore."

Gabriella experiences leaving her child during the day as problematic, while Jean, who gave up her professional career to be with her children, has to cope with negative reactions from her former colleagues and acquaintances. While Gabriella and Jean have different relationships to motherhood, they each negotiate complex and contradictory ideas about the nature and value of both motherhood and paid work. Despite decades of feminist gains, we have not resolved these contradictions between paid work and motherwork. Until such time as child rearing is understood as a shared and parental social responsibility, this "damned if you do and damned if you don't" scenario will continue.

Significantly, it was the one lesbian co-mother in our study, Susan, who did not experience these kinds of conflicts. Susan, a university professor, does, however, describe learning a great deal about "gender relations in child raising" as she observes the "really hard choices" that many hetero-sexual women around her are making to "balance their career and their kids," noting that in almost every case, these negotiations take place at the expense of the women's careers and not their male partners'. As Craig (2006) found, even the increased involvement of fathers does not result in shared parental responsibility for child care; fathers overwhelmingly engage in child care that is centred around playing, while mothers continue to carry the responsibility for the ongoing physical and emotional care of their children.

The social construction of motherhood also affects the social construction of fatherhood. As Doucet (2006) has documented in detail, even when men are the primary caregivers, their work is significantly different from that of mothers because their social context is different. Mithreal commented that when he is trying to find out useful information by reading *Good Housekeeping, Reader's Digest,* and other such publications, they are all geared toward women (and, of course, a particular version of womanhood that is not reflective of many women). He said, "You pick up the magazine and all the ads are for women's stuff, lipstick and everything. It's supposed to be about households, I think.... They should change the name to *Women's Household.*" Although he finds that he has an easier time than stay-at-home fathers did 20 years ago, he still experiences a certain amount of social alienation being a male leading what he describes as "an alternative lifestyle."

Gendered ideologies regarding carework are not only experienced in relation to parenting and child care, despite the prevalence of these examples above. Rather, our emphasis on child care here reflects the strength of dominant social understandings of carework. One consequence of the construction of caring as "natural" for women is that carework becomes invisible; in fact, the ideology of naturalness so strongly shaped a normative notion of carework among our respondents that when asked about the carework they did, some of them (especially men) initially said that they did none! Morgan, a 22-year-old university student who lives by himself, was quite typical of other respondents when he stated that he understood carework to involve only children, elders, or people who need assistance. He remarked:

> I've never really had to do any unpaid carework, in my under-standing of it…. I don't consider helping my friends carework. It's not work. I'm kind of a very helpful guy…. I think work is something you're asked to do, whereas I don't ever think of being asked to help my friends. I just help my friends.

For some, however, and especially for women, the gendered nature of carework was quite apparent. Sheila describes how she became responsible for the care of her two elderly parents, eventually moving in with them when maintaining two households became too much work:

> There's no support for women who are caregivers…. At first you're thanked, but then after a while, I get told by my two brothers, "Well, you're living rent free." Not that you gave up your income, that you gave up your life. And then my father, after my mother died, was very depressed, so that was really hard, living with him. And I finally lost it. And he moved into a seniors' home, but I still was the sole person in town, up until this year, when he passed away.

Sheila's situation demonstrates the extent to which the social organization of caring labour is deeply gendered and naturalized in ways that obscure both its demands and effects. While Sheila expresses that she would have liked to share responsibility for caregiving with her brothers, her story is in fact instructive in that the public social value of the labour she is providing remains quite invisible even while she reflects on the inequitable division of that labour. This is not unusual. Carework, as we will show in the next section, is both a complex and constant social need that, while performed disproportionately by women, actually involves a wide variety of different people, relationships, and responsibilities.

The Nature of Carework in Everyday Life

Carework is provided to a large range of people. In our study, child care and care for aged parents were, of course, prominent, but there were also many others whom people cared for: adult siblings (usually brothers), other relatives or fictive relatives, friends, colleagues, even pets.

CAREWORK WITHIN FAMILIES

We received innumerable examples of women providing material and emotional support for others, and some examples of men doing the same, although to a significantly lesser degree. Some women took on loads that seemed overwhelming. One Aboriginal woman, for example, reported that she looked after her brother, who had schizophrenia, for several months, "and nobody in the family would even accept the fact that he has a mental illness, let alone deal with it." She also took on her ex-husband's 13-year-old step-grandchild as a foster son and, at the same time, the 16-year-old daughter of her best friend, who, it turned out, also had schizophrenia.

As children get older, they may still require considerable care, although of a different nature than when they are younger. Some women also described the sense of obligation they feel as part of the "sandwich generation," referring to people who are sandwiched between young children and aging parents, and who must care for both.

Parents with disabled children face particular challenges in a society that constructs disability as an individual problem requiring individual solutions (Titchkosky 2007). Jackie, for example, has a six-year-old son with ADHD and a somewhat older daughter. Caring for her children was not always an easy task. Frequently, when she needed to get her son to therapy:

> He didn't want to go.… Some days, he'd wake up and say, "Am I going?" and I'd say, "Yes," and he'd say, "I'm not, and if I do, I'm not speaking." And even when we get to therapy, he would lock me out of the car when I got out.

Jackie was working part-time, and taking him to daycare was equally challenging. Her daughter would sometimes misbehave, and when Jackie told her, "Well, that's not a good way to get my attention," she replied, "But Mom, that's the only way I can get your attention." There was also the issue of how much to tell her daughter about her brother's situation. Jackie decided not to inform her when her brother was put on medication, and described how guilty she still feels about giving her son medication.

In other words, caring can be very complex, with entangled relationships and with high demands on the care provider. It may affect not only the care provider and the care recipient, but others who also rely on the care provided by someone who is caring for more than one person. Disability, like other forms of social marginalization, interacts with the gendered nature of carework in particularly complicated ways. As Bennett (2007: 107) points out, "ADHD brings to the fore the inequalities of already established gendered subject positions, which include child care and primary responsibility for children." The experience of caring is thus firmly embedded within gendered social conditions that position disability as a problem at the same time as they fail to address the systems of exclusion which produce disability in the first place.[9]

CARING FOR FRIENDS, NEIGHBOURS, AND PETS

People went to considerable lengths to care for friends, and not just family members. Allison took time off work to be with a friend who had been diagnosed with breast cancer, and who needed emotional support. Margie telephoned her friend in Bermuda several times a day when her friend went through a separation and divorce and was depressed. For others, the boundaries of family definitions were stretched in the absence of biological family. Nzanzi, who is single, in his mid-thirties, and immigrated to Canada from the Congo about 10 years ago, remarked that:

> When you live outside your native country and especially when, like me, I'm almost on my own here, your friends become your family, so you are there for each other. Whenever something

happens, you rely on each other, like when I want to do my groceries, my friends pick me up and we do that. When I used to drive and volunteer for newcomers, I [did] the same thing.

This is one way in which the force of familial ideology is disrupted, a phenomenon that is common not just among immigrant communities but also among queer communities. As Aronson (1998: 506) points out, "we live much of our lives outside kinship structures where exchanges of care and support are not framed by the assumptions and obligations associated with heterosexual kin ties." Caring also took place among roommates and neighbours, as was the case for Marie, who agreed to feed an elderly neighbour who lived in her building and was too frail to feed himself after he returned home from hospital.

Not just people require care. Pets were also mentioned. Jimmy remarked that after separating from his girlfriend, who previously performed most of the tasks related to the physical care of their two dogs, he became solely responsible for them. As a result, his relationship to his pets changed:

> I had a deeper appreciation for the dogs themselves because they became dependent on me ... whereas before, I would just be like the fun guy that takes them to the park, or throws tennis balls around with them, that sort of thing.

The gendered division of labour often apparent in child care extends, in this case, to pet care. It was only in the absence of his girlfriend that the considerable amount of day-to-day care required by their two dogs became visible to Jimmy, and thus valuable as a site of work and learning.

CARING FOR THE SELF

We also included self-care in our understanding of carework. Questions about it often brought immediate reactions of disbelief. "I suck at self-care" was one type of response, along with descriptions of what the women did *not* do for themselves. This contrasted with others who provided detailed descriptions of how they looked after themselves. This included taking several hours every week to sit alone in a coffee shop, praying, meditating, calling friends to chat, going to the gym, practising yoga, walking, dancing to records, reading, going to Chinatown, eating at a favourite vegan restaurant, sleeping in, taking a bath with jazz and candles, taking a lot of supplements, turning off the phone, watching videos from the home country, and much more. These examples reflect a particular kind of self-care, however; namely, those predicated upon leisure and the replenishment of energy. As we saw in Chapter 3, both the meanings and practices associated with self-care depend greatly upon the social location and context of those involved.

Often women established a hierarchy, where the needs of their family members always trumped their own. One disabled woman reported that she can justify spending money on her son's needs, but not on her own needs: "It's always a juggling act, trying to prioritize. I find that I'm always at the bottom of the needs ladder because my children and obviously my spouse come first, right?" Because of this priority list, she could not afford therapy, and got her doctor to refer her to a psychiatrist, which, in this instance, turned out to be very helpful: "I was shocked because it took just three office visits, and he gave me enough tools to manage on my own."

Another disabled woman found that helping others is actually also a way of helping oneself. Finding herself in a rather desperate situation, she started caring for others, even in tiny ways, and it helped reaffirm her value as a human being and re-established an important part of her identity.

CARING ACROSS BORDERS: LONG-DISTANCE AND TRANSNATIONAL CARE

A considerable number of people engaged in long-distance and transnational care. This was particularly true for first-generation immigrants, many of whom had children, parents, parents-in-law, and other relatives in their country of origin or elsewhere around the world, but it was also true for Canadians whose children, parents, siblings, or friends lived a long distance away. For instance, Maggie, a graduate student with no family in Toronto, described extensive "support calls" with her sisters and mother, particularly with one sister whose young son was having difficulties at school. She said:

> I think she phones not because I necessarily have anything really insightful to say, but just to be able to know, "Wow, this is really hard" and "It's really difficult." So it's more as an emotional support than having any child care knowledge.

Maggie also travels to her sister's home in northern Ontario from time to time, which she says is "not even approaching a holiday" because she spends her time cleaning and helping her sister with child care.

In particular, the Black women talked about providing care across long distances. Sometimes their children (and occasionally other family members) still lived in their home countries in Africa or the Caribbean while they were trying to build enough of a life in Canada to bring them here. The nature of care clearly changes when there are long distances between the care provider and the care recipient. Rendering services, such as driving someone to the doctor, cooking for them, etc., are not possible. The care therefore shifts to providing emotional support or long-distance advice, some of which may be of minute detail. When Speranza was arranging for her daughter to immigrate to Canada, she organized the medical exam, the interview with the school principal, and the interactions with the Canadian embassy, all as if she had been in Kenya, only with considerably more difficulty because she was doing all this from her home here in Canada.[10]

The negotiations involved in the provision of carework across borders vividly reveal the complexity and fluidity of this work as it is mediated by the social contexts shaping its existence. In this sense, then, another kind of border is being disrupted when we highlight this complexity: the theoretical border, or dualism, which characterizes the experience of migration as leaving one home to arrive at and establish another (Trotz 2006).[11] In effect, the transnational carework we describe above involves the maintenance of multiple homes and the social reproduction of many different lives in different places.

Notions of home and household, then, take on different meanings within their particular contexts as they are shaped by wider social and economic structures. While much has been written about the extent to which women's paid service work propels the global economy (e.g., Sassen 2000), highlighting unpaid transnational carework demonstrates that global economic policies increasingly rest upon the largely invisible unpaid labour of women working to navigate, and often ameliorate, the social inequalities produced through these same global economic arrangements. (Chapter 6 elaborates upon this issue through its discussion of the paid carework performed by nannies.) In this way, the reproduction of the national market economy through unpaid carework is mirrored at the global level.[12]

Carework thus takes multiple forms: it is rendered to kin and non-kin, it may range from relatively small contributions to life-absorbing ones, and it impacts not only those who receive and provide care, but also others who may rely on the same care provider. The toll the work takes on care providers can be great, which may become most obvious when the burden is removed. For instance, Sheila, in her sixties, had a full-time paid job, did a great deal of "babysitting for special-needs grandchildren who could not be with regular babysitters," and "was taking care of an elderly husband, who needed caregiving on an ongoing basis." When she was 70, she retired from her job and became a full-time caregiver. Then her husband died, the grandchildren grew up, and "for the first time in 70 years in my entire life, my time was mine. And I'm enjoying every single moment of it! Trying not to feel guilty about how happy I am."

In spite of—or perhaps because of—the demanding nature of carework, considerable learning takes place through caring. Having expanded our understanding of carework and recognizing its complexity and value to social life, we will now shift our attention to explore the pedagogical dimensions of carework through the metaphor of choreography.

Choreographing Care: Learning through Unpaid Carework

When we think of choreography, we tend to imagine a dance, the movement of bodies through a particular space and set to a particular rhythm. Sometimes this dance is joyful, sometimes it is difficult; often it involves a mixture of emotions, which, in turn, can shape the emotions of other people around. Sometimes a person dances alone, and sometimes groups of people dance together. Sometimes this dance involves specific techniques and has been designed and rehearsed for a particular occasion or performance, while at other times the dance is spontaneous, but incorporates movements or sequences from the past. Dancing, then, like caring, engages the whole person in relation to others across time and space; it is embodied, dynamic, and intersubjective.

As Jean remarks, a kind of "choreography" of learning takes place *through* carework that is simultaneously required to *perform* that carework throughout the life course. For Jean, like many of our other respondents, this choreography involves a day-to-day blending of reading about child development, talking with friends in her book club, conducting research on the Internet, critically assessing the advice she is given, and putting it all into practice—and reflecting upon it as she does it over and over again.

Following Hocking, Haskell, and Linds (2001), choreography is a useful metaphor for learning because it highlights learning as a kind of doing, a social activity that engages the body, mind, and spirit. Choreography, as they point out, requires that "one must be involved in it both on the inside and the outside in order to realize what it feels like" (Hocking, Haskell, and Linds 2001: 83). This is similar to caring, which also requires a certain level of active, self-reflective engagement with others even while particular skills or techniques are being acquired and put into practice. Let us now look at the choreography of caring described by our research respondents a little more closely.

"I NEED A HUGE TREASURE CHEST OF COPING SKILLS"

People spoke about learning a wide range of skills and knowledge through their unpaid carework. For parents, information about pregnancy, infant care, and child development was prevalent, acquired most often through reading, Internet research, and conversations with health and education professionals. Caring for children is, of course, challenging and entails a constantly shifting set of tasks amid continually changing conditions. Parenting effectively, in response to these changing demands, requires ongoing education and learning. As one parent remarked with respect to parenting three young children, "I haven't finished learning … because it never stops. They're always changing." Similarly, Jackie reflects upon how learning about her son's disability and developing her communication skills have made her a better parent:

> Instead of saying "You're bad" or "You're not listening," [we say]
> "That wasn't a very good choice." It's just education. It's made me
> be educated. I've gone out and had to find the research, and so
> there is the silver lining in the cloud, I guess. I'm more tolerant and
> a better parent, I think.

For some people, learning to parent meant learning to do so differently than they themselves were parented. Several of our participants were brought up in ways with which they do not agree. For example, one woman shared that even though she was hit as a child, she does not want to use physical punishment with her own child:

> How can I do it better? How can I not hit? … What I need [is]
> a huge treasure chest of coping skills that I was never taught, so
> that's why I ask other people, read, and find out a different way of
> doing things.

Parents overwhelmingly identified discussion with other parents as a major source of learning about issues related to their children, community and educational resources, and daily household management strategies, pointing to the significance of informal social networks for information sharing, networking, and problem solving.

Societal norms regarding parenting come into sharp relief for immigrants who may learn different parenting styles. Our Chinese immigrant respondents, in particular, commented on the differences between parent-child interactions in Canada and China. Liu (2008a: 2) argues that: "The Chinese parenting style is deeply influenced by the Chinese culture, which values collectivism, conformity to norms, and puts a strong emphasis on family harmony." This can result in an expectation of greater parental authority and child obedience than is the norm in Canada. Wei, for instance, says that in China, "the children must obey the parents. Here, like, more, we are equal."

Learning in instances such as the ones above reminds us that parenting is highly contingent upon the varied social contexts and discourses that ground the daily work of caring for children. Wider cultural ideologies, together with social structures and relationships, operate across temporal-spatial boundaries to shape and reshape people's understandings and practices of parenting within and across generations.

Carework can also lead to reciprocal learning between parents and children. For example, parents learn to do new things at their children's request. Mithreal learned new techniques from cooking with his children: "The kids watch the TV shows about cooking and say 'Let's try that, Dad' and we'll go and try it." Ardea recounted camping with her young son while pregnant with her daughter, in the rain, despite never being interested in camping herself, "because you want them to experience the joy of what life has to bring." Perhaps most significantly, parents of school-age children indicated that they have become more knowledgeable about environmental issues themselves when their children come home from school, excited to be learning about global warming, extinction of species, and energy conservation. As one parent remarked, "You can't ignore it when your kids are talking about it."

Learning also emerged when people provided care for others who were dealing with health-related problems. Respondents described learning about community health resources, as well as new knowledge about specific health conditions, such as endometriosis, allergies, and cancer, most often through a combination of independent research and conversations with health professionals, although some people did attend support groups and seminars. Significantly, concrete and transferable skills were also developed through the experience of caring for someone (including oneself) who was ill. These skills ranged from cooking food for special diets to dealing with health bureaucracies and providing emotional support to others. Al, who had cancer himself and helped support one of his children, Jane, through two experiences of cancer while parenting his other child, described learning "practical skills" through all this:

> One of the difficulties is looking after the other sibling too, I think! They can't feel left out, they can't be at the hospital all the time. You learn skills being at the hospital, being optimistic, dealing with doctors. Even now, Jane probably goes to the Hospital for Sick Children once a month for follow-ups, but there's still a lot of stress, still a lot of doctors. Every time you go to the hospital, it's like a day that she misses from school.

THE SQUEAKY WHEEL GETS THE GREASE

Many people also talked about the absence of adequate health and social resources, and the skills they learned in the face of these inadequacies. As Jackie remarked, "I learned that you have to be persistent, that it's not good enough to put in a call. And the squeaky wheel gets the grease. That's what I've learned."

Sometimes, people organized within their communities to address issues at the systemic level. Mithreal, for example, worked with a group of parents to advocate for both a park and a French-language school in their neighbourhood. He reflects upon this experience, saying:

> I've learned that if you get enough people together, you can get

the systems to do stuff. Our kids go to a French-language school system, and they were on the other side of the city, and we got a bunch of parents together on the sidewalk the first time. Then we had barbecues and got more and more, and we managed to get about 110 parents together. And we pressured for a school and got a school. I've learned that if you work at it hard enough, and it's something worthy of doing and you get enough people involved, the politicians will listen to you and you'll get it.

Thus carework can lead to individuals learning outside their home setting. A number of people described learning new skills, or developing existing ones, through the community work they perform as an extension of their parenting and child-care responsibilities. Al, for example, learned strategies for dealing with children through training provided by his son's Boy Scouts group. Many other parents described how having children motivated them to learn more about community issues, particularly those related to the environment, as they developed a sense of responsibility for other people. Jackie learned from news media about the links between air pollution and increased allergy rates among children, while Gabriella researched diaper options to minimize her environmental impact. As Jean remarked, "I consider, in the realm of caring for my children, becoming involved in any way that I can with organizations or groups that they are involved with." For Jean and for others, caring for her children and the responsibility she feels toward her family can become a commitment to social responsibility within her community.

SOMETIMES YOU JUST NEED TO TALK TO THEM

People also learned to maintain their relationships with others in different ways, developing valuable emotion work skills that were often transferable across different contexts and situations. Emotions are socially produced and mediated. While there is certainly an experiential dimension to our emotions, these feelings are steeped in the culture that surrounds us and gives meaning to them. In Chapter 2, we demonstrated that emotion work involves an interplay between oneself and others, regardless of the form that work takes. Dealing with emotions is central to the practice of carework and involves a pedagogical dimension as people develop the necessary skills to perform emotional labour (Erickson 2005; James 1989).

While the gendered organization of emotional and caring labour has made it appear as if it is naturally the domain of women, our research reveals a more complex picture. As James (1989: 26) points out, "Emotional labour does not exist in isolation from the conditions under which it is carried out, rather the circumstances under which it takes place influence the content and form of emotional labour." The same might be said about learning to do emotion work. The skills and knowledge people described varied, depending on their particular context, experience, and access to resources.

Many people, for example, learned to adapt their communication skills in the face of changing circumstances. Jane, a 32-year-old single professional, explained how she learned to maintain a close relationship with her friend after they no longer lived together as roommates:

> We certainly had to make a real conscious decision about how to stay connected so I relearned how to be supportive at a bit more of a distance. [Before] I would see her every day and could be supportive just by being there, but now it's more of a conscious effort of making sure to call or connect.

Gabriella, like many other respondents, now relies more on email to keep in touch with people, a strategy that doubles as a time-management technique. Nzanzi, whose parents live in the Congo, began to telephone them more regularly after his mother became ill:

> Before, I used to call every two, three months. I would tell them, "Look, if you really need to get in touch with me, email me or call me or leave a message." But since my mom's sickness, I keep in touch. I call them almost every week. I just try to find out

how they're doing. Is there anything I can do? Stuff like that. I've learned to do that and that it's important. Sometimes you just need to talk to them.

Nzanzi's reflection is not unusual; many people described how personal or family crises ultimately improved the quality of their relationships with others as they learned new emotion work skills. Jeffrey, for instance, lived alone and was employed full-time as a postal worker. His divorce five years prior had precipitated a crisis for him, causing him to "lose everything" and leaving him homeless and quite vulnerable, without full-time employment, health benefits, or other forms of security. He turned to a sister with whom he had not spoken for 10 years because of "a little spat" that he had stubbornly refused to resolve, and they are now in close contact. Although it was out of desperation that Jeffrey reconnected with his sister, since then he has begun to provide emotional support to others because of his experience:

> I'll reach out now a lot more easily because of the situation I went through. I wanted somebody to really talk to, but there was no one. So if I can help someone else, yeah, I'll do that. I don't want them to go through what I went through.

Jeffrey also describes learning to resolve conflicts differently—he is less apt to "blow up" now—and talk through his problems more with friends, family, and colleagues. More difficult to pinpoint is precisely how he learned these new techniques. Like many people, learning emotion work skills seems to have occurred informally and experientially through a complex combination of experience, reflection, discussion, and more experience. Although some respondents did mention other, more formal means of learning emotion work skills—therapy, workshops, and reading, for example—people were often at a loss when asked to explain how they learned these skills: "I just do it!" or "I just know!" were regular refrains. As George, the father of two young daughters, says:

> I think a whole series of learnings come together and form a feeling about things.... Some people just put it together in their minds without being able to describe it, without being able to say it's because of this, and this, and this. It's a series of things, which you learn and somehow together, inside you—you just know.

And so people do learn, and it appears that this learning has a kind of sedimentary quality to it, as new layers of experience build upon previous layers of experience, interacting with one another to create different insights and understandings.

I'VE LEARNED THAT I NEED TO APPRECIATE LIFE

The performance of carework is strongly predicated upon relationships between the self and others, which at times can facilitate spiritual learning about the meaning of life. As Miller (2002: 89) has written: "When we view life from a spiritual perspective, we see ourselves connected to something larger than ourselves." For many of our respondents, this sense of interrelatedness—to other people, their communities, and the world around them—gave way to changing priorities and values, and a sense of responsibility for life (or lives) beyond their own.

English (2000: 30) outlines three components of spirituality that can be fostered through informal learning experiences in everyday life: (1) a strong sense of self; (2) care, concern, and outreach to others; and (3) the continuous construction of meaning and knowledge. The spiritual learning that respondents described with respect to their carework similarly involved learning new insights about oneself, others, and the meaning of life in general—often at the same time.

Through their engagement with others—supporting, caring for, witnessing, talking with them—people learned a great deal about themselves. For the most part, this learning was expressed as a source of strength amid complex lives and situations. (We will address exceptions to this through our critique of what people should not have to learn in the following section of this chapter.) For example, Francine, a disabled woman who was no longer employed, described her struggle to reconcile a perceived gap between her professional and personal identities. Eventually, she learned that "I had intrinsic value as a human being, that I was not my work, and I was not my position, job, [or] function in the union."

Although Francine, like many oth er respondents, learned this informally through experience and reflection, other respondents described spiritual learning through participation in organized groups. One Aboriginal woman, for example, recounts how she learned to value herself as a person through her participation in a healing program. Although it was initially a personal crisis—separation from her husband of 20 years—that led her to seek out such a program, her story suggests that she gained a new perspective about herself *in relation* to her family through the experience. She says:

> I learned how to love myself from the inside, and to see [that] what was important to me is me. Like, even though my children and my husband [with whom she has reconciled] are still [my] number one priority and I'm below that, I still know who I am, so through that program I really learned a lot. And I learned all about how to meditate, and your chakras, and all these different awesome things.… I just loved it.

Many women talked about their struggle to find a balance between their responsibility to others (especially to their children) and the need to care for themselves. At the same time, many respondents also identified understanding that "life is about more than me" as a key spiritual dimension to their carework-related learning. There is thus a tension here between learning to value oneself and learning that the value of oneself and one's life is inextricably linked to wider social relationships.

For some, this sense of responsibility beyond the self emerged through familial carework, but extended outwards to shape the character of other caring relationships. Munaza's narrative (Chapter 2) illustrates this interplay between learning about the meaning of one's own life through carework responsibilities and increased care and responsibility for others when she discussed how her struggle to remake her life here in Canada as a single parent made her more patient and compassionate about the lives of others, which, she believes, will shape her interactions with patients when she practises medicine again.

Carework associated with experiences of loss, illness, and disability was particularly generative of spiritual learning. Many respondents described learning to "appreciate life" and find a greater balance between their paid work, unpaid work, leisure activities, and time with family and friends. After supporting several family members through a series of major health crises, Gabriella began to reflect upon her own mortality and priorities in life, realizing that "life changes just like that." Describing herself as a "type A" person, Gabriella learned to pause and reflect, saying, "I've learned that I need to appreciate life, and that everything doesn't have to be perfect."

Alesia, who is 30 years old and lives alone, tells a similar story. Employed full-time as a software consultant, Alesia is a self-described "workaholic." Her parents live in Taiwan, and after her father became ill, she travelled back and forth to care for him. While Alesia was raised to be fiercely independent, witnessing her father's experience caused her to reflect upon her own life and relationships with others:

> I think it made me look at life differently.... It made me slow down.... I think happiness is important, and life is so short that you have to make the present worth everything.... It's what fulfills [you] rather than "I need more money now" and forget about family and friends.... My life is more balanced.

In this way, the intimacies of caring labour were often accompanied by an awareness of the vulnerability of life itself. As Alexander (2005: 309) writes, spiritual learning occurs through a complex combination of reflection and experience as people reach back in time, shaping their understandings of the present and hopes for the future:

Spirit brings knowledge from past, present, and future to a particular moment called a now. Time becomes a moment, an instant, experienced in the now, but also a space crammed with moments of wisdom about an event or series of events already having inhabited different moments, or with the intention of inhabiting them, while all occurring simultaneously in this instant, in this space, as well as in other instants and the spaces of which we are not immediately aware.

As Alexander argues, however, spiritual knowledge is generally marginalized in Western society, which she traces to processes of secularization that value concrete, observable experience over experience and knowledge that are not easily explicable or demonstrable. One consequence of this, Alexander suggests, has been the privatization of spiritual work and spiritual knowledge such that spirituality is stripped of its relationship to social life. Our analysis here similarly suggests that spiritual work, and the learning that flows from it, is not only firmly located within the realm of the social, but also *animates* social life as it engages people in processes of meaning-making.

I DON'T USE ALL THE SKILLS I HAVE

Of course, learning does not always take place in straightforward ways, and sometimes it does not take place at all. At times, people were not able to draw upon knowledge that they had already acquired because of the complexity of the situations in which they found themselves. For example, not everyone was successful at maintaining relationships amid the demands and constraints of their lives. Many parents, in particular, described the loss of family and social relationships with some regret when the demands of becoming a parent made it difficult to balance these other relationships.

The changing context of family life thus impacts wider social relationships in complicated ways. For some women, caring for a new baby meant structural changes to daily life, which both restricted their flexibility and availability to maintain friendships and other relationships, as well as prevented others from contacting them for fear of disturbing a sleeping child. Many parents, particularly women, also noted that friendships with people who did not have children themselves tended to fall away as their contexts diverged dramatically, pointing to the intermingling of different social relationships and carework through the activities that people engage in.

Many people also identified gaps in their learning, or expressed the need to learn more, for instance, about conflict resolution with children and dealing with the competing demands of parenting amid busy, complicated lives. Both men and women commented that they would like to learn to manage their own emotions and resolve conflicts with children more effectively. Mithreal is keenly aware of the need for learning in this area because he has worked professionally in the field of conflict resolution:

> When I try to do it on my family, I don't use all the skills I have. I just forget about them in the panic of the situation, so I guess what I'm saying is that the skills that I have, that I know how to use in a professional setting, they seem to not be available in the course of trying to cook a meal, trying to resolve a conflict…. I've learned that the skill is not as easily transferable as you think.

Often, when people identified a desire to learn more in this area, they were actually highlighting the need for further support and resources; the scenarios they described were typically ones in which it seemed unlikely that people would always be able to mobilize the emotional management and conflict-resolution skills they already had. Ardea, for example, talked about her struggle to parent two young children while working full-time as a teacher. Her husband has a progressive physical disability, and she increasingly provides care for him and is required to take on aspects of household work that he previously performed. Ardea's life is extremely busy with enormous demands on her time and energy, which began to affect how she reacted to her children:

... I was getting to the point where I was so stressed that I was screaming at my children all the time. I said, "You know what? You don't like it when I do that, so how about we try to treat each other with a little bit more respect? And I will try to do that. When I don't, you have to remind me." Because it's not the way I want to raise my children ... and it's amazing—that little bit of change— how much that changed our whole outlook.

Ardea indicates here that she has found a way of handling stressful family dynamics to create a more respectful home environment; however, when asked about areas she would still like to work on, she replied "my temper," and went on to describe, with some regret, that "my children don't always get my full attention." Ardea's story is not unique. Like other women, she carries primary responsibility for the maintenance of her family's household and she is often overwhelmed. Also, like other women, she represents her situation through a largely individualizing narrative, which places the burden of responsibility for addressing problems emanating from broader social conditions back upon herself. This is a familiar narrative in Western society, and one that focuses on the demand to learn new ways of coping rather than on the need for collective forms of carework and increased resources to support people. We will now explore this issue further through an examination of what people should not have to learn through their unpaid carework.

What People Should Not Have to Learn

There is a general assumption that learning is good. And indeed, as we have seen, people learn highly valuable skills through providing care to others and themselves. However, as Pratt (2008) reminds us in her discussion of the limits to transnational mothering circumscribed by structural violence, sometimes people learn things no one should have to learn. Particularly those who are socially marginalized demonstrate that learning can be a way of coping with the normative demands of social inequality and the absence of appropriate social supports. In this sense, both the content and form of the learning accomplished through carework may at times reproduce wider social inequalities.

People learned to cope with ageism, sexism, racism, and ableism, in particular, when dealing with social institutions and programs. They learned to cope with insufficient or faulty services, unequal access to resources, and to adapt to living in poverty. Here are a few examples.

SEXISM: "THEY CONVINCED ME THAT IT WAS MY FAULT"

Sexism functions at the institutional level, as well as at the personal level. Hilda described a history of being battered. When she went to the police, they just were not interested: "The comment of the particular police officer I went to was, 'Well, I can't see any signs of the battering. Come back, you know, when you're bleeding or your arm is broken.' I mean, this is what he said!" She adds sadly: "They convinced me that it was my fault" that her husband had battered her. Fortunately, she learned through a slow process of "evolution" to value herself enough to change things.

Other, less lethal but still very life-shaping forms of sexism involve a division of labour in which the husband (and sometimes the children) expect the wife (mother) to render asymmetrical services—to function as the emotional shock absorber, to bring a beer to the husband who sits in front of the TV while she is preparing dinner, having worked at a demanding job all day long. As we were discussing this situation in a focus group, one Aboriginal woman pinpointed how deeply embedded these gender roles are: "I think it's something that's natural. We're naturals at it. It's something that was taught to us, and it's been given to us for a long time." This is a form of learning that we, the authors, think should better be unlearned.

LIVING IN POVERTY: "DO I MAKE A PHONE CALL OR DO I HAVE A CUP OF COFFEE?"

A significant portion of respondents were poor, mostly because they had experienced disabilities within their families or were recent immigrants to

Canada who had not found the type of job they had expected when they applied for immigration; sometimes they were students, or single mothers (none of these categories are mutually exclusive).

A disabled woman who was a student, a wife, and a mother said:

> It really takes a lot of energy if you have to struggle for that money. You're going to school and ... you're getting some help and you're really appreciative of that, maybe your tuition was paid or whatever. But when you get there, do I make a phone call home to see if my husband and son are killing each other, or do I have a cup of coffee? And can I get through till the end of the month? And I'll bum enough rides because I don't have money to put gas in the car.

People were "incredibly resourceful" in coping with poverty because "you have to be." In 2006, 10.5 percent of all people in Canada were poor, with women being somewhat more likely to be poor than men.[13] In a rich country like Canada, it should not be acceptable that one-tenth of the population is living in poverty. People with disabilities and single mothers are disproportionately among those who are poor.

ABLEISM: "I'VE LEARNED THAT THERE ARE NOT ENOUGH RESOURCES OUT THERE"

Many disabled people talked about the ableism they experienced in their daily lives. Narcissa, for example, described how she had to learn to teach other people how to "handle" her visual impairment so that she could remain a full and active participant in social life. Participants who were disabled or who had children or husbands with disabilities[14] were unanimous in stating that there were simply not enough resources available to help them deal with the problems they confronted. For instance, Jackie, who has a child with ADHD, describes the situation as follows:

> I've learned that there's not enough resources out there ... because

from the time you make your initial call, quite often it's six months to a year. And the wait is far too long, and there's way too many people out there that need the help.

She goes on to describe that her son was recommended to receive speech therapy, and still had not seen a therapist after a lengthy wait when we talked with her. The effects of inadequate support (and sometimes no support) are not only experienced by the child, but also by their mother. Jackie says about herself:

Myself, I was very stressed out, so I went on a medication for depression and anxiety attacks, which I've recently come off. And because I was just losing it—frustration—I would be crying because he was upsetting me so much.

This is a clear example of what Aronson (1998: 516) has identified as a problem within the carework literature that focuses upon "individual experiences of stress and burden rather than on the broader conditions that isolate them and curtail the options available to them and to those who rely on their care." In Jackie's case, this reductionist approach leads to the medicalization and individualization of a social problem. It also reflects naturalized notions of caring as necessarily located within nuclear family structures, and thus precludes the development of alternative models of carework provision.

INSUFFICIENT HEALTH CARE: "I LEARNED THAT THE HOSPITALS DON'T DO THEIR JOB"

Marie was twice widowed, with few friends. During her husband's illness, she visited him eight hours a day to look after him: "They don't feed them properly. Even when you tag your clothes, they go missing." When the laundry came up, she would grab two flannelette sheets for him rather than the regulation one since he felt cold even though she had bought him a jogging suit to keep warm. She also brought a blanket to keep him a little bit warmer, but had to watch that it did not "walk away."

Such experiences must, of course, be put into the larger context of inadequate health care funding and social policies that emphasize private responsibility for care (Luxton 2006). Neo-liberal ideology has also influenced the structure and delivery of health care, leading to an intensification of carework provision through the application of business model strategies to the public health care sector, influencing many aspects of care from policy and funding to staffing levels, assessment, and discharge of patients (Armstrong et al. 2001; Armstrong and Armstrong 2005; Bourgeault et al. 2001). The effects of this are acutely gendered because it is primarily nursing (and other health care) staff who bear the burden of this within hospitals, and women who provide unpaid carework within the private sphere as the care of patients increasingly shifts from hospitals to homes (Armstrong and Armstrong 2005).

RACISM AND DISCRIMINATION AGAINST IMMIGRANTS: "I'M LOSING MY EXPERIENCE, MY EDUCATION"

Many of the recent immigrants in our study talked about having to cope with discrimination and racism. As Dobrak, an engineer who immigrated to Canada from Slovakia, commented, the struggle to find employment in his field has had an impact on his sense of self and hopes for the future:

> I'm a little bit sad on myself because I'm losing my experience, my education.... I do not want to be a loser.... In Slovakia, I was significantly more concentrated on career.... Right now, because my career is nowhere, I'm just trying to enjoy my family.... My future is my kids. If they are going to be okay, I am okay, even if I do a dirty job.

All of our Chinese focus group participants were highly educated professionals; all of them had experienced significant downward social mobility, which required them to learn to adapt to work below their level of expertise, and to find solace in family relationships rather than their professional status. In the past 20 years, the economic situation of immigrants of colour has declined, due in part to discrimination within the paid labour force (Tran 2004).[15] While the discrimination occurred in the paid work sphere, it had noticeable effects on the household work of respondents, who had to adjust to living with fewer financial resources than they had expected, and to learn to bolster each other's egos, as well as their own, in the face of unexpected downward social mobility. This situation is mediated by gender. As we saw in Chapter 4, the household work of Chinese immigrant respondents increased after immigration, and along with it, there was an intensification of traditional gender roles.[16] This is exemplified by the cases of two women, formerly employed as professionals in China. One became a full-time housewife; the other went back to college as a student while being responsible for all the housework.

The examples we have provided here are in no way exhaustive. They do indicate, however, that sometimes people learn things that, in a just and fair society, they should not have to learn. To view *all* learning, therefore, as by definition positive neglects the social context within which it is located, and can unwittingly lead to an implicit endorsement of oppressive practices by failing to challenge the hierarchies that result in social inequalities. Implicitly, this is a way to maintain existing hierarchies (Burke and Eichler 2006). Notably, as Munaza points out, "it is not that *we* are losing, people [in Canadian society] are losing," suggesting that as a society, we need to take greater responsibility for progressive social change in these areas.

Conclusion

In this chapter, we have explored the social organization of unpaid carework and the learning that occurs both *through* this work and that is required in order to *do* this work. By expanding normative understandings of carework that emphasize relationships of dependency and the "naturalness" of women's responsibility for caring labour, we have painted a picture of carework that reflects the reciprocity and learning that shape the vast array of carework performed. As we have shown through the stories of our research participants, carework is a complex social activity that takes place across a variety of contexts and is mediated by the diverse social locations people bring to their experiences of caring labour and relationships. Rather like choreographing a dance, carework is often both demanding and enriching for the people involved, and just as the work itself engages people physically, mentally, emotionally, and spiritually, so too are the skills and knowledge required to perform it.

Carework performed for others is inextricably bound up with work on the self and not only as a form of self-care, although this represents an important and often overlooked site of carework as well. Rather, carework demands internal reflection, negotiation, and learning in order to perform one's carework responsibilities for others (Colley 2006). This suggests that there is a pedagogical dimension to carework, and that the capacity to care for others is far from natural. Rather, the social organization of unpaid carework is deeply influenced by gendered ideologies and practices, which shape the way that the unpaid provision of care is delivered and understood. It is performed disproportionately by women, devalued socially and economically despite its substantial contribution to society, perceived to be "natural" rather than skilled labour, and assumed to take place within the private sphere and nuclear family structures as opposed to running across households, paid and unpaid spheres of work, and geographical boundaries. These assumptions are reflected within Canadian social policy, which has further intensified the privatization and devaluing of unpaid carework, with particular implications for women and racialized communities through the more recent influence of neo-liberal ideology.

At the same time, dominant ways of understanding and organizing carework in Canadian society are often grounded in oppressive social relations and ideologies. Learning related to carework, then, cannot be taken as a self-evident good. As other chapters throughout this book have discussed, learning often emerges through inequitable social conditions that require individuals to develop new skills and knowledge and renegotiate meaning in their lives in order to make the conditions of social life more livable.

Recognizing this, it becomes important to reflect upon those taken-for-granted ways of doing carework such that we might imagine doing it differently. Whether through policy initiatives that recognize the value of unpaid carework and the skills and knowledge fostered through this work, the development of a national child-care program, or the communities of care model advocated among disabled communities as a way of shifting from individual to collective forms of carework provision, we hope that this chapter might encourage reflection that allows for equitable and socially responsible ways of understanding and organizing carework within Canadian society.

Portrait: Dee

I cannot afford to pay someone else to babysit my son.... It's a sac-rifice.... I cannot take care of my own son, and I'm taking good care of other people's children.

As a nanny, Dee takes care of someone else's children, while her own child is in the Philippines being looked after by her mother. Dee came to Canada after completing a university degree and a six-month caregiving course in the Philippines. She has fulfilled the mandatory two-year live-in requirement and is now awaiting her landed immigrant status, which will allow her to sponsor her husband and 18-month-old son.

When Dee tells her story, she acknowledges that she would rather be mothering her own child than the children of others. She demonstrates an understanding of the economic and global forces that have positioned her in such a way that she finds herself in the situation she is in. Dee is doing everything she can to reunite with her husband and son, and recognizes what she refers to as "the good life" that Canada can offer them as a family unit. In the meantime, Dee portrays the complexity of transnational mother-ing and states that at least by mothering other children, she feels as though she is "being active."

Dee came to Canada under the Live-in Caregiver Program. However, she was sponsored by relatives, who paid her very little. With their permission, she took on two other jobs, which included caring for children and other household work. Legally this is not supposed to happen, although in the quest for her per-manent residence status, she put up with exploitative requests for late-night babysitting and ironing. After two years of this, Dee was able to work legally as a live-out nanny and secured a job with a Canadian family with three children aged seven, six, and two. After some time with the family, Dee was fired over the phone, without notice and without any offer of severance pay. Dee acted quickly and visited the agency through which she obtained this job and then visited the Ministry of Labour. Dee now knows her rights, but in telling her story, it is obvious that this was a very stressful time for her.

Dee's story demonstrates the significant amount of learning that happens in and around her paid household work. In addition to the formal credentialed education that she has received, Dee's story tells us about the many things she learned on the job, some of which have been positive, and some have been prompted by negative situations. Examples of Dee's on-the-job learning are: time management, organizational skills, communication and conflict-resolution skills, learning to cook food from another culture, learning to discipline and play with the children in her care in a way that corresponds to dominant social models of mothering in Canada, and how to navigate various institutions to stand up for her rights. She also learned to manage her own emotions, particularly with regard to her own child's absence.

Chapter 6
THE CASE OF NANNIES:
SHIFTING UNPAID WORK ONTO PAID WORK
Nicky Hyndman

As I sit here at my desk writing this chapter, there is a cleaning woman in my house and my youngest son is at daycare. This is me outsourcing so that I can write about outsourcing. How ironic. I have said in conversation that I LOVE these women. I think, perhaps, it's more likely gratitude I feel that they are allowing me to pursue this other work that I love.

I am engaging in one type of work by letting go of another—work that I have experienced as being undervalued. I first experienced this shortly after my first child was born. I made the decision to quit my teaching job so that I could be a full-time caregiver to my son. I came to dread the question "What do you do?" My answer seemed to be an instant turn-off to whomever I was talking with when I answered that I was a stay-at-home mother. It also exposed my own ambivalence about the decisions I was making about paid and unpaid work. I quickly came to realize that our society devalues unpaid household work. A decade later, with two more children and periods of paid work combined with my unpaid household work, I am still working toward an elusive balance between the two. Under the weight of it all, I remain perplexed that we as a society can be so misguided as to devalue both paid and unpaid household work.

It is not without a significant amount of guilt that I outsource. I pass some of that unpaid work that I have experienced as undervalued on to other women, who do the work for pay. Why do I attach guilt to this? Certainly part of the reason is that I believe that although I am paying for someone to clean my home and look after my child, deep down I know that their work is undervalued, both monetarily and attitudinally. And so here I am writing about it while Ruth cleans my house and Barbara takes care of my three-year-old—a complicated way to resist something I know is not right in our society.

Nannies: An Alternative Focus

Dee's story brings to life the discussion of household work and learning. Here we have a young woman from the Philippines, a mother who has left her home, her 18-month-old child and husband, to come to Canada to work as a nanny under the Live-in Caregiver Program. This program did not allow her to bring her child and husband with her, so consequently she has had to learn to manage her emotions in order to deal with this separation and with the complexity of caring for other people's children. To qualify to work as a nanny, Dee obtained a university degree in the Philippines and did a six-month training program, yet she experiences her work here as looked-down upon—degraded. She has experienced being taken advantage of due to the live-in component of her employment. This experience has been complicated, but Dee and others do not necessarily view it as exploitation because of the complexity that caring brings to paid work. Dee's story brings up many issues that need to be considered in our consideration of household work and learning. It also prompts us to think about how the work of nannies may provide an alternative lens with which to view all household work and learning.

Thus far the discussion in this book has been focused on exposing and examining connections between learning and work in the context of *unpaid* household work. This chapter takes a somewhat different approach by examining the work and learning that occurs in one form of *paid* household work, specifically, the work and learning of nannies. Ten nannies were interviewed about their work and the learning related to household work. The nannies came from a variety of backgrounds. Five came from the Philippines, three came from the United Kingdom, and two came from the Caribbean. They ranged in age from 26 years old to 45 years old. Four were married and six of the nannies had children of their own. Of these, only two had young children who were living with them in Canada. The children of the other four nannies were living in their mothers' country of origin. The number of years of experience working as nannies varied between 18 months and 15 years. Six of the nannies came to Canada through the Live in Caregiver Program.

A focus on nannies makes it clear that working as a nanny is a site of rich learning, both formal and informal. Before moving onto specific examples of this learning, it is important to understand some of the structures of nannies' work and how this work is both different and similar to unpaid household work.

THE LIVE-IN-CAREGIVER PROGRAM

Like Dee, many nannies working in Canada are from other countries and come under the immigration program called the Live-in Caregiver Program. Over the past four decades, demand for domestic workers in Canada has developed substantially, undoubtedly coinciding with the increased numbers of women with young children entering the paid workforce (cited in Cohen 2000; Stasiulis and Bakan 1997; England and Stiel 1997). Demand for low-wage service workers, particularly domestic workers, arises partially from persisting gender inequalities in families (Nakano Glenn, Chang, and Forcey 1994). Some middle-class families are turning to racialized, working-class women, often from the "economically developing" South to fill the gap. These women are used to transform unpaid work into paid work, all the while leaving the gender division of household labour in middle-class families relatively untouched. There is essentially a buying of gender equality within these homes (Parreñas 2001) by shifting the household work onto other women.

This approach to dealing with the household work dilemma reinforces the sense that this work and division of labour is a private problem for individual households to address. It is a problem that is compounded by the lack of larger-scale, public efforts such as the creation of an affordable, comprehensive child-care system in Canada. However, Canadian governments have opted to deal with the insufficient public option for child care and numbers of Canadians willing to work as nannies by establishing a separate immigration program aimed at importing foreign domestic workers.

Foreign domestic workers have come into Canada under various immigration policies to meet the demand. A detailed history of immigration policies for domestic workers is outlined by Cohen (2000). In brief, in 1967 the Immigration Act replaced ethnic quotas with a points system. Household labour was not considered to be a significant skill under the Immigration Act, so consequently domestic workers encountered difficulties qualifying as independent immigrants despite the constant demand for their services. As a remedy to this, various Canadian governments created programs over the years to meet the demand for domestic workers. In 1992 the Live-in Caregiver Program, a special program to allow the import of needed domestic labour, was developed and is still in place today. Domestics are allowed to sponsor their children and/or spouses *only* after they receive landed immigrant status, which they are allowed to apply for after working as a live-in caregiver for two out of three consecutive years.

This program has proven to be problematic. The *Toronto Star* published a three-part investigative series in spring 2009, which effectively highlighted serious issues of abuse and exploitation, and went so far as to suggest that due to the lack of regulation regarding nanny recruitment, the program is effectively allowing exploitation and human trafficking. The Ontario Ministry of Labour has since announced that they intend to license Ontario's vast and unregulated nanny recruitment industry, ban placement fees charged to foreign caregivers, create a hotline to receive complaints of abuses, and begin "targeted enforcement" of agencies that breach labour laws (*Toronto Star*, October 15, 2009). Proposed federal changes also come in the wake of the *Star* investigations to deal with employers who hire workers under false pretenses. Any employers shown to have violated the Temporary Foreign Workers Program and the Live-in Caregiver Program will have their names and addresses posted on a government website so foreign workers will know these employers are ineligible to hire them. The problem here is that we continue, for the most part, to treat "abuses" and other "misuses" of the system as individual-level problems rather than address systemic problems and assumptions underlying these programs, including the undervaluing of this work and these workers.

UNDERSTANDING NANNIES AS PAID MOTHERS

Dominant ideas about motherhood make nannies' work and learning, even though it is paid, difficult to see. These dominant, entrenched ideas frame the paid work of nannies as a labour of love in ways similar to unpaid mothering. Conceiving of nannies' work as paid mothering and mothering as doing rather than being helps to highlight the skill and labour involved.

There is little doubt that nannies are acting as substitute mothers in the paid work that they do. In fact, the nannies in this study describe themselves as second mothers and talk about treating the children in their care as if they were their own. Miranda, from the Philippines, is a nanny to four children ages 11, eight, six, and four. She says, "They are very close to me because, well, they grow up with me.... I'm their second mother."

Miller draws a comparison between her relationship with the children she cares for as a nanny and her own children, who are now grown. She says, "The bonding that goes on with the children—they are the exact same as the bonding I had with my own children."

This was echoed by Rose, from the Philippines, who has children of her own, ages 22 and 15, who are still living in the Philippines. She cares for three children ages 10, nine, and five as a nanny. She says, "I feel that the kids I'm looking after … they are my own … so I treat them like my own as well."

Is there a difference between unpaid and paid mothering? Does the fact that it is paid make the work of mothering more visible? Conceptualizing nannies as paid mothers can lead us to understanding all mothering as *doing*, mothering as a set of skills, something that can be learned. Maher (2004) suggests that in our common/everyday thinking about and understanding of mothering, the notion of *being* rather than *doing* is predominant. She cites DiQuinzio (1999: xv), who argues that the key defining account of mothering in public discourse and in many theorized accounts is one where motherhood is an all-encompassing identity or a "state of being." Maher argues that if motherhood is a state of being, then the labour that women do and the skills they employ to mother are rendered invisible. By contrast, she says, if we describe mothering as a trade or as "doing," we foreground the skills and labour of women.

I take up this notion of nannies being paid mothers, who are "doing" and learning mothering, to highlight the skills and labour involved in nannies' work. As we know, and have clearly seen in this research, like mothering, the skills and responsibilities of nannies are devalued. For instance, Rose says, "Being a nanny is like being a garbage collector. They think we are uneducated, lazy … but this is my profession."

April gives expression to this same sense of devaluation when she says, "There's a frowning upon being a nanny. It's a feeling that you are lesser, that there is inferiority, that I should be embarrassed. There is a feeling that you are not doing enough and yet you're doing everything!"

Miranda's description of a typical day gives us an idea of what the work of a nanny looks like, the doing of paid mothering. Within the doing, and perceiving it as such, we can more readily examine the learning involved. Miranda says:

> I get there at 8 o'clock, I have to get ready with their lunch bag, their backpack, and help them to eat their breakfast because they have to leave, like, 8:30 in the morning, so I have to be in a rush

in half an hour. After they leave, then that's the time that I have to tidy up, first the kitchen because it is messy. I clean up the kitchen and at the same time I can do the laundry. I have one child that only does half-days, so I need to drop her off at 9 o'clock. I have to stop the water because I am not in the house, drop her, then go back again. I make it fast, and then I get back home, start the laundry again, and keep going. It's a lot. I do groceries and some errands and cleaning like vacuuming and bedding, so I have to budget all the work within a week. When the kids get home, somebody is cranky, somebody is hungry, you never know. I unpack all of the backpacks, give them a snack, and do some playing or helping with homework. Around 5 o'clock, it's time to start getting ready for dinner.

The description of Miranda's day is likely very familiar to anyone who has done this work without pay—a stay-at-home parent. It is demanding work that requires physical stamina and mental agility for the multi-tasking required in any given day. The nannies described scenarios in which they may be cooking dinner, helping one child with homework, and resolving a sibling spat—all at the same time.

The other nannies gave descriptions of a typical day that were very similar to Miranda's. In their descriptions, the nannies had clearly worked out a routine to their days that allowed them to fit in all of the work required of them. The number and ages of the children the nannies cared for varied and therefore dictated different schedules and requirements for the day. Nevertheless, all of the nannies described their job as including aspects of tidying and/or cleaning, laundry, cooking, and shopping. Some mentioned helping with the planning of meals and driving children to school or activities. Their days were very full with little to no downtime. Almost all reported working 10 hours a day or 50 hours a week. The long list of their daily tasks demonstrates the physical, mental, and emotional dimensions of their work.

Planning, budgeting time, and organizing their schedule are examples of the mental work present in nannies' daily work. Nannies spoke of this in terms of learning. They learned how to fit in all of their work by learning to budget their time, work efficiently, and multi-task. In order to complete their required daily work and have their day run smoothly, it was imperative that they acquire these skills. The nannies spoke of the learning as coming primarily through trial and error, and that they became better at it as they did the work. This is an example of experiential learning, which was common to all the nannies in this study.

THE BLURRING BETWEEN THE BOUNDARIES OF PAID AND UNPAID WORK

Nannies present us with a site in which there is a shifting of boundaries. Unlike almost all other paid work, the work of nannies takes place primarily in the *private* space of the home. This alone shakes up dominant ideas of work. When we think of paid work, we tend to think of it with distinct boundaries between work and not work; a clear beginning to the working day and a clear end; a physical space of work and not work. We think of being paid for work done overtime. We think of distinctions between being at work and being at home. We think of scheduled breaks through the day for lunch or coffee. For most nannies, these seemingly clear boundaries do not fit or exist, and there is much more blurring between when they are "on" and "off" work. This is particularly true for nannies living with their employers.

For example, Miller has been a nanny for 15 years. She has worked as both a live-in nanny and a live-out nanny. She is currently caring for three children. Miller has learned over the years of being a nanny that this work is demanding and that it is not structured the way that most other paid work is structured; there are no defined coffee breaks and lunch breaks, and often daily work hours are stretched. She says, "The thing about a nanny is you don't get a specific allocated lunch break. And you find that you can start a 10-hour day and your 10-hour day goes non-stop."

Jade has worked for eight years as a nanny and is currently caring for two children ages seven and nine. She too speaks of the long hours and days that often go into overtime, for which she is not compensated. Jade says, "On a good week I work 50 hours. I'm supposed to be off at 6 p.m., but often my employers are not home until 6:30 or 6:45. Sometimes I get paid overtime and sometimes I don't. It's the one thing I really dislike about the job and that is the inconsistency in our work."

These quotes are examples of the blurring between paid and unpaid work and how the private nature and the structure of the Live-in Caregiver Program creates a situation where nannies may be taken advantage of, as we also saw in Dee's case. Time and space are not their own, particularly in the case where a nanny is living with the employer.

Nannies perform carework in a private setting, similar to mothering, but are paid for it. Paid and unpaid work becomes blurred for many live-in nannies and this is often exacerbated by the care component of their work. Aronson (1996) examines exploitation of home-care workers, and much of what she discusses and describes can be said for the work of nannies as well. She describes highly personalized caring labour that often goes beyond its formal, paid boundaries into informal, unpaid activities. She argues that this can come to represent uncompensated and exploited labour (Aronson 1996). Because this work is undertaken in the privacy and informality of care recipients' homes, the labour is less open to observation and regulation. We see the similarity to the work of nannies, particularly because they are also often emotionally connected to the people they care for. Lucy, for instance, describes a strong connection toward the children she is caring for: "I just love the children. I just look at each kid and treat them as I would my own."

This particular positioning of labour in the privacy and informality of homes makes the separation of practical and emotional labour and the distinction between formality and informality especially ambiguous and problematic. The overlap of paid and unpaid work draws upon, and sometimes exploits, the love or care that nannies develop with the children, and is perhaps exaggerated also by being made to feel like they are part of the family. Several of the nannies spoke of evenings when they were technically off work, and the children would come into their rooms for a visit, or there were times when they might be invited along for a family weekend away and left to babysit the children. The boundary between paid work and love or connection to a family becomes blurred. As Dee says, "So many times they treat us like part of the family. It's not just work. That's the hard thing about being a nanny. I mean even though the employer is treating you tough and rough, … once you get attached to the children, that's the hard part, you know."

Miranda similarly states: "The most important thing there, too, is not that you're a nanny, [but] … that you are part of the family."

Some of the nannies did experience situations where they felt they were being taken advantage of, or where they had to defend their rights vis-à-vis their employers. They spoke of the difficulty in drawing a clear line between "work" and care provided because of an emotional bond given the connection that they developed with the children they were caring for. Many also expressed a feeling of "being part of the family," which also complicated and blurred the lines of work and personal relations. Navigating this is something that the nannies needed to learn.

Learning

Nannies present an interesting site when looking at household work and learning because in their case, we see elements of both formal and informal learning. The most obvious learning is the formal learning required to qualify for the Live-in Caregiver Program. As is usual with formal learning, it has clear objectives and outcomes, is credentialed, and takes place in an educational institution.

In addition to this formal learning requirement, we found that there is significant learning that occurs on the job. This learning is informal, on-the-job training that is not credentialed and does not take place in an institutional setting, yet it is learning that is required of the nannies if they want to keep their jobs.

FORMAL EDUCATION OF NANNIES

A detailed description of the formal education requirements for acceptance into the Live-in Caregiver Program is evidence that a particular level of education is demanded. To qualify for the Live-in Caregiver Program, applicants must obtain the equivalent of successful completion of secondary school in Canada; successful completion of six months of full-time caregiver training in a classroom setting; and the ability to speak, read, and understand English or French at a level sufficient to communicate effectively in an unsupervised setting.

An outline of the six-month Caregiver Course, as described by the Philippine government organization TESDA (Technical Education and Skills Development Authority) is as follows:

The Caregiver Course covers several topics that will provide the trainees the opportunity to learn and experience the various skills and working knowledge vital in the performance of a job of a caregiver. The course modules specifically for Canada generally focus on the following:

- Overview of Live-in Caregiver Program of Canada
- Introduction to the Live-in Caregiver Skills Enhancement Program
- Basic first aid
- Basic life support
- CPR
- Home and client safety management
- Home management and client care
- Nutrition and food preparation
- Care of the child
- Care of the elderly
- Canada: People, culture, traits
- English as a second language
- Personality development
- On-the-job training in caregiving institutions

Here is clearly a paradox: in spite of these requirements, the Live-in Caregiver Program policy states specifically that this is classified as *unskilled work*. How is this possible? I suggest that, as discussed above, nannies constitute a version of paid mothers, and that this explains the discrepancy between the actual formal requirements of the job and the general perception that this is unskilled work.

INFORMAL LEARNING ON THE JOB

As we have seen, there is a considerable amount of formal training required of nannies in order to be admitted to Canada. In addition, we found a large amount of informal learning that took place on the job once they had arrived, and that was structured by their working conditions.

The informal learning that nannies do is much harder to see, describe, and quantify, just like the informal learning that takes place in the unpaid household work, which has been described in the preceding chapters; the difference between the informal learning that nannies do and what has been presented in other chapters is that the nannies' learning is part of on-the-job training.

One type of on-the-job learning that I have already discussed is in the description of the nannies' day: learning to be organized, to schedule and budget time, and to multi-task. These skills are usually learned experientially, as the nannies told us. Another major area of learning is around cooking and food-related work.

LEARNING ABOUT FOOD AND COOKING

Food is such a necessary and constant component in our lives. However, how often do we step back and think about the work and learning we are doing regarding food? In my own household work, I sometimes joke that my day would be so much easier if only we didn't need to eat! And yet, I fully appreciate the nourishment and pleasure that food brings and the social aspect of sitting down to a meal together.

When the nannies were asked whether they had to learn anything new when they started working as a nanny, the most spontaneous references were made to the work regarding food. Some referred to needing to learn how to cook recipes that were culturally different, or to cook something from scratch. Others reported being asked to plan meals for the week as well as prepare them. Miller comments about her learning about food: "I think one of the biggest things is just initially the actual doing it itself. No one says, 'Sit down and we'll show you how to make spaghetti Bolognese.' And for the kids, balancing out the kinds of foods, so making sure they get enough fruits and vegetables [and] not taking the easy way out with the fast snacking stuff."

Marianna comments on learning about food from a different culture: "I needed to learn different recipes. The family I work for is Jewish and their Friday meal is important to them. They invite friends and have a very formal dinner. I learned through my employer and also through cookbooks."

April also talks about needing to adjust her previous way of cooking: "In my West Indian culture, it [the cooking] was totally different, so there are things you have to readjust, tone it down. You have to get a feel for what people like and what they don't. Now I have a basic knowledge of Canadian foods."

The above quotes reflect the significant amount of work and learning that happens regarding food. Chapter 4 gives us good insights on understanding the dimensions of work involved when we consider food. I, too, draw on DeVault (1991) to show that while there is the obvious physical dimension of food work, which includes the preparation, cooking, and cleaning associated with a meal, there is also the mental dimension of food work, which includes planning and organizing a meal. As well, there is the emotional dimension of food work, which may involve the social negotiations of having a meal together, and there is the spiritual dimension of food work, which may represent the comfort and ritual that food often brings.

There is also learning that coincides with each of these dimensions of food work. The nannies speak of learning to cook from scratch and to plan meals. Jade, for instance, relates: "My employer expects me to cook everything from scratch, and I've never done that before. I'm getting better at it as I go. I have a calendar each week with what I'm going to make each day, so I look through recipe books and everything so I can buy the right food and make it up."

In the above example we see Jade learning to physically do the work, learning to mentally plan the tasks before her, and learning to emotionally deal with her employer's expectation. Miller learned to provide balanced meals. Marianna and April needed to learn about preparing food from a culture other than their own. This represents significant learning along many different dimensions—physical, mental, and emotional.

Nannies reported learning about food in various ways. Sometimes they learned by doing, sometimes they were taught directly by their employer, sometimes they learned through cookbooks and magazines, and sometimes through sharing with other nannies. While they may come to enjoy some of this food-related learning, it is also required by their employment. Much of the learning they do is therefore not simply self-initiated learning, done for fun or out of personal interest. They are learning informally, out of necessity, and as part of a job requirement.

Learning elements of mothering: Patience, discipline, and play

An interesting theme that arose in the discussions about care was learning patience. Learning patience came up in the interviews in response to the question we asked about advice that nannies would give to others who were considering becoming a nanny. Rose said, "I think that being a nanny with three kids, you have to be more patient. I have to learn to be more patient." Jade similarly stated: "I'm more patient with the kids that I work for during the day than I am when I'm meeting with my own family."

Patience is something that we do not often think of as a skill to be learned. Instead, it is often considered to be part of one's personality, or emotional makeup, and stereotypically, it is a trait more often "naturally" attributed to women. The concept of learning emotion, specifically patience, as an important caring skill is captured well by Colley (2006). Comparing theorizations of emotional capital and emotional labour, Colley suggests we need social rather than individualized understandings of how feelings are put to work. The concept of emotional labour helps us to understand how this work is learned and performed (Hochschild 1983).

Dee speaks about her patience being tested by children who do not respect her authority, and how she has learned to manage this better. Her advice to someone considering becoming a nanny is simple: "They would need lots and lots of patience." When the nannies talk about needing to be patient and learning patience, they remind us of the emotional work being done, and that within this work there is learning. Their words of advice about *learning* patience to anyone thinking of becoming a nanny also challenge the seemingly "natural" nature of emotional work.

Another major part of their emotion work that required learning and that did not simply "come naturally" had to do with disciplining children. The most common disciplinary tool among the nannies was the time-out and counting method. The time-out method of discipline removes the child from the situation temporarily and the counting method gives the child a certain amount of time to stop what he or she is doing. For example, "Stop jumping on the bed, Jonny. I'm going to count to five and if you haven't stopped by then, you are going to your room for a time out." Both of these disciplinary tools represent the most currently socially accepted forms of discipline in middle-class Canadian mothering. Dee learned that spanking was not socially acceptable in Canada, and learned from her employer and other nannies about counting and time outs as an alternative disciplinary tool. Rose gave examples of learning to give verbal warnings and if those were ignored, she then gave time outs or used grounding. Again, we see here that nannies had to (informally) learn to manage their own emotions and the behaviour and emotions of the children for whom they had responsibility.

Nannies talked about learning and engaging in play that had educational value. This also represents an element of a particular way of mothering. When asked how she plays with the children in her care, Lucy's comments show the educative element of play that many of the other nannies also spoke of: "We do a lot of arts and crafts. I'm currently teaching the four-year-old to read, write, and do phonics—she loves it. I do a lot of reading with the children too. We go to the park, they have classes, and we have play dates."

These nannies were quite consistent in the way they discussed how they played with the children in their care. When talking about getting together with another child and caregiver, they used the term "play date." Learning this language and practice was another clear example of the informal learning that nannies did, and again demonstrated the physical (the doing), emotional (the managing of their own and the children's feelings), and mental (the planning) dimensions of their work and learning.

That Dee had to *learn* that spanking was not an acceptable method of discipline is evidence that aspects of mothering are learned and not "innate" or "natural." That the nannies all spoke with the same language and described the same educative play with the children in their care is also evidence that this is *learned* and not "natural."

Learning patience, learning discipline, and learning play are examples of nannies learning a particular way of mothering. Nannies all used similar language and reported playing with and disciplining the children under their care in very similar ways. This leads me to believe that they were learning the dominant social norms of mothering through informal on-the-job training and formal learning. I would also suggest that nannies are learning the dominant social norms of middle-class mothering.

The social norms of mothering and what childhood represents at any given moment in history are subject to change, and norms differ from one cultural context to another. There has been much written about the social construction of motherhood (Chodorow 1978; DiQuinzio 1999; Hays 1996; Abbey and O'Reilly 1998; Ruddick 1989). Bringing this back to the nannies, it makes sense that nannies are learning and conforming to the ways of mothering that their employers demand. This changing and learning imply that what we perceive to be "natural," innate traits of mothering are, in fact, skill-laden social constructs and not "natural" or inevitable to women.

What Does a Focus on Nannies' Learning Add?

The focus on the learning within and surrounding the work that nannies do is what this chapter adds to the discussion about nannies in general, to the discussion of lifelong learning, and to discussions of motherhood and feminism. The most important contributions that a focus on nannies' learning brings are the following: a broadening of lifelong learning theory to include the private sphere and household work as a significant space and source of learning; a denaturalization of the work involved in mothering, both paid and unpaid; a challenge to the classification of paid household work as unskilled; and finally an additional voice in the demand that household work be revalued.

ADDING TO LIFELONG LEARNING THEORY

As we saw in Chapter 2, lifelong learning literature ignores unpaid household work almost completely. Extending this, it is fair to say that lifelong learning literature also ignores paid household work. Like Gouthro (2005) and Livingstone (2001), I believe that the home is an important site of learning. The examination of the work and consequent learning that nannies do shows this to be true. What is interesting, and what adds to the lifelong learning literature, is that nannies are learning in the private space of the home, but for employment reasons. Beyond the formal training that qualifies them for their jobs, there is a lot of informal learning, some of it self-initiated, some employer-initiated, some acquired individually (e.g., by studying cookbooks), and some acquired socially (e.g., through exchange of information with other nannies).

It is important to include learning through household work as a central aspect of lifelong learning. This allows us to approach the premise of understanding learning as life-wide and lifelong. Nannies offer a site to more readily see that which is often rendered invisible in household work and learning.

DENATURALIZING CARING WORK

Within the ideology of motherhood, there is an essentialist assumption that women are naturally predisposed to be mothers. As Courtenay-Hall (1998) explains, the myth of the "natural" mother involves the representation of mothering as "natural" to women, essential to their being, an engagement of love and instinct that is utterly distant from the world of paid work and formal education. According to this view, we do not learn to mother, we *become* mothers. And yet, in our interviews we discovered that the nannies were learning in significant ways about how to mother in accordance with the dominant social norms regarding Canadian, middle-class mothering.

Continuing with the idea of nannies as paid mothers, a focus on learning within and around the work of nannies denaturalizes their work and motherwork in particular. This is very important in exposing the work as work. It allows for a critique and challenge to the notion of a "labour of love," which, as we have seen in Chapter 5, make invisible and devalues caring work. When this happens, in the case of nannies, it has the potential to result in exploitation, lack of compensation, a diminished sense of self-worth, and unfair government policies.

CHALLENGING POLICY

Unpaid caring work assumed by women is seen as women's "natural" and unremarkable activity in the private domestic sphere. Unfortunately, when this work is paid, its imagery as just an extension of ordinary domestic labour means that it is accorded little value or status and is seen as fairly unskilled. We know that this is the assumption made by the Canadian government as evidenced in the Live-in Caregiver Program.

This policy is problematic on many fronts. The structure of the program prevents women's skills as caregivers from being recognized as "real" skills that would make them eligible to apply for immigration as independent immigrants through the points system. It also prevents them from immigrating with their husbands and children. The required live-in component further structures nannies' employment in a way that exposes them to exploitation. The two-year continuous employment rule keeps them vulnerable (fearing job loss) to the whims and demands of employers. The focus on nannies' learning challenges the basis for the existence of this separate immigration program by showing that the work of nannies is not unskilled.

WHAT SHOULD NOT HAVE BEEN LEARNED

Nannies have learned some things they should not have had to learn because of a negative situation brought on primarily because of how the Live-in Caregiver Program policy is structured.

"I have learned my rights"

Among the nannies there was a recognition of their vulnerability. This was at times unspoken and, at other times, referred to obliquely. They did not speak directly about feeling vulnerable, but there were many comments made about being "lucky" to be with a good family. Many of the nannies mentioned having friends or acquaintances who were not so lucky and found themselves in difficult situations, situations that exploited their labour and rights.

Marianna says, "Yeah, because I got, I'm lucky also because they're [a] nice family.… Some of my friends, they try to break with another family because … they cannot … their employers are not easy to work with."

April tells us:

> I've been pretty lucky with the people you get to sponsor you and work with. But there are lots of dark sides to it, which I think the government doesn't … I think they are aware of it, but they don't go deeper … 'cause what it is basically is cheap labour, but they don't tell you that. And then with the cheap labour comes a lot of abuses, which I know personally because I've encountered a lot of people who've gone through it.

April goes on to discuss what she sees as a problem with the Live-in Caregiver Program: "There's another dark aspect, where you have to live in for two years before you qualify for residence, which I think they should definitely do a review of because some people endure abuses just because they want to stay. It's all these things that I discover along the way! So, if you don't know your rights, or if you're not able to speak up for yourself, then you're toasted."

Miller, after being asked to work long hours and doing cleaning that she felt was unreasonable, ended up inquiring and learning about labour laws: "I called up Immigration and I spoke to them, and they gave me this pamphlet, and everything is clearly written, so you know."

A non-profit community-based organization called INTERCEDE has a mandate to educate domestic workers about their rights (among other services). None of our participants directly cited INTERCEDE. However, it is an example of an organization that provides support to nannies through learning opportunities.

"I learned how to deal with separation of my own family"

Dee speaks about learning to deal with being separated from her child. She says, "I could not afford to pay someone else to babysit my son. It's a sacrifice.… You cannot take care of your own son, and you're taking good care of other people's children." The frustration that she feels is evident in her use of the word "sacrifice." As a way to cope with this situation, she has learned to manage her emotions. When asked why she has chosen to work as a nanny, she gives an answer that is quite complex. She talks about missing her own son, but that this work allows her to still be a mother: "… dealing with kids is just like being a mother.… It makes you feel more active."

The challenges and the social ramifications of transnational mothering have been written about extensively elsewhere. Parreñas (2001) documents the creation of a division of reproductive labour in the global economy. She describes the formation of a three-tier transfer of reproductive labour. One group of women in Canada transfer care of their children to another group of women (nannies), many of whom have left children in their home countries to be taken care of by yet another group of women. As Dee's situation shows us, this transfer of reproductive labour is one with negative consequences for some groups of women.

ADDING A VOICE IN CALLING FOR A REVALUATION OF HOUSEHOLD WORK

A focus on nannies brings different aspects of household work and learning into view. Examining both paid and unpaid household work as work, and understanding that within this work there is much learning, encourages a reassessment of what is valuable and transferable in household work. The case of nannies tells us that adding a small price tag to household work does not make it more valued because it remains largely invisible, hidden in private homes, underscoring the "naturalness" that is too often linked to motherhood. By unveiling the informal learning that happens on a daily basis in the lives of nannies, which happens on top of the required formal learning, we aimed to magnify and bring to light the scope of the work and learning.

Viewing household work as being much more than physical work is of utmost importance, as we have all been arguing throughout this book. The inclusion of the mental and emotional components of paid household work allows the complexity of the work to be seen and consequently allows us to better recognize and understand the learning that goes along with the work. Nannies' paid household work more readily enables us to see unpaid household work as work and the learning of dominant methods of mothering makes it possible for us to see that there are definable skills in mothering, whether paid or unpaid.

Conclusion

Women continue to shoulder most of the domestic labour associated with caring for children and running a household. Household labour, both paid and unpaid, is an area of women's gendered lives that poses challenges for theorists, policy-makers, and courts alike, and the need to address it properly is vital in promoting equality for all women. Household work for pay in our society remains highly gendered, poorly paid, and often precarious.

The struggle for recognition of women's household work has been part of the feminist discourse for many years now, but household work is still largely invisible and thus unrecognized in many ways. The combination of economics and ideology has led us to a point in which household work, whether paid or unpaid, is devalued in both monetary terms and attitudinally. This chapter adds a voice to what Doucet (2006: 207) describes as "a chorus of generations of women who have argued for the valuing of unpaid work (Crittenden 2001; Luxton 1997; Luxton and Vosko 1998; Waring 1998)."

As more (White, middle-class) women participate in the paid workforce, there is a shifting of household work onto other women, what we can refer to as an outsourcing of household work or a buying of equality. When this is done along lines of race and class and involves the shifting of devalued work, it is obvious that this is problematic. When devalued household work is transferred from women who do it without pay to women who do it for pay, little is done to challenge existing gender hierarchies. We are effectively shifting the invisibility of unpaid household work onto paid work. There is discomfort among some in the racialization of outsourced domestic work. Pratt (2004) helps to identify this discomfort: "The figure of the racialized domestic worker forces white middle-class feminists to face their privilege and think concretely about the difficulties of feminist alliance, especially because their gains in gender equity in the labour market often rest on the availability of low-waged domestic labour" (Pratt 2004: 3).

Lan (2003) suggests that we need new ways of conceptualizing domestic work that transcend constructed oppositions. She offers a helpful way to examine paid and unpaid household work by viewing them not as dichotomous categories but as structural continuities across the public and private spheres. She argues that to separate unpaid and paid household work blinds us to women's multiple roles and fluid trajectories and ignores their articulation and embeddedness.

Nannies have presented an interesting case to examine concepts of work, private/public, labour and love, and value/devaluation. Making the work/learning connection is a new approach to an old problem. It has the potential to not only make the invisible visible, but also to address policy in various ways that can revalue this devalued work.

CONCLUSIONS
Patrizia Albanese

Introduction

We began this book with an old Hindu tale about an elephant's invisibility and partial understanding. Our intention was to show that so much of what we *think* we know about some large and seemingly mundane aspects of the world around us are only partial understandings until we see the thing in more of its entirety. While we do not profess to have surveyed the entire elephant, we believe we have taken a step closer to a different, broader, and more comprehensive understanding of household work and learning, their inseparability, and their social worth. At the very least, we believe we have uncloaked a few more parts of the elephant, paving the way for others to continue to expand and broaden our understanding of the nature of this work and learning.

In Canada, as in many other capitalist, industrialized nations, we tend to (over)value "things." These are often things purchased with money acquired from the paid work that in most cases follows formal training and education. At the same time, these societies continue to undervalue and devalue the unpaid (re)production of life—household work—that takes place on a daily basis within and across households, and which involves a considerable amount of informal learning. Despite some changes, this work continues to be treated as women's work and remains hidden within private households. The mostly informal learning associated with it is almost always unrecognized, and the skills learned and needed to maintain life are underestimated.

Rarely do we as a society think of household work as anything more than necessary toil, or as unskilled work, easily done by anyone. But in this book, we set out to make visible some of its invisible dimensions by challenging some of the taken-for-granted assumptions about what this work entails, and where and how it is performed. In doing this, we sought to denaturalize entrenched or fixed ideas about household work by showing that it involves and requires a considerable amount of learning. When this learning is revealed, we are able to see that household work is not "natural" for women, and that it should not be inevitable that women must be the chief custodians of household labour. By uncloaking more of the work and learning in household work, we take our place among those who seek to reclaim the notion of lifelong learning, to make it truly lifelong and life-wide in scope.

This chapter presents an overview of a number of the findings and arguments discussed throughout this book. We documented some of household work's devaluation and importance by looking at household work and learning through the perspective of recent immigrants, people who have experienced other significant life changes, people who have a disability, and those who do carework with and without pay. Through these different lenses (disability, immigration, unpaid and paid carework) we were better able to highlight some of the learning in household work.

We suggest a new definition and approach to understanding household work through our unique dual focus on household work and learning. Without wishing to glorify household work, we hope that by making the learning related to it visible, we make the work and its value visible as well. This chapter ends with a section on the project's policy implications and suggestions for future research.

Another Way of Thinking about Work

We rarely think of global economic restructuring (globalization) and household work in the same sentence, but in fact they go hand in hand. Over the past few decades, women, particularly those with young children, have been entering the paid labour force in large numbers. At the same time, expectations about household work have changed very little. People still need to eat, homes need to be cleaned, clothes need to be washed, tears need to be wiped, schedules and appointments need to be managed, and care and advice still need to be doled out—and society still mostly expects women to do this work. But household work *has* changed: people live longer, but not necessarily healthier; we spend more hours doing paid work; governments make cuts to social services, families find themselves dispersed across national borders; and there are different and increased expectations about how we parent and care, for whom, and for how long. With some of these changes we are forced to do more planning, managing, and juggling within and across households, and as we do so, we (re)learn.

Throughout this book, we argue and show that household work is an important and valuable part of social reproduction—the daily production and maintenance of a population—that entwines with and supports all other aspects of life, including paid work. Recognizing household work as *work* necessitates not only a revision of operational definitions for statistical and analytical purposes, but also a redefinition, or at least a more profound look at what makes any work "work." In Chapter 1, Eichler unpacked various traditional and academic uses of the term "work," and showed how people who perform household work tend to reinforce these in their own understanding of household work.

Interestingly, for some participants in this study, the simple fact that it is not paid made household work non-work. Nevertheless, with probing, most began to recognize the large amount of work involved in household work. They also recognized that much of this work involves more than a physical dimension. We found, both expectedly and unexpectedly (in the case of the spiritual dimension), that unpaid household work, like paid work, involves physical, emotional, mental, and spiritual dimensions for the people performing it. This also showed that, contrary to the common rhetoric surrounding household work, it is work, and it is *not* simple, strictly private, and "natural." Our study participants clearly helped expose household work as multi-dimensional, complex, skilled, and socially valuable.

After our study participants' experiences revealed that household work is often multi-faceted, and involves a plurality of dimensions, we redefined household work as the sum of all physical, mental, emotional, and spiritual tasks that are performed for one's own or someone else's household and that maintain the daily life of those for whom one has responsibility. By broadening its definition, we believe we have made household work, including carework, more recognizable and visible.

This work needs to be recognized as a precondition to having it more equitably redistributed on a broader social level and within households, particularly as it applies to men. After all, as we have seen throughout this book, much of this work continues to be treated as women's private or individual responsibility. It also needs to be visible in order for it to be valued.

We challenged the devaluation of household work by showing that much learning takes place around this complex, frustrating, exhausting, and, at times, rewarding work. We believe that having done this, there is no justification in the future to ignore it as a site of learning. In showing that it changes over time and throughout the life course, with changing social and economic circumstances, we also saw that people have to learn, relearn, and unlearn as necessary to meet new challenges and demands. This was clearly the case for individuals who acquired a disability, as we saw in Chapter 3, and recent Chinese immigrants, in Chapter 4. Change is also the only constant in carework, whether unpaid or paid (chapters 5 and 6).

Another Way of Thinking about Learning

In changing global economies more emphasis has been placed on the importance of learning for life. In fact, much of this has actually been interpreted as a need for formal education and retraining in adulthood as a response to job losses, economic shifts, and changing economic and social circumstances. Lifelong learning as a term, for the most part, has been used by governments and policy-makers here and abroad to refer to lifelong education and formal skills (re)training to fill specific economic needs.

We found that regardless of which mainstream account of lifelong learning we encountered, as we saw in Chapter 2, most of the approaches focus on the educator, not the learner; deal with paid work, not unpaid work; and deal with formal or non-formal education created or fostered by the state, not self-initiated, informal learning.[1] In this book, we took a different approach to learning. We approached it from the experiences of the learner, through and for unpaid work, as self-initiated and usually informal, and as arising through opportunities and circumstances in people's everyday lives.

By taking the notion of lifelong learning, which we believe has been used mostly in restricted ways, and applying it to a large-scale study of household work, we sought to *widen* the site of learning to include everyday life and households, and *lengthen* it to include the entire life cycle, between and beyond paid work. We wanted to reclaim the concept of lifelong learning and show that it could and should be seen as lifelong and life-wide. We believe this came through in each of the chapters in this book.

We learned that people needed to learn *how* to do household work and how to do it *differently* with changing life circumstances. At times, as we saw in the case of some Chinese immigrants, nannies, people with disabilities, and some unpaid caregivers, people learned new roles or readjusted their roles as they engaged in household work. Interestingly, we saw that while it was obligatory that nannies engaged in both formal and informal learning to be able to do carework for (relatively low) pay, as a society, for the most part, we continue to deny that any learning takes place or is required when caregivers in general, and especially mothers, do the same work and are not paid. We showed that carework involves learning whether it is done for the self or for others, and whether it is paid or unpaid.

This book confirmed that despite some individuals' initial difficulties in identifying the learning involved in their household work, with probing, almost all came to identify some. People learned to do, undo, and redo many household-related skills, consciously and unconsciously, on a daily basis. Some learned to cook differently, as we saw in the case of Chinese immigrants and nannies. While they were forced to (re)learn the same activity—cooking—recent immigrants and nannies did so under very different circumstances and to fulfill very different needs. At the same time, both recent immigrants and nannies, through a great deal of learning, changed *what* they cooked and for *whom*, and *how* they budgeted, shopped for, and prepared food. They did it in new places, in new ways, and under new, sometimes strained circumstances.

On top of more obvious skills like cooking, many of our study participants, throughout the course of their household work, noted that they learned to multi-task, budget time and money, and manage complex relationships. They learned patience, time management, self-care, conflict resolution, how to work with and for younger and older family members, friends and neighbours, how to interface with government agencies, and how to access resources and organizations. Some learned about their rights, often denied to them, and the rights of those they cared for.

Having said that, while so much of what was learned was positive, we found that there were many cases where people learned things they should not have had to learn. We saw, in all contexts—in the case of nannies, unpaid caregivers, recent Chinese immigrants, people with disabilities, older people, and those who were sick or caring for sick family members or friends—that people should not have to learn to adjust to poverty, loss of status, and a diminishing or precarious standard of living. Individuals should also not have to learn to deal with a sense of worthlessness and/or isolation because they cannot find or do not participate in paid work. Many who performed household work as their primary responsibility should not have to apologize for "not working" when some of the household work that they do may, in fact, be both socially and publicly useful. While we argue that all household work *is* work, and the learning associated with it is important and valuable, some of this work, like the care of an ailing and aging parent or neighbour, is clearly socially and publicly useful and should be recognized as such. Gaining this recognition should not, however, preclude women from being or becoming financially independent, which often requires, among other things, access to publicly funded (affordable), high-quality child, adult, and/or elder care.

Pulling It Together

Throughout this book we have seen that household work is complex and demanding, involving physical, mental, emotional, and spiritual effort, and it is part of what provides meaning for life, at least for some people or under some circumstances. At the same time, we are not trying to glorify household work as it is often forced onto individuals due to lack of other social supports. Rather, we have shown that it is valuable work, it is more than it seems, and it involves a considerable amount of learning.

We found that the typical assumptions evident in most of the household literature are limiting and problematic, and do not allow us to see large parts of our elephant. Since household work has been conceptualized, measured, and understood largely as a static set of repetitive and low-level tasks performed within one household by wives and some husbands, it has not been seen and understood as complex, difficult, demanding, and requiring significant learning. Traditional approaches to defining and measuring it have not reflected its breadth, dynamic nature, the locations in which it takes place (across households), the complex relationships it often involves, its personal and individual nature (self-care), and the learning it requires.

We believe our approach and new definition are steps toward a broader and more comprehensive understanding of household work and life-long learning. We hope that others will build upon this, and expand our understanding further to include more on children, the work of resident and non-resident adults (adult children living with their parents, for instance), and individuals involved in other types of paid and unpaid help. We also hope that our approach can lead to some social change, no matter how small. To take some steps toward this, we have identified some policy implications that arise from this research. No doubt many others exist.

General Policy Implications and Recommendations

Boychuk (2004) suggests that there are four sources of well-being for citizens: (1) market income; (2) non-market care and support within the family; (3) state-sponsored services and income transfers; and (4) community services and supports.[2] If we accept these, then equitable policy and practice can emerge only from a framework informed by a better and more complex understanding of household work and the learning that goes along with it. This helps us recontextualize women's and some men's experience as workers and learners in ways that recognize both the increasing commonalities of women's efforts to mediate their productive and reproductive work, and the constraints imposed by variables that include race, immigration status, age, income, (dis)ability, and gender on individual and household decision making.

SOCIAL RESTRUCTURING

We believe there are some obvious policy implications emerging from this project, particularly in light of recent cuts and announcements of further cuts, to social services—hallmarks of a neo-liberal agenda that impacts on public policy in this country. The findings from this project conceivably lead to calls for programs and approaches that restructure social relations of production and reduce the economic inequality that has been consistently growing over the last few decades in Canada. To begin with, we must stop accepting the state's downloading of social services onto the backs of its citizens. We should begin to envision and/or revive and emulate societies that provide more social supports to individuals, families, and communities, so that the burden of household work, in its broadest sense, is more equally distributed between private individuals and public organizations.

Toward this end, we might include such things as a resuscitated health care system that supports and maintains the physical, emotional, and mental well-being of its citizens. As it stands, Skinner (2008) notes that there is considerable doubt within the public service restructuring literature about whether the voluntary sector and private individuals and households should or even could bear an increasing share of responsibilities for the direct delivery of health and social care. Increasingly many have argued that we can cut the need and cost of health care services while still improving health outcomes by reducing social inequalities. The World Health Organization's Commission on the Social Determinants of Health (2008) notes that generous family policies that provide social protection across the life course result in better population health. They add that a number of things can be done toward this goal, including that states "ensure that social protection systems include those normally excluded: those in precarious work, including informal work and household or care work" (Commission on the Social Determinants of Health 2008: 7). At the same time, elder care, and care and support for those with disabilities should be enhanced to include programs and services that promote dignity; inclusion; and access to people, places, and paid work, where desired.

We should also adequately fund high-quality, universal early learning and child-care programs that recognize and value the work of paid child-care providers. In this area, Canada, excluding Quebec, has been characterized as an international laggard (Boychuk 2004; Organisation for Economic Co-operation and Development 2006). The Organisation for Economic Co-operation and Development (OECD) recently published *Starting Strong II* (2006), a report comparing early childhood education and care (ECEC) across economically "advanced" nations. The report notes that there is a growing need for non-parental care across nations, and it is increasingly seen as a public good. Most striking in the report was that of the 14 countries compared, Canada ranked the lowest (even below the

US) in public expenditure on ECEC services as a percent of gross domestic product (Organisation for Economic Co-operation and Development 2006). There is mounting recognition that improvements in the provision of high-quality, affordable child care serve a variety of goals, including improving child outcomes and promoting gender equality. Both of these are achieved through improving women's opportunities to pursue education and paid work, and fostering more egalitarian household division of labour (Canadian Policy Research Networks 2002). These and many other social programs, including those that foster community building, would go a long way toward producing healthy and more productive individuals (including paid workers), families, and communities.

DOING OUR FAIR SHARE

We seek social change that leads to a more equitable division of household labour. To begin with, more social emphasis needs to be placed on men doing their fair share. While a necessary first step, we need to move beyond individual men and women privately renegotiating their workloads. A more equitable division of labour needs to be supported by social structures like those named above (affordable, high-quality child care; accessible and universal health care, elder care, and adult care), which would be funded through a taxation system that draws revenue from improved basic wages and access to decently paid, stable jobs. We believe that an environmentally sustainable and improved quality of life will inevitably lead to substantial improvements for all workers and learners, paid and unpaid.

RECOGNIZING THE WORK AND LEARNING

All Canadians should be allowed to enjoy a minimum standard of living. Combining a wide range of income-support measures into a single basic income program offers an efficient and just means to recognize the social and economic contribution made by every individual through his or her unpaid and paid work (see Wax 2009; Malul, Gal, and Greenstein 2009).

Alstott (2004) has recently suggested that governments earmark special benefits for individuals who care for dependants—most commonly their minor children. However, in light of recent demographic and social trends (including fewer people living in nuclear family arrangements; rising childlessness; a delayed child launch and "boomeranging" adult children; a rising number making up the sandwich generation; increased longevity, etc.), and an ongoing commitment to family diversity, some recommend that we not simply extend eligibility for such assistance to a broader array of arrangements, encompassing many combinations of caretakers and dependants, but rather promote an alternative—a guaranteed basic income for all (Wax 2009). Given our broader definition of household work, and the recognition that household work takes place across households and social arrangements, a guaranteed basic income would prevent states from selectively rewarding social relationships they deem "fit" and appropriate to the detriment of all others. We believe that our expanded definition of household work and many of our key findings warrant further discussion of the possibility of a single basic income program, as well as wages for those who care for others who cannot care for themselves.

Overall, our broader and more inclusive definition of household work that recognizes the mental, emotional, physical, and spiritual dimensions of this work and its learning should lead to a better understanding, measuring, and valuation of household work on the part of individuals and states. This new recognition and valuation would also contribute to a more equitable division of labour by substantially increasing the recognition of the volume and value of this work and learning. As a result, women would be even more aware of what they do, how they do it, and for whom, and men could and should learn to do more.

In applying our new definition, we would recognize that carework, including self-care, is work. In doing this we would begin to see more clearly that there is a great deal of carework being done—certainly beyond child care—which should then translate into an adequate level of recognition when it is privately useful, and state support when the work is socially and publicly useful, in the form of respite care for caregivers whenever possible, as well as some form of recognition of this work in the pension system. Understanding "motherwork" and carework (whether paid or unpaid) as a site of learning and as more than a "natural" labour of love should move us toward improved pay when it is done for pay, or increased social (including financial) support when it is unpaid.

Our project's emphasis on learning should help us recognize and value the plethora of skills learned and performed in the home and encourage the recognition of skills gained in and through household work. This should also help us recognize that many of these skills enhance and spill over into paid work, not just the other way around.

RAISING AWARENESS

All of this would require a change in consciousness and some awareness-raising, which could begin early in life, through the public school system. We propose the development of curriculum at both the primary and secondary school levels about the nature and value of household work, and how it relates to paid work, for boys as well as girls. This should include discussions about the management, organization, and other social skills learned through doing household work, and how these skills can be transferred to other work. Our own DVD and accompanying CD, *More Than It Seems*, is part of our effort toward this. This could be followed or supplemented by the development of broader public education materials and campaigns encouraging understanding of the nature and value of household work, and the skills learned through doing it.

Other Policy Implications and Recommendations

Beyond the suggestions identified above, our own unique approach, which dissects household work and learning into dimensions, and filters our understanding through the experiences of immigrants, people with disabilities, people experiencing other major life transitions, and paid and unpaid caregivers, has allowed us to consider an additional set of policy implications (presented below). As a result of this new approach, we believe there are other, less obvious but important policy implications that result from our research.

DISABILITIES, UNDERSTANDING, AND ACCESSIBILITY

Work on and with disabled study participants reminds us that we are all only "temporarily able-bodied" because, as some respondents revealed to us, their disabilities were acquired or developed later in their lives. We should all expect, either through the aging process, accidents, and other incidents, that our bodies will transform and require us to unlearn and relearn some of the taken-for-granted tasks associated with maintaining daily life and household work. Chapter 3's focus on the social model over the medical model of disability also reminds us that *societies* create barriers to bodies, especially those that do not meet our normative expectations. It follows that societies can also deconstruct and recreate themselves with fewer barriers, if they so choose. We call for such a restructuring.

Sherri Torjman (2009), from the Caledon Institute of Social Policy, recently wrote about the "three ghosts of poverty." She explained that the three ghosts stalk too many Canadian households involved in providing care and support for relatives with severe disabilities or sick and aging parents. She states that many people with disabilities, seniors living on low incomes, and caregivers spend too much for basic food, heat, and shelter (Ghost no. 1). Torjman (2009) adds that caregivers' own employment status and income can be jeopardized by the pressures of caregiving responsibilities (Ghost no. 2), and caregivers often pay the additional costs of disability—an array of goods and services not covered by medicare or private insurance (Ghost no. 3). Her paper considers various policy solutions, including reforming the disability income system, expanding the Compassionate Care Leave under Employment Insurance, providing a modest caregiver allowance, turning caregiver tax measures into refundable tax credits, and investing in the supply of disability supports (the same or similar could be expanded to child and elder care). Having said this, as we noted throughout this book, people with disabilities are also caregivers and should be recognized and valued as such.

Research on disability, household work, and learning reminds us that we all need to think about how we care and for whom, and how we are cared for by others. In Chapter 3, we were introduced to a large amount of work and learning associated with self-care. We saw self-care as a source of empowerment, and at times a source of frustration, due mostly to lack of mechanisms, supports, and programs that make everyday things accessible. Better access to well-paid and well-trained care providers, and more user-friendly and environmentally sustainable transportation, would go a long way toward creating healthier and more inclusive communities. It may also help reshape social attitudes toward the recognition of the "ability" (to care for self and others, for example) in "disability." After all, although the unique and previously unexplored focus of this chapter was self-care, people with disabilities are also care providers.

SETTLEMENT AND ACCULTURATION FOR IMMIGRANTS

Chapter 4 demonstrated that household work, particularly food-related household work, has contributed to Chinese immigrants' positive and negative understanding and experiences of Canadian society. The too-common drop in standard of living, and very limited access to paid work showed recent Chinese immigrants a negative side of the Canadian experience, which resulted in many having to learn to budget, shop, and cook differently. They became familiar with new and different cooking styles, utensils, appliances, ingredients, ways of shopping for and storing ingredients, and food. At the same time, food-related household work was, in part, a way to help preserve elements of their own culture. Therefore, food-related household work is simultaneously about both cultural preservation and acculturation. Local and federal bodies working with immigrants may do well to recognize that household work is a locus of a considerable amount of learning and acculturation.

Although they were writing on non-formal learning, we, like Shrestha, Wilson, and Singh (2008) found that non-formal and informal learning provides a mechanism by which fragmented or marginalized communities may be (partly) repositioned socially and economically. As we saw in

Chapter 4, non-formal and informal learning through food-related household work builds and/or reinforces social networks, social capital, and the norms of reciprocity (as was found by Shrestha, Wilson, and Singh 2008). Food-related learning and sharing of know-how within and across cultures helps build confidence, connections to others, rootedness to Canada, language, and budgeting skills. As a result, non-formal learning opportunities—such as workshops, community events, classes, etc.—around food-related household work (and particularly those that involve learner-initiated, two-way knowledge exchange, not just top-down approaches to teaching and learning) may help foster social inclusion, community participation, language skills, and "conscientization" (where individuals and communities become aware of factors that help and impede their sustainable development [Shrestha, Wilson, and Singh 2008]). Informal learning that is part of household work, particularly when it involves food, can and does have comparable benefits, as we have seen among Chinese immigrants. Increased funding and support for non-formal and informal learning and sharing surrounding food-related household work is a simple, positive, empowering, and co-operative way of facilitating social inclusion, particularly among older, perhaps more isolated immigrant women, and improving social capital and lifelong learning outcomes. This can and should also include school-aged children to help effect change early in life.

NANNIES AND IMMIGRATION POLICY

Race and economic status clearly play an important role in the experience of both paid and unpaid household work as we have seen in the case of caregivers and nannies. As we saw in Chapter 6, Canada has created a separate immigration program aimed at taking advantage of a large source of relatively cheap feminized labour from parts of the world like the Philippines and the Caribbean, as well as other countries. In setting up this program, the Government of Canada was able to bypass its own immigration rules and restrictions and establish additional criteria and regulation of workers, for example, the live-in requirement for foreign domestic workers. In doing this, Canada has also sent out the message that the training and skills required of these women to perform household work for pay are not valued in the same way as other training and skills required of other economic immigrants to enter Canada through the merit point system. In effect, there is a double standard that reinforces the low value of household work.

The existing policy and program reiterates that the skills related to maintaining life are not important enough to qualify nannies to enter Canada through the same route as other independent-class immigrants. Ironically, while some of these women need formal education to qualify for entry to Canada through this foreign live-in caregiver program, it is the unrecognized informal learning associated with the household work they do on a daily basis that keeps them employed in Canada.

The aim of this part of our research was to understand if the work, skills, and learning associated with paid household work were treated and experienced differently than unpaid household work. We found that paid household work was still highly undervalued, even by governments, and that the informal learning that took place on a daily basis was as invisible as ever. We believe governments need to remedy this by recognizing the skills and formal, non-formal, and informal learning associated with household work when it comes to immigration and employment of caregivers. In doing this, we would hope that nannies and other caregivers could apply for and be granted entry into Canada through the regular merit point system, allowing them to bypass, like all other immigrants, the live-in component of the current caregiver program. This would allow them to immigrate with and care for their own children if they have them, and make them less vulnerable to exploitation by some employers.

LIFELONG CHALLENGES AND LIFELONG LEARNING

Through this book, we not only wanted to contribute to a body of literature that discusses what lifelong learning is, but also to what it can be. Our work suggests that we broaden our understanding of what is learned, where it is learned, how it is learned, when it is learned, and for what purpose. We came to this by shifting our thinking about lifelong learning from the teacher and the classroom to the learner and her or his lifeworld.

This allowed us to identify and value the learning that takes place within and across households through household work.

We conclude this section by noting that policies regarding household work and learning should promote gender equality, recognize the diverse and changing nature of families, support all women in their roles as paid and unpaid workers, encourage the sharing of responsibility for unpaid work within families and across sectors of society, and recognize the home-place as a site of learning. Having said this, there is no doubt that, among other things, men must be drawn further into this discussion as paid and unpaid workers, and as partners for change. We hope we have moved this debate and discussion beyond static, limited, and often unproductive traditional approaches to understanding household work and learning toward larger, more inclusive, and dynamic approaches and future debates.

A Final Thought

This research sheds light on the diversity of women's and some men's life situations, and the many dynamic manifestations of household work and learning they experience. We encountered women and men of different backgrounds, including new immigrants, Aboriginal women, women and men of different ages, cultures, and physical and mental abilities, with and without younger and older children, and from different geographic and demographic locations. By sharing their experiences, they helped uncloak more of the work and learning so often ignored in household work. They helped us tease out and uncover multiple dimensions of their household work and learning, which led to our new and more inclusive definition of household work. Through them, the research team learned a great deal. We also believe that many study participants walked away from this research with a better sense of the personal and wider social value of the household work they perform. We hope a bit of the same has happened to you, the reader.

APPENDIX 1:
METHODOLOGICAL OVERVIEW
Ann Matthews

The Unpaid Housework and Lifelong Learning study is part of a larger project on The Changing Nature of Work and Lifelong Learning (WALL), funded by the Social Sciences and Humanities Research Council (SSHRC), from 2002 through 2006, as a Collaborative Research Initiative on the New Economy (Project no. 512-2002-1011). The community partner for this study was Mothers Are Women (MAW), represented by Kathryn Spracklin. The aim was to reveal the informal learning that happens in the context of unpaid household work. The study was conducted in four phases from 2002 through 2007 (see Table 1 below, for a demographic breakdown of participants). Each phase was ethically reviewed by the University of Toronto. Participants signed consent letters and were promised confidentiality. We used pseudonyms throughout and have omitted or altered other potentially identifying information whenever necessary. A report-back conference was held for and with participants after the data were collected.

An additional Public Outreach Grant from SSHRC (Project no. 502-2005-0021) made it possible to produce a DVD and teacher's guide,

TABLE 1: UNPAID HOUSEWORK AND LIFELONG LEARNING STUDY DEMOGRAPHICS					
	TOTAL	Phase 1	Phase 2	Phase 3	Phase 4
SEX	[435]	[254]	[86]	[75]	[20]
Sex Female	82%	215	77	44	20
Sex Male	18%	39	9	31	0
DISABILITY					
Disability	N/A	N/A	33	15	0
RACE					
Race White	76%	241	43	42	3
Race Black	5%	0	14	4	3
Race Chinese	7%	0	10	20	0
Race Aboriginal	3%	3	9	0	0
Other	5%	5	4	9	6
No Response/Not Known	4%	5	6	0	8
AGE					
Age to 39	28%	53	26	34	9
Age 40-64	52%	132	47	37	9
Age 65-74	8%	29	3	3	0
Age 75+	9%	35	5	1	0
No Response	3%	5	5	0	2
MARITAL STATUS					
Never Married/Co-habit	14%	22	15	18	7
Married/Partner	64%	182	46	39	9
Divorced/Separated	13%	21	22	12	3
Widow	8%	24	3	6	1
No Response	1%	5	0	0	0
CHILDREN					
Children at Home	53%	151	41	32	8
No Child at Home/No Children	47%	103	45	43	12
PAID/UNPAID WORK					
No Work Pay	40%	120	31	25	0
Work for Pay Full/Part Time	56%	133	40	50	20
Student Full Time	2%	0	8	0	0
No Response	2%	1	7	0	0

	TOTAL	Phase 1	Phase 2	Phase 3	Phase 4
EDUCATION					
High School/incl. some	12%	27	7	14	5
Community College Diploma incl. some Comm. Col, University	22%	53	18	13	10
University Undergrad Degree	23%	48	21	29*	1
Professional Degree/incl. some	19%	64	10	5	4
Graduate Degree/incl. some	22%	60	22	14	0
No Response	2%	2	8	0	0
INCOME Dollars					
Personal 20,000 less	35%	91	40	13	9
Household 20,000 less	10%	15	11	12	5
Personal 20,001-60,000	33%	87	24	25	9
Household 20,001-60,000	28%	68	26	23	6
Personal 60,001-100,000	10%	30	3	10	0
Household 60,001-100,000	22%	70	11	14	0
Personal 100,001 and over	4%	11	3	1	0
Household 100,001 and over	15%	47	9	10	0
Personal No Response	18%	35	16	26	2
Household No Response	25%	54	29	16	9
NOTES					
Phase 1 - the disability question was not asked in all questionnaires					
Phase 2 - includes 11 focus groups and 1 online focus group					
*Phase 3 only - University Undergraduate Degree includes some university					

based on the research findings, for use in high school and undergraduate classrooms. Since participants were credited for their participation, with their consent, they have no anonymity in the DVD.

Phase 1

In 2003, questionnaires were mailed across Canada to members of six women's groups: Mothers Are Women (MAW), the National Council of Women of Canada (NCWC), the Disabled Women's Network (DAWN), the Older Women's Network (OWN), Eta Zeta Sorority (EZ), and the National Farmers' Union (NFU). Questionnaires were also mailed to the partners of women in the MAW group. The response rate was 31 percent.

Respondents were asked about the housework, carework, and community work they perform and the learning associated with this work. We also inquired about housework and carework that was performed by people (unpaid and paid) other than the respondent. The closed-ended questions in the questionnaire were coded and analyzed using SPSS. The open-ended questions were coded using a template designed to capture the housework and carework done by the respondent and others (unpaid and paid) and the learning related to these activities.

Phase 2

During the fall and winter of 2003–2004, 11 focus groups were held in three Ontario cities. In addition, a member of DAWN, who participated in our focus group, established an online discussion group on her own initiative, with 20 women with disabilities from across Canada.

Some of the participants in the 11 focus groups were recruited from respondents in Phase 1 who indicated that they would like to participate in further research. However, since the Phase 1 sample was not sufficiently diverse, we recruited other participants to increase diversity. Focus groups were held with White women, women with disabilities, Black women, Aboriginal women, Chinese women, and predominately White men (there was one Chinese male participant). The group discussion was taped, transcribed, and coded into the N6 software program.

Phase 2 questions focused on the cognitive and emotional aspects of household work, and whether people considered the activities work or not. We also asked about changes in participants' household work during the past five years, what they learned because of these changes, and how they learned what they learned. The disabled women, Aboriginal women, and Black women spoke of spirituality in their focus groups. We subsequently asked a question referring to this dimension of learning in the Phase 3 interviews.

Phase 3

During the fall and winter of 2004–2005, 75 individual interviews were conducted using a sample of people who had participated in the national WALL survey (n = 9,023), had experienced a life-changing event, and had expressed an interest in participating in further research. As there were not enough recent Chinese immigrants available from the WALL survey, 12 additional Chinese participants were recruited by the interviewer, Lichun Willa Liu. Six female graduate students conducted the interviews after participating in a one-day training session.

TABLE 2: NUMBER OF INTERVIEWS BY SEX AND EVENT IN PHASE 3		
Life Change Event	Female	Male
New Job	5	5
Lost Job	5	5
New Child (birth, adoption, etc.)	5	5
Lost Partner (divorce, separation, death)	5	5
Disability (at any time in their lives)	10	5
Chinese (recent immigrants)	14	6
Total	*44*	*31*

The Phase 3 interviews focused on learning: "What" is learned in unpaid housework and carework because of the life change event and "how" it is learned. Interviews were taped, transcribed, and coded into the N6 software program.

Phase 4

In the spring of 2005 we conducted individual interviews with 20 women: 10 paid housecleaners and 10 paid nannies. Most participants were recruited through personal and participant contacts. In this phase we wanted to find out if housework, carework, and learning are experienced differently when they are done for pay rather than without pay. We also wanted to know if/how knowledge and learning transfer between paid and unpaid sites of household work.

Report-Back Conference

On October 1, 2005 we held a full-day report-back conference at the University of Toronto for and with our participants. Thirty-one participants and project members attended. The conference was designed to give participants an overview of the findings to date. We also wanted to get participant feedback on our new definition of housework and the saliency of our analyses. The feedback we received is integrated into our publications.

DVD: Household Work: More Than It Seems

In the spring of 2006 a dissemination grant from SSHRC was used to hire Sky Works, a non-profit production company that focuses on social justice issues, to co-produce a film based on the research findings that would be suitable for classroom use. A teacher's guide for the DVD was written by a group of Ontario high school teachers. Participants included White, Chinese, Black, and disabled women; Chinese and White men; and the children of some of the participants.

The research network on The Changing Nature of Work and Lifelong Learning (WALL) was funded by the Social Sciences and Humanities Research Council of Canada (SSHRC) from 2003 through 2007 as a Major Collaborative Research Initiative on the New Economy (Project no. 512-2002-1011). The WALL network is based in the Centre for the Study of Education and Work (CSEW) at the Ontario Institute of Studies in Education/University of Toronto. The WALL research focus includes paid employment, housework, and community volunteer work, as well as formal schooling, adult education courses, and informal learning activities, and the interrelations of all of these forms of learning and work.

WALL research builds on the pioneering studies of the prior SSHRC network on New Approaches to Lifelong Learning (NALL), which developed this expanded framework and conducted the first national survey in 1998 of all forms of learning and work, as well as a series of over 30 exploratory case studies between 1997 and 2002. The WALL research team conducted a large-scale national survey in 2004 and 12 closely related case studies to provide unprecedented documentation of lifelong learning and work relations in Canada. The specific projects and team leaders are:

- National Survey of the Changing Nature of Work and Lifelong Learning (D.W. Livingstone, Ontario Institute for Studies in Education/University of Toronto; Pierre Doray, Université du Québec à Montréal; John Myles, University of Toronto and Statistics Canada).
- The 12 case studies have five interrelated foci: (1) industrial sectors; (2) at-risk workers; (3) unpaid work; (4) learning-work transitions; and (5) labour education:
- Pharmaceutical industry (1, 2) (Paul Bélanger, Université du Québec à Montréal)
- Manufacturing and nursing homes (1, 2) (Anil Verma, University of Toronto)
- Public Sector (1, 2, 5) (Peter Sawchuk, Ontario Institute for Studies in Education/University of Toronto)
- Public school teachers (1, 2, 3) (Harry Smaller, York University, and Rosemary Clark, Ontario Secondary School Teachers' Federation)
- Disabled bank employees (1, 2, 5) (Kathryn Church, Melanie Panitch, Catherine Frazee, Ryerson University)
- Women in information technology (1, 2, 3, 4, 5) (Shauna Butterwick, University of British Columbia and A Commitment to Training and Employment for Women)
- Immigrant workers (1, 2, 4, 5) (Eric Shragge, Concordia University)
- Housework and carework (2, 3, 4) (Margrit Eichler, Ontario Institute for Studies in Education/University of Toronto)
- Volunteer workers (2, 3, 4) (Daniel Schugurensky, Ontario Institute for Studies in Education/University of Toronto)
- School-to-work youth transition (2, 4, 5) (Alison Taylor, University of Alberta)

- Critical transitions throughout the life course (2, 4) (P. Doray and P. Bélanger, Université du Québec à Montréal)
- Labour education (2, 5) (Nancy Jackson, Ontario Institute for Studies in Education/University of Toronto)

Further information about WALL, the national survey, and the case studies may be found at the network website: http://www.wallnetwork.ca. Detailed information on the prior NALL survey may also be found through this site or www.nall.ca. Publications include the special December 2007 issue on lifelong learning and work of *The Canadian Journal for the Study of Adult Education*, *The Future of Lifelong Learning and Work* (Sense Publishers, 2008) and a series of other forthcoming books. See also the WALL Resource Base, an extensive annotated bibliography on work and lifelong learning on the WALL website. For continuing related research, see the CSEW website: www.learningwork.ca/csew.

APPENDIX 3:
MOTHERS ARE WOMEN
Kathryn Spracklin

Mothers Are Women (MAW), an organization for mothers who have chosen to be the primary caregivers of our children and believe that the ability to exercise this choice without the threat of social or economic penalties is part of the struggle for equality, was formed in 1985 by a group of Ottawa stay-at-home feminist mothers as a forum to express their concerns and explore their interests as women. Within a few years, MAW had grown into a national volunteer-run organization supporting and engaging women in social, economic, and political issues through a quarterly magazine *Homebase*, an online discussion group, and local workshops and events in Ottawa and other Canadian cities.

In the 1990s, MAW became increasingly politically active, collaborating with other women's organizations to bring issues of particular concern for mothers who do not have regular paid employment—including child care and women's economic insecurity—to the attention of Canada's policy-makers. For much of the decade, the organization focused on the issue of unpaid work, undertaking three projects funded by the Women's and Disabled Persons Program, Government of Canada (Count Us In, Step by

Step, and When Women Count). Through these projects, MAW played a central role in the successful national grassroots advocacy campaign to have unpaid domestic work counted in the 1996 Census of Population, and then to explore strategies for ensuring that women and women's organizations would be directly involved in policy development using the data collected. Statistics Canada responded to our collective sustained demand for Census data on unpaid work by retaining the questions on the 2001 and 2006 censuses.

Over this period, MAW members conducted research, held workshops; hosted symposia; wrote plain-language newsletters for members, resource manuals for women's organizations, and policy briefs for government; and participated in official consultations and national coalitions and working groups. MAW's public profile grew—enhanced by interviews on "Morningside" and "As It Happens," debates on the Women's Television Network, articles in magazines from *Homemakers* to *Ms*—drawing the attention of women across Canada. MAW became, as one long-time member explains, "a voice of women I could hear, with whom I felt I could identify, and who had something to teach me about being a woman—and how to be a woman and a mother at the same time." Or, in the words of another member, MAW mattered because "it helped me feel that I still mattered even though I didn't have a business card, corporate job title, or pay cheque.... It meant sanity.... The MAW Toronto meeting group ... was a regular re-affirmation that my work was valuable."

MAW's research, its politicized membership, and its connections with diverse Canadian women's organizations regarding the issue of unpaid work made the organization a good match for the Household Work project. MAW eagerly agreed to join the project as community partner in 2001, hoping to both continue its work on the issue and to re-energize the organization, which was facing a decline.

What MAW Did

Throughout its history, MAW struggled with feminism, externally battling to be accepted within the mainstream feminist movement and internally struggling with finding consensus around the "f-word." MAW members faced ongoing tension between their support and activist roles, and growing concern that its strong feminist stance was discouraging members who were less political, members who were needed to keep the organization alive.

Although MAW sought a diverse membership, most members were educated, married, middle-class women who were able to choose to be mothers at home for a period of time. Turnover in membership was high—mothers joined when their children were babies or preschoolers and drifted away as they returned to paid work. Many long-standing members had moved on by the early 2000s, while the political issues that had driven their activism the decade before were no longer attracting new members—mothers had become "hot," but feminism was not. When asked recently why MAW could not be sustained, one member replied, "The tide had turned."

In fall 2003, MAW published what turned out to be the last *Homebase*. Four years later, 32 boxes of MAW records became part of the Women's Movement Collection at the University of Ottawa Archives. MAW's work, however, isn't done. Describing what MAW meant to her, a member says, "MAW provided a network and a connection to a different way of thinking about work in the home.… I withdrew from the paid workforce at the age of 38 thinking that the feminist battles had been won … but was totally caught off guard in 1998 when I stayed home with my son to discover I was entering a time warp.… *Homebase* connected me to others who didn't see a conflict in their role as mothers and as women; who celebrated the work they did in the house but weren't defined by their shining floors and their clean bathrooms." The surveys and focus groups conducted as part of this project show that women still experience this "time warp." Fortunately, projects like this one continue to bring us together to advance our understanding of work and, perhaps, to encourage lasting change.

NOTES

INTRODUCTION

1. The various phases of this study included other recent immigrants. See Appendix 1 for details.

2. Two participants in this group were not disabled.

3. Sixty-three participated in the larger WALL questionnaire, while 12 Chinese immigrants/respondents were recruited separately.

4. We continue to use "housework" whenever the literature we draw upon uses that term.

5. Robyn Bourgeois, Mary Bullen, Alexia Dyer, Lingqin Feng, Young-Hwa Hong, Gada Mahrouse, Carly Manion, Tracey Matthews, Gayle McIntyre, Thara Mohanathas, Sam Rahimi, Milosh Raykov, Susan Stowe, Carole Trainor, and Natalie ZurNedden have also contributed to the project at various stages.

6. Social reproduction refers to the daily and generational production and maintenance of a population (Bezanson 2006). Also see Bezanson and Carter (2006).

7. The DVD (with CD) is available through Vtape, 401 Richmond St. W., Suite 452, Toronto, ON, Canada, M5V 3A8, tel.: 416-351-1317; fax: 416-351-1509.

CHAPTER 1

1. Throughout the book, all names of research participants have been changed to protect their anonymity, with the exception of members of the research team and their family members.

2. Statistics Canada defines housework in terms of core and non-core activities. Core housework consists only of "meal preparation, meal clean-up, indoor cleaning, and laundry.... Non-core housework includes things such as outdoor cleaning, mending or sewing, interior or exterior maintenance and repair, gardening, pet and plant care, household paperwork, or unpacking groceries." Their measure of total housework consists of core and non-core activities. "Primary child care ... is separated out from household activities. It includes activities directly involving children, such as feeding, helping, teaching, reading to, talking or playing with, medical care, and any related travel such as taking children to school or driving them to sports or other activities" (Marshall 2006: 6).

   I have added up Statistics Canada data on housework and primary child care and shopping for goods and services in order to arrive at the figures cited (Marshall 2006: 5, chart A). Nevertheless, this still vastly under-represents the amount and diversity of work that is actually performed on an unpaid basis within households, including, in particular, care of adults, self-care, and many of the mental and emotional tasks that constitute such an important part of household work.

3. "Replacement costs are based on the average hourly earnings of people employed full-year/full-time in occupations within each equivalency group, weighted by the number of people employed in each occupation" (Chandler 1994: 3.3).

4. Informal caregiving is defined "as help and care provided by individuals to members of their household and to people who reside in other households as well as travel related to the provision of this help and care" (Zukewich 2003: 15). However, it *excludes* some of the help and care activities such as cleaning the house, cooking a meal, fixing a broken appliance when provided to someone living within the same household (Zukewich 2003: 16). Furthermore, because only one activity at a time is counted, much care that

is provided while simultaneously doing something else (e.g., cooking and listening to someone) is also excluded.

5. A small sampling includes Armstrong and Armstrong (1990); Baxter (1997); Benéria (1992); Benéria and Roldán (1987); Benin and Agostinelli (1988); Bianchi et al. (2000); Bierman (2007); Bond and Sales (2001); Chandler (1994); Coverman (1983); Delphy (1984); Eichler (1985, 1997); Ferber and Green (1985); Ferree (1991); Folbre (2001); Gather (2004); Glucksmann (2005); Luxton (1997); Pettinger et al. (2005); Stevens, Kiger, and Riley (2001); Waring (1988); Windebank (2001); Wong (2005); Zuo and Bian (2001).

6. For a longer discussion of this issue, see Eichler and Albanese (2007).

7. While there is a small literature on lesbian and gay couples and household work (Chan et al. 1998; Goldberg and Perry Jenkins 2007; Kurdeck 2007; Oerton 1997; Patterson and Surfin 2004; Solomon, Rothblum, and Balsom 2005), most of the literature concentrates on heterosexual couples.

8. These are the different quarters in my wallet as I am writing this.

9. See Eichler (2008a) for a longer discussion of this issue.

10. We interviewed the Very Reverend Lois Wilson, past moderator of the United Church of Canada, past president of the World Council of Churches and, at the time of the interview, senator of the Senate of Canada on this issue.

11. To understand the conceptual focus of the sociology of work, we surveyed a selection of books and articles in sociological journals (Abbot 1993; Bender and Leone 1995; Auster 1996; Caplow 1954; Castillo 1999b, 1999a; Cornfield and Hodson 2002; Berger 1964; Grint 1998; Lowe and Krahn 1993; Nosow and Form 1962; Ritzer 1989; Simpson and Simpson 1983; Vallas 2001; Watson 1987; Wipper 1984; Cornfield, Campbell, and McCammon 2001; Pettinger et al. 2005; Edgell 2006). We disregarded publications that discussed work in a specific context. Our intent was to find out the way in which the sociology of work discusses unpaid housework and carework.

For instance, Grint (1998) indicates at the beginning of his book that he "considers work in a rather wider perspective which includes unpaid domestic labour" (Grint 1998: 1). Nevertheless he, like other authors (Bender and Leone 1995; Caplow 1954; Cornfield and Hodson 2002; Lowe and Krahn

1993; Simpson and Mutran 1981) continues to focus on paid work. The problem, therefore, is not so much with the definition of work, but rather with the way that it is operationalized within the sociology of work. The exception to this general trend is the book by Pettinger et al. (2005), discussed in the text.

12. This criterion is usually employed by economists; see Ironmonger (1996); Chandler (1994: 3.1); see also Grint (1998: 30) and Marshall (1998: 706).

13. The classic example is the wife of the "corporation man" of the 1950s–1960s (Whyte 1956), but it includes many other occupations. While it seems that the number of two-person careers has somewhat diminished because most wives today have their own job or career, it is by no means dead (Frame and Shehan 1994; Mederer and Weinstein 1992).

14. Compare also the discussion in Edgell (2006), Chapter 9.

CHAPTER 2

1. Since we did our individual follow-up interviews one year after the WALL survey was completed, as many as six years might have passed since respondents had experienced the life changes mentioned.

2. We asked respondents "If you look back over the last five years, what would you say were events in your life that in some way changed the way you live?" Some of them mentioned the event on the basis of which they had been selected, but others mentioned other events. In either case, we were guaranteed that something important had changed in people's lives. Garfield, for instance, had been selected because he had taken a new job, but in the meantime, he had married and the couple had adopted a daughter. Those two events, especially the arrival of his daughter, by far trumped the new job in importance. All subsequent questions regarding household work and the learning accompanying this work were centred on the changes that had been occasioned by whatever event respondents had selected as the most significant one during the past five years. We did not apply the five-year time frame to disability for several reasons.

The WALL survey, from which we drew our respondents, did not ask those who self-identified as having a disability about when they acquired the impairment, or the nature of the impairment. Disability may be temporary, permanent, or progressive, and the immediacy of the need to change or do things differently varies from person to person.

3. We engaged in multiple computer searches, interviews with experts, etc., to find relevant literature, but at the design stage of our own study had been able to locate only the Livingstone study. The other references came to light in three more years of diligent searching, using multiple sources of information. Some of the literature was published only after our own study was already underway.

4. The studies demonstrate that both positive and negative spillover from work to family and from family to work are common for both women and men. Here, we have concentrated only on positive spillover from family to work. Positive spillover depends on a number of variables, including the nature of the job—for instance, a managerial job (Kirchmeyer 1995) vs. nursing as an occupation (Cohen and Kirchmeyer 1995)—and large samples of employees vs. small ones (Hill 2005). The same is true for the nature of the family work, such as parent care (Stephens, Franks, and Atienza 1997) vs. child care (Ruderman et al. 2002). Gender (Hill 2005; Rothbard 2001) and age (Grzywacz, Almeida, and McDonald 2002) are obviously important. Likewise, the personality of the individuals affects the nature of the spillover (Wayne, Musisca, and Fleeson 2004; Sumer and Knight 2001), as does the response of the employer (Kirchmeyer 1995). For an excellent summary of the literature, see Greenhaus and Powell (2006). For a longer discussion of this issue, see Eichler (forthcoming)

5. Except in the case of nannies, who are paid. However, their paid work is heavily influenced by the unpaid work (housework and carework) that they do, as we will see in Chapter 6.

6. This section draws heavily on Eichler (2008a).

7. Managing one's emotions for the sake of a job or other people (Hochschild 1983: 7); providing support to others (Erickson 1993, 2005: 338; Strazdins and Broom 2004: 357); carrying emotional baggage on behalf of others (England and Farkas 1986: 91); managing one's emotions for oneself (Hochschild 1979: 562).

8. English, Fenwick, and Parsons (2003: 2) note that there has been "an increase in texts acknowledging the significance of spirituality in learning and teaching." See also Bai (2001) and (Ng 1998).

9. See Gouthro and Plumb (2003). To date discussions related to adult learning have taken place primarily in the context of formal education.

10. Schugurensky (2000) suggests that we can understand informal learning better when we look at it through the concepts of intentionality and awareness at the time of the learning experience. He identifies three types of informal learning: self-directed, incidental, and socialization. Bova and Kroth (2001) describe incidental learning as learning that occurs as a by-product of other learning. Foley (2001: 85) says that "most learning is informal and incidental, embedded in other activities, and tacit." Colley, Hodkinson, and Malcolm (2003) maintain that the categories of formal and informal learning are not necessarily distinct and see a blurring of the lines between the two. For instance, informal learning takes place in formal and non-formal learning settings, and what we learn informally influences the way we make meaning in other learning contexts.

11. Jarvis (2006b: 85) would call these primary experiences.

12. Jarvis (2006b: 85) refers to these as secondary experiences.

13. In this example we are using the experiential learning model of Kolb (1984) to illustrate some of the elements involved in learning from and through a primary experience. Kolb identifies four interrelated cyclical phases in his model: (1) *concrete experience*, which is learning through "experience"; (2) *reflective observation*, which provides an opportunity to reflect on what happened in the experience and relate it to prior knowledge and experiences; (3) *abstract conceptualization* in which the person creates an understanding of the experience and generates new meaning and theory that will inform action; and (4) *active experimentation* in which the person learns through "application" of the theory or processes that have been conceptualized. While Kolb's model has been useful in this example, we recognize that it has been critiqued by many theorists of adult learning. These critiques bring out aspects of the learning process that became evident in our study but are not built into the Kolb model. Jarvis (2006b: 85) suggests that experiential

learning is about primary experiences, but that "most of what we learn about the world comes from secondary experience." Fenwick (2003: 124–125) argues that there is a mentalist bias to understanding experiential learning, and that the body has been rendered completely invisible by experiential learning theory. This is a comment on how educators have tried to integrate experiential learning into classroom practices. If we move our gaze from the educators to people whom we ask how they learn about aspects of their daily lives, we find, as we have seen above, that the body is present, especially if it cannot be taken for granted to do everything people would like it to do.

14. Merriam and Caffarella (1999: 293) define self-directed learning as "a process of learning, in which people take the primary initiative for planning, carrying out, and evaluating their own learning experiences.... [T]his form of learning can take place both inside and outside institutionally based learning programs.... [B]eing self directed in one's learning is a natural part of adult life."

15. See Eichler (forthcoming) for a detailed discussion of this issue.

CHAPTER 3

1. Taken from a Statistics Canada Report, Profile of disability in 2001, in *Canadian Social Trends* (Spring 2004): 14–18.

2. Personal email communication with Stephen Billet, June 20, 2006.

3. Personal conversation with Stephen Billet, June 5, 2006.

CHAPTER 4

1. As part of my doctoral research, I interviewed 20 Chinese immigrants from mainland China, who had immigrated to Canada within five years prior to their participation in my research. Of the 20 people interviewed, 14 are women and six are men, who were residing in the Greater Toronto Area. Eight of the interviewees (four men and four women) were from the WALL survey, and 12 (10 women and two men) were from my own contacts, due to a lack of recent Chinese immigrants/participants in the Greater Toronto Area from the original survey. The interviewees were between the ages of 25 to 58, most were married, and had one child in their family who varied in

age from a few months to young adults in their twenties. All the interviewees had at least a university or college degree and worked as professionals before immigration.

I chose more women for the interviews because literature on housework has repeatedly indicated that women continue to do most of the household work despite their increased participation in the labour force. I chose new immigrants with five years of residence in Canada because literature on lifelong learning suggests that major life transitions, such as getting married, having a child or become disabled, etc., lead to significant learning for those involved in such transitions. My research presumes that international migration is one of the major events in a person's life, and thus poses great potential and opportunities for lifelong learning.

2. *Yuan* is a unit of Chinese currency. Currently 1 yuan equals about 0.14 Canadian dollars.

3. All the interviews were conducted in either English or Mandarin or in a mixture of both languages. All the Chinese transcripts were translated into English, and some of the English quotations cited in this chapter were slightly edited for grammar.

4. LINC is the abbreviation for Language Instruction for Newcomers to Canada, a government-funded language training program for new immigrants to Canada.

5. For more detailed discussion about different ways and forms of adult learning, please see P. Jarvis, *Towards a comprehensive theory of human learning* (New York: Routledge, 2006); S.B. Merriam and R.S. Caffarella, *Learning in adulthood: A comprehensive guide*, 2nded. (San Francisco: Jossey-Bass, 1999).

CHAPTER 5

1. Boubalina is my family's nickname for me.

2. Statistics Canada, *The Daily*, July 31, 2006, http://www.statcan.ca/Daily/English/060731/d060731b.htm. The Canadian fertility rate has hovered around 1.5–1.7 since 2000.

3. A noticeable number of our respondents had children with disabilities, in particular ADHD or Asperger's Syndrome, which reflects the steep rise in the

number of children diagnosed with learning disabilities. "The latest statistics indicate that 1 in 200 Canadian children are affected by autism, an increase of 600% in the past 10 years. What was once viewed as a rare disorder is now recognized as the most common neurological disorder affecting children" (The Geneva Centre for Autism, http://www.autismcentre.ns.ca/aboutAutism/incidence/, accessed June 20, 2008). However, some of the increase may be due to clearer and broader diagnostic criteria.

4. Many respondents did describe, however, performing unpaid carework within hospitals and other institutional settings as part of the care they provide for ill family members and friends, for example.

5. Informal caregiving is defined "as help and care provided by individuals to members of their household and to people who reside in other households as well as travel related to the provision of this help and care" (Zukewich 2003: 15). However, it *excludes* some of the help and care activities such as cleaning the house, cooking a meal, fixing a broken appliance when provided to someone living within the same household (Zukewich 203: 16). Furthermore, because only one activity at a time is counted, much care that is provided while simultaneously doing something else (e.g., cooking and listening to someone) is also excluded.

6. This is higher than the labour income "generated by the health care and social assistance industry ($42.1 billion), education services ($40.1 billion) or the finance, insurance and real estate industry ($43.4 billion)" (Zukewich 2003: 18).

7. Given that there are some universal demogrants such as Old Age Security, Canada's system is a mixed one.

8. Interestingly, in their study of first-year nursing students' reasons for pursuing nursing as a career, Poole and Isaacs (1997) found that maternal and familial ideologies strongly influence not just unpaid carework but also provide the rationale for choosing a career in paid caring professions such as nursing.

9. Disability studies argues that disability is a social phenomenon that can be distinguished from impairment insofar as disability is produced through social environments and structures that disable individuals who have impairments; disability is, in effect, the result of social conditions imposed on top of impairments (Oliver 1996).

10. This example is taken from the DVD/documentary film *Household Work: More Than It Seems,* based on this research. On the DVD, see the portrait "Speranza."

11. As much transnational feminist scholarship asserts, the emphasis on migration as a linear trajectory obscures the embodied realities of transnational lives, which so often involve multiple forms of movement within different diasporic formations (e.g., Kaplan 1996). By allowing for a recognition of the intimate and the global as mutually constitutive, and the fluidity of movement between these different social spaces, as Pratt and Rosner (2006) suggest, we might begin to disrupt those familiar dualisms—public/private, personal/political, etc.—which are foundational to Western thought, and which often function as received analytical categories.

12. This is similar to what Lan (2003: 188) argues are "structural continuities across the public/private divide."

13. Statistics Canada reported that 10.9 percent of women lived in poverty versus 10.1 percent of men (Statistics Canada, http://www40.statcan.ca/l01/cst01/famil19a.htm).

14. We had no case of a husband with a disabled wife.

15. Tran reports: "The gap in labour market outcomes for foreign-born visible minorities may be related to incidents of discrimination or unfair treatment. According to the Ethnic Diversity Survey, about 20% of visible minorities aged 15 and over said that they had sometimes or often experienced discrimination or unfair treatment in the previous five years because of their ethnicity, culture, race, skin colour, accent, language, or religion. These incidents most often occur at work when applying for a job or promotion" (Tran 2004: 11).

16. In their study of the effects of migration upon immigrant women's caregiving, Spitzer et al. (2003: 282) similarly found that "female migrants were afforded fewer opportunities to renegotiate caregiving responsibilities" after immigration due to their lack of extended family networks and conditions of low-wage employment.

CONCLUSION

1. To recap, formal learning or education refers to accredited learning that is provided through authorized educational establishments and institutions (schools, colleges, universities). Non-formal learning is made up of non-mandatory, supplemental activities that are part of intentional/purposeful structured learning opportunities outside formal educational systems. They include attending courses, workshops, and related activities aimed at teaching literacy, numeracy, hobbies, etc., usually done for employability, life skills, and/or pleasure. Informal learning refers to unstructured and unintended knowledge or skills that people acquire incidentally through everyday experiences (Shrestha, Wilson, and Singh, 2008).

2. There are others who offer a more complex, multidimensional, dynamic, and relational model of well-being (see Burke et al. 2000).

REFERENCES

Abbey, Sharon, and Andrea O'Reilly, eds. 1998. *Redefining motherhood: Changing identities and patterns.* Toronto: Second Story Press.

Abbot, Andrew. 1993. The sociology of work and occupations. *Annual Review of Sociology* 19: 187–209.

Ahmed, Sara. 2004. *The cultural politics of emotion.* New York: Routledge.

Alexander, M. Jacqui. 2005. *Pedagogies of crossing: Meditations on feminism, sexual politics, memory, and the sacred.* Durham: Duke University Press.

Alstott, Anne. 2004. *No exit: What parents owe their children and what society owes parents.* Oxford: Oxford University Press.

Appleby, Yvon, and Ann Marie Bathmaker. 2006. The new skills agenda: Increased lifelong learning or new sites of inequality? *British Educational Research Journal* 32 (5): 703–717.

Armstrong, Pat, and Hugh Armstrong. 1990. *Theorizing women's work, network basics series.* Toronto: Garamond Press.

Armstrong, Pat, Carol Amaratunga, Jocelyne Bernier, Karen Grant, Ann Pederson, and Kay Willson. 2001. *Exposing privatization: Women and health care reform in Canada.* Aurora: Garamond Press.

Armstrong, Pat, and Hugh Armstrong. 2005. Public and private: Implications for care work. *Sociological Review* 53 (2): 169–187.

Aronson, Jane and Sheila M. Neysmith. 1996. You're not just in there to do the work: Depersonalizing policies and the exploitation of home care workers' labor. *Gender & Society* 10 (1): 56–77.

Aronson, Jane. 1998. Lesbians giving and receiving care: Stretching conceptualizations of caring and community. *Women's Studies International Forum* 21 (5): 505–519.

Auster, Carol J. 1996. *The sociology of work: Concepts and cases.* Thousand Oaks: Pine Forge Press.

Avoseh, M.B.M. 2001. Learning to be active citizens: Lessons of traditional Africa for lifelong learning. *International Journal of Lifelong Education* 29 (6): 479–486.

Bai, H. 2001. Beyond the educated mind: Toward a pedagogy of mindfulness. In *Unfolding bodymind: Exploring possibility through education*, edited by B. Hocking, J. Haskell & W. Linds, 86–99. Brandon, VT: Foundation of Education.

Baker, Lois K., and Mary J. Denyes. 2008. Predictors of self-care in adolescents with cystic fibrosis: A test of Orem's theories of self-care and self-care deficit. *Journal of Pediatric Nursing* 23 (1): 37–47.

Barnes, Colin, Geof Mercer, and Tom Shakespeare. 1999. *Exploring disability: A sociological introduction.* Cambridge: Polity Press.

Baxter, Janeen. 1997. Gender equality and participation in housework: A cross-national perspective. *Journal of Comparative Family Studies* 28 (3): 220–247.

Bender, David, and Bruno Leone, eds. 1995. *Work: Opposing viewpoints.* San Diego: Greenhaven Press.

Benéria, Lourdes. 1992. Accounting for women's work: The progress of two decades. *World Development* 20 (11): 1547–1560.

Benéria, L., and M. Roldán. 1987. *The crossroads of class and gender: Industrial homework, subcontracting, and household dynamics in Mexico City.* Chicago: University of Chicago Press.

Benin, M.H., and J. Agostinelli. 1988. Husbands' and wives' satisfaction with the division of labour. *Journal of Marriage and the Family* 50: 349–361.

Bennett, Janette. 2007. (Dis)ordering motherhood: Mothering a child with attention-deficit/hyperactivity disorder. *Body & Society* 13 (4): 97–110.

Benston, Margaret. 1969. The political economy of women's liberation. *Monthly Review* 21 (4): 13–27.

Berger, Peter, ed. 1964. *The human shape or work: Studies in the sociology of occupations*. New York: Macmillan Co.

Bezanson, Kate. 2006. *Gender, the state, and social reproduction: Household insecurity in neo-liberal times*. Toronto: University of Toronto Press.

Bezanson, Kate, and Ellen Carter. 2006. *Public policy and social reproduction: Gendering social capital*. Ottawa: Status of Women Canada.

Bianchi, Suzanne M., Melissa A. Milkie, Liana C. Sayer, and John P. Robinson. 2000. Is anyone doing the housework? Trends in the gender division of household labor. *Social Forces* 79 (1): 191–228.

Bierman, Arlene S. 2007. Sex matters. Gender disparities in quality and outcomes of care. *CMJA* 177 (12): 1520–1522.

Bond, Sue, and Jill Sales. 2001. Household work in the UK: An analysis of the British Household Panel Survey 1994. *Work, Employment & Society* 15 (2): 233–250.

Bourgeault, Ivy Lynn, Pat Armstrong, Hugh Armstrong, Jacqueline Choinière, Joel Lexchin, Eric Mykhalovskiy, Suzanne Peters, and Jerry White. 2001. Everyday experiences of an implicit rationing: Comparing the voices of nurses in California and British Columbia. *Sociology of Health & Illness* 23 (5): 633–653.

Bova, Breda, and Michael Kroth. 2001. Workplace learning and generation X. *Journal of Workplace Learning* 13 (2): 57–65.

Boychuk, Gerrard. 2004. *The Canadian social model: The logics of policy development*. CPRN Social Architecture Papers, Research Report F 36 Family Network. Ottawa: Canadian Policy Research Networks Inc.

Budgeon, Shelley. 2003. Identity as an embodied event. *Body & Society* 9 (1): 35–55.

Burke, Mary Anne, and Margrit Eichler. 2006. *The BIAS FREE Framework: A practical tool for identifying and eliminating social biases in health research*. Geneva: Global Forum for Health Research.

Burke, Mary Anne, Craig McKie, Ron Colman, Gail Ward Stewart, and Michael

Bach. 2000. *Dynamic Model of Health*. Ottawa: Commonwealth Working Group on Gender Equality and Health Indicators.

Burstow, B. 1994. Problematizing adult education: A feminist perspective. *The Canadian Journal for the Study of Adult Education* 8 (1): 1–14.

Butler, Linda. 1993. Unpaid work in the home and accreditation. In *Culture and processes of adult learning: A reader*, edited by M. Thorpe, R. Edwards, and A. Hanson, 66–83. London and New York: Routledge.

Canadian Policy Research Networks. 2002. *Final report: Child care policy conference*. October 18, 2002. Ottawa: Canadian Policy Research Network Inc.

Caplow, T. 1954. *The sociology of work*. New York: McGraw-Hill Book Company.

Castillo, Juan Jose. 1999a. Which way forward for the sociology of work? An introduction. *Current Sociology* 47 (2): 1–4.

Castillo, Juan Jose. 1999b. Sociology of work at the crossroad. *Current Sociology* 47 (2): 21–46.

Chan, Raymond W., Risa C. Brooks, Charlotte J. Patterson, and Barbara Raboy. 1998. Division of labor among lesbians and heterosexual parents: Associations with children's adjustment. *Journal of Family Psychology* 12 (3): 402–419.

Chandler, William. 1994. The value of household work in Canada, 1992. *Canadian Economic Observer* 3 (1–3): 9.

Chang, K.C., ed. 1977. *Food in Chinese culture*. New Haven: Yale University Press.

Charles, Nickie, and Manion Kerr. 1988. *Women, food, and families*. Manchester: Manchester University Press.

Chau, Pauline, Hen-shin Lee, Rose Tseng, and Norma Jean Downes. 1990. Dietary habits, health beliefs, and food practices of elderly Chinese women. *Journal of the American Dietetic Association* 90 (4): 579–580.

Chodorow, Nancy. 1978. *The reproduction of mothering: Psychoanalysis and the sociology of gender*. Berkeley: University of California Press.

Cohen, Aaron, and Catherine Kirchmeyer. 1995. A multidimensional approach to the relations between organizational commitment and nonwork participation. *Journal of Vocational Behavior* 46: 189–202.

Cohen, Rina. 2000. "Mom is a stranger": The negative impact of immigration policies on the family life of Filipina domestic workers. *Canadian Ethnic Studies* 32 (3): 76–88.

Colley, Helen. 2006. Learning to labour with feeling: Class, gender, and emotion in childcare education and training. *Contemporary Issues in Early Childhood* 7 (1): 15–29.

Colley, Helen, Phil Hodkinson, and Janice Malcolm. 2003. *Informality and formality in learning: A report for the Learning and Skills Research Centre.* London: The Learning and Skills Research Centre.

Collins, Michael. 1998. Critical returns: From andragogy to lifelong education. In *Learning for life: Canadian readings in adult education*, edited by S.M. Scott, B. Spencer, and A.M. Thomas, 46–58. Toronto: Thompson Educational Publishing.

Colman, Ronald. 1998. Module Two: The Economic Value of Unpaid Housework and Child Care in Nova Scotia. (Part of Measuring Sustainable Development – Application of the Genuine Progress Index to Nova Scotia). Halifax: GPI Atlantic. http://www.gpiatlantic.org/pdf/housework/housework.pdf

Coltrane, Scott. 2000. Research on household labor: Modeling and measuring the social embeddedness of routine family work. *Journal of Marriage and the Family* 62 (4): 1208–1233.

Commission on the Social Determinants of Health (CSDH). 2008. *Closing the gap in a generation: Health equity through action on the social determinants of health: Final report of the Commission on Social Determinants of Health.* Geneva: World Health Organization.

Connell, R.W. 2002. *Gender: Short Introductions.* Cambridge: Polity Press.

Corker, Mairian, and Sally French. 1999. Reclaiming discourse in disability studies. *Disability Discourses*, edited by M. Corker and S. French (eds.), 1–11, Buckingham: Open University Press.

Cornfield, Daniel B., Karen E. Campbell, and Holly J. McCammon, eds. 2001. *Working in restructured workplaces: Challenges and new directions for the sociology of work.* Thousand Oaks: Sage.

Cornfield, Daniel B., and Randy Hodson, eds. 2002. *Worlds of work: Building an international sociology of work.* New York: Kluwer Academic/Plenum Publishers.

Counihan, Carole M. 1999. *The Anthropology of Food and Body: Gender, Meaning and Power*. New York: Routledge.

Courtenay-Hall, Pamela. (1998). Mothering in the late 20th century: Science, gender lore, and celebratory narrative. *Canadian Women Studies* 18 (2): 16–21.

Coverman, Shelley. 1983. Gender, domestic labor time, and wage inequality. *American Sociological Review* 48 (5): 623–637.

Craig, Lyn. 2006. Does father care mean fathers share? A comparison of how mothers and fathers in intact families spend time with children. *Gender & Society* 20 (2): 259–281.

Crittenden, Ann. 2001. *The price of motherhood: Why the most important job in the world is still the least valued*, 1st ed. New York: Metropolitan Books.

Cruikshank, Jane. 2002. Lifelong learning or re-training for life: Scapegoating the worker. *Studies in the Education of Adults* 34 (2): 140–155.

Dei, George J. Sefa. 2002. Spiritual knowing and transformative learning. In *Expanding the boundaries of transformative learning*, edited by E.V. O'Sullivan, A. Morrell, and A. O'Connor, 121–133. New York: Palgrave.

Delphy, Christine. 1984. *Close to home: A materialist analysis of women's oppression*. London: Hutchinson in Association with The Explorations in Feminism Collective.

DeVault, Marjorie L. 1991. *Feeding the family: The social organization of caring as gendered work*. Chicago: University of Chicago Press.

DeVault, M.L. 1999. Comfort and Struggle: Emotion Work in Family Life. *Annals of the American academy of political and social science*. 561: 52–63.

DiQuinzio, Patrice. 1999. *The impossibility of motherhood: Feminisn, individualism, and the problem of mothering*. New York: Routledge.

Doucet, Andrea. 2006. *Do men mother? Fathering, care, and domestic responsibility*. Toronto: University of Toronto Press.

Edgell, Stephen. 2006. *The sociology of work: Continuity and change in paid and unpaid work*. Thousand Oaks: Sage.

Eichler, Margrit. 1980. *The double standard: A feminist critique of feminist social science*. London: Croom Helm.

Eichler, Margrit. [1983] 1991. *Families in Canada today: Recent changes and their policy consequences*. Toronto: Gage, reissued by Routledge.

Eichler, Margrit. 1985. *The connection between paid and unpaid labor and its implication for creating equality for women in employment. Research studies of the Commission on Equality in Employment*, series edited by R.S. Abella. Ottawa: Minister of Supply and Services.

Eichler, Margrit. 1997. *Family shifts: Families, policies, and gender equality.* Toronto: Oxford University Press.

Eichler, Margrit. 2005. The other half (or more) of the story: Unpaid household and care work and lifelong learning. In *International handbook of educational policy*, edited by N. Bascia, A. Cumming, A. Batnow, K. Leithwood, and D. Livingston, 1023–1042. Dordrecht, the Netherlands: Springer.

Eichler, Margrit. 2008a. Integrating carework and housework into household work: A conceptual clarification. *Journal of the Association for Research on Mothering: Mothering* 10 (1): 9–19.

Eichler, Margrit. 2008b. Just women's stuff: Lifelong learning through unpaid household work. In *The future of lifelong learning and work: Critical perspectives*, edited by D. Livingstone, K. Merchandani, and P. Sawchuk, 27–46. Rotterdam and Taipei: Sense Publishers.

Eichler, Margrit. Forthcoming. "I am the patient and compassionate cashier": Learning through unpaid household work for paid work. In *Demystifying family/paid work contradiction: Challenges and possibilities*, edited by C. Krull, TBA. Vancouver: UBC Press.

Eichler, Margrit, and Patrizia Albanese. 2007. What is household work? A critique of assumptions underlying empirical studies of housework and an alternative approach. *Canadian Journal of Sociology* 32 (2): 227–258.

England, K., and Stiel, B. 1997. They think that you are as stupid as your English is: Constructing foreign domestic workers in Canada. *Environment and Planning*, 29: 195–215.

England, P., and G. Farkas. 1986. *Households, employment, and gender: A social, economic, and demographic view.* New York: Aldine.

English, Leona M. 2000. Spiritual dimensions of informal learning. *New directions for adult and continuing education*, 85, 29–38.

English, Leona M., Tara Fenwick, and J. Parsons. 2003. *Spirituality of adult education and training.* Malabar: Krieger Publishing.

Erickson, Rebecca J. 1993. Reconceptualizing family work: The effect of emotion work on perceptions of marital quality. *Journal of Marriage and the Family* 55: 888–900.

Erickson, Rebecca J. 2005. Why emotion work matters: Sex, gender, and the division of household labor. *Journal of Marriage and Family* 55 (4): 337–351.

Faure, E. 1972. *Learning to be*. Paris: UNESCO.

Fenwick, Tara. 2003. Reclaiming and re-embodying experiential learning through complexity science. *Studies in the Education of Adults* 35 (2): 123–141.

Ferber, Marianne A., and Carole A. Green. 1985. Homemakers' imputed wages: Results of the Heckman Technique compared with women's own estimates. *Journal of Human Resources* 20 (1): 90–99.

Ferree, Myra Marx. 1991. The gender division of labor in two-earner marriages: Dimensions of variability and change. *Journal of Family Issues* 12: 158–180.

Field, John. 2001. Lifelong education. *International Journal of Lifelong Education* 20 (1/2): 3–15.

Flannery, D.D. 2000. Connection. In *Women as learners: The significance of gender in adult learning*, edited by E. Hayes and D.D. Flannery, 111–137. San Francisco: Jossey-Bass.

Folbre, Nancy. 2001. *The invisible heart: Economics and family values*. New York: New Press.

Foley, Griff. 2001. Radical adult education and learning. *International Journal of Lifelong Education* 20 (1/2): 71–88.

Fournier-Savard, Patric. 2006. Women with disabilities. In *Women in Canada: A gender-based statistical report*, edited by StatsCan, 291–298. Ottawa: Statistics Canada.

Fox, Bonnie. 2006. Motherhood as a class act: The many ways in which "intensive mothering" is entangled with social class. In *Social reproduction: Feminist political economy challenges neoliberalism*, edited by K. Bezanson and M. Luxton, 231–262. Montreal and Kingston: McGill-Queen's University Press.

Frame, Marsha Wiggins, and Constance L. Shehan. 1994. Work and well-being in the two-person-career: Relocation stress and coping among clergy husbands and wives. *Family Relations* 43: 196–205.

Frank, Arthur W. 1995. *The wounded storyteller: Body, illness, and ethics*. Chicago: University of Chicago Press.

Furst, Elisabeth L'Orange 1997. Cooking and femininity. *Women's Studies International Forum* 20 (3): 441–449.

Gather, Claudia. 2004. Paid and unpaid housework and social inequality in Germany. *Atlantis* 28 (2): 61–71.

Gerzer-Sass, Annemarie. 2004. Familienkompetenzen als Potential einer innovativen Personalpolitik. In *Kometenzentwicklung im Wandle. Auf dem Weg zu einer informellen Lernkultur?*, edited by B. Hungerland and B. Overwien, 87–127. Wiesbaden: V.S. Verlag fuer Sozialwissenschaften.

Glucksmann, M.A. 1995. Why "work": Gender and the total social organization of labour. *Gender, Work, and Organization* 2 (2): 63–75.

Glucksmann, Miriam. 2005. Shifting boundaries and interconnections: Extending the "total social organisation of labour." In *A new sociology of work?*, edited by L. Pettinger, J. Parry, and R. Taylor, 19–36. Malden: Blackwell Publishing.

Goldberg, Abbie E., and Maureen Perry-Jenkins. 2007. The division of labor and perceptions of parental roles: Lesbian couples across the transition to parenthood. *Journal of Social and Personal Relationships* 24 (2): 297–318.

Goleman, Daniel. 1995. *Emotional intelligence*. New York: Bantam Books.

Gouthro, Patricia A. 2000. Globalization, civil society, and the homeplace. *Convergence* 33 (1/2): 57–76, nweb:hwwilsonweb.com/hww/results/results_single_ftPES,jhtml.

Gouthro, Patricia A. 2005. A critical feminist analysis of the homeplace as learning site: Expanding the discourse of lifelong learning to consider adult women learners. *International Journal of Lifelong Education* 24 (1): 5–19.

Gouthro, Patricia A., and Donovan Plumb. 2003. Remapping the tripartite register: Moving beyond formal, nonformal, and informal learning. Paper read at Canadian Association for the Study of Adult Education, Halifax. May 29–31.

Grace, Andre P. 2004. Lifelong learning as a chameleonic concepts and versatile practice: Y2K perspectives and trends. *International Journal of Lifelong Education* 23 (4): 385–404.

Greenhaus, Jeffrey, and Gary N. Powell. 2006. When work and family are allies:

A theory of work-family enrichment. *Academy of Management Review* 31 (1): 72–92.

Grint, K. 1998. *The sociology of work: An introduction*, 2nd ed. Cambridge: Polity Press.

Grzywacz, Joseph G., David M. Almeida, and Daniel McDonald. 2002. Work-family spillover and daily reports of work and family stress in the adult labor force. *Family Relations* 51: 28–36.

Grzywacz, Joseph G., and Adam B. Butler. 2005. The impact of job characteristics on work-to-family facilitation: Testing a theory and distinguishing a construct. *Journal of Occupational Health Psychology* 10 (2): 97–109.

Gupta, Sanjiv. 1999. The effects of transitions in marital status on men's performance of housework. *Journal of Marriage and Family* 61: 700–711.

Hamdad, Malika. 2003. *Valuing households' unpaid work in Canada, 1992 and 1998: Trends and sources of change.* Ottawa: Statistics Canada.

Hart, Mechthild U. 1992. *Working and educating for life: Feminist and international perspectives on adult education, international perspectives on adult and continuing education.* London: Routledge.

Hasselkus, Betty R., and Robert O. Ray. 1988. Informal learning in family caregiving: A worm's eye view. *Adult Education Quarterly* 39 (1): 31–40.

Hayes, Elisabeth, and Daniele Flannery. 2000. *Women as learners: The significance of gender in adult learning.* San Francisco: Jossey-Bass Publishers.

Hays, Sharon. 1996. *The cultural contradictions of motherhood.* New Haven: Yale University Press.

Heo, Seongkum, Debra K. Moser, Terry A. Lennie, Barbara Riegel, and Misook L. Chung. 2008. Gender differences in and factors related to self-care behaviors: A cross-sectional, correlational study of patients with heart failure. *International Journal of Nursing Studies* 45: 1807–1815.

Hiemstra, R. 1994. *Self-directed learning.* Retrieved from http://www-distance.syr.edu/sdlhdbk.html.

Hill, E. Jeffrey. 2005. Work-family facilitation and conflict, working fathers and mothers, work-family stressors and support. *Journal of Family Issues* 26 (6): 793–819.

Hochschild, Arlie Russell. 1979. Emotion work, feeling rules, and social structure. *The American Journal of Sociology* 85 (3): 551–575.

Hochschild, Arlie Russell. 1983. *The managed heart: Commercialization of human feeling*. Berkeley: University of California Press.

Hocking, Brent, Johanna Haskell, and Warren Linds, eds. 2001. *Unfolding body/mind: Exploring the possibility through education*. Brandon: Foundation for Educational Renewal.

Hughes, Christina, Loraine Blaxter, Jacky Brine, and Sue Jackson. 2006. Gender, class and "race" in lifelong learning: Policy and practice in the UK and EU. *British Educational Research Journal* 32 (5): 643–648.

Illeris, Knud. 2002. *The three dimensions of learning*. Copenhagen: Roskilde University Press.

Ingadottir, Brynja, and Sigridur Halldorsdottir. 2008. To discipline a "dog": The essential structure of mastering diabetes. *Qualitative Health Research* 18 (5): 606–619.

Ironmonger, Duncan. 1996. Counting outputs, capital inputs, and caring labour: Estimating gross household product. *Feminist Economics* 2 (3): 37–64.

James, Nicky. 1989. Emotional labour: Skill and work in the social regulation of feelings. *Sociological Review* 37: 15–42.

Jarvis, Peter. 1987. *Adult learning in the social context*. Beckenham: Croom Helm.

Jarvis, Peter. 1992. *Paradoxes of learning: On becoming an individual in society*. San Francisco: Jossey-Bass.

Jarvis, Peter. 2004. *Adult education & lifelong learning: Theory and practice*, 3rd ed. London: RoutledgeFalmer.

Jarvis, Peter. 2006a. Beyond the learning society: Globalisation and the moral imperative for reflective social change. *International Journal of Lifelong Education* 25 (3): 201–211.

Jarvis, Peter. 2006b. *Towards a comprehensive theory of human learning*. New York: Routledge.

Juster, F. Thomas, and Frank P. Stafford. 1991. The allocation of time: Empirical findings, behavioral models, and problems of measurement. *Journal of Economic Literature* 29 (2): 471–522.

Kaplan, Caren. 1996. *Questions of travel: Postmodern discourses of displacement.* Durham and London: Duke University Press.

Kiger, Gary, and Pamela J. Riley. 1996. Gender differences in perceptions of household labor. *Journal of Psychology* 130: 357–370.

Kirchmeyer, Catherine. 1992a. Nonwork participation and work attitudes: A test of scarcity vs. expansion models of personal resources. *Human Relations* 45 (8): 775–795.

Kirchmeyer, Catherine. 1992b. Perceptions of nonwork-to-work spillover: Challenging the common view of conflict-ridden domain relationships. *Basic and Applied Social Psychology* 13 (2): 231–249.

Kirchmeyer, Catherine. 1995. Managing the work-nonwork boundary: An assessment of organizational responses. *Human Relations* 48 (5): 515–536.

Koc, Mustafa, Rod MacRae, Luc J.A. Mougeot, and Jennifer Welsh. 1999. Introduction: Food security is a global concern. In *For hunger-proof cities: Sustainable urban food systems,* edited by M. Koc, R. MacRae, L.J.A. Mougeot, and J. Welsh. Ottawa: International Development Research Centre.

Koc, Mustafa, and Jennifer Welsh. 2002. Food, identity, and immigrant experience. *Canadian Diversity* 1 (1): 46–48.

Kolb, D.A. 1984. *Experiential learning: Experience as the source of learning and development.* Englewood Cliffs: Prentice-Hall.

Kostiainen, Juha. 2002. Learning and the "ba" in the development network of an urban region. *European Planning Studies* 10 (5): 613–637.

Kurdeck, Larence A. 2007. The allocation of household labor by partners in gay and lesbian couples. *Journal of Family Issues* 28 (1): 132–148.

Lan, Pei-Chia. 2003. Maid or madam? Filipina migrant workers and the continuity of domestic labor. *Gender & Society* 17 (2): 187–208.

Leathwood, Carole. 2006. Gendered constructions of lifelong learning and the learner in the UK policy context. In *Gender and Lifelong Learning: Critical Feminist Engagements.* Edited by C. Leathwood and B. Francis. New York: Routledge, pages 40–53.

Leathwood, Carole, and Becky Francis, eds. 2006. *Gender and Lifelong Learning: Critical Feminist Engangesmens.* New York: Routledge.

Lessa, Iara, Cecilia Rocha, and Debbie Fields. 2007. *Women's identities and food:*

Practices of settlement and resistance in immigrant Toronto. CERIS-funded RFP: Final Report. Toronto: Ryerson University.

Li, Peter S. 1998. *The Chinese in Canada,* 2nd ed. Toronto: Oxford University Press.

Liu, Lichun. 2007. Unveiling the invisible learning from unpaid household work: Chinese immigrants' perspective. *The Canadian Journal for the Study of Adult Education* 20 (2): 25–40.

Liu, Lichun. 2008a. Carework in a transnational context among new Chinese immigrants in Canada. Paper presented at the 43rd Conference of the Canadian Sociology Association, Congress of the Humanities and Social Sciences, University of British Columbia, Vancouver, Canada, June 3–6.

Liu, Lichun. 2008b. Food work, acculturation, and health: Chinese immigrants' perspective. Paper presented at the *3rd Conference of the Canadian Association for Food Studies (CAFS), Congress of the Humanities and Social Sciences,* University of British Columbia, Vancouver, Canada, May 30–June 1.

Livingstone, David W. 1999. Lifelong learning and underemployment in the knowledge society: A north perspective. *Comparative Education* 35 (2): 163–186.

Livingstone, David W. 2001. Basic patterns of work and learning in Canada: Findings from the 1998 NALL survey of informal learning and related Statistics Canada surveys. Retrieved from http://www.oise.utoronto.ca/depts/sese/csew/nall/res/33working&learning.htm.

Livingstone, David W. 2004. *The education-jobs gap: Underemployment or economic democracy,* 2nd ed. Aurora: Garamond Press.

Livingstone, David W. 2005. Expanding conception of work and learning: Recent research and policy implications. In *International handbook of educational policy,* edited by N. Bascia, A. Cumming, A. Datnow, K. Leithwood, and D. Livingstone, Vol. 2, 977–995. Dordrecht: Springer.

Livingstone, D.W., and Antonie Scholtz. 2006. *Work and lifelong learning in Canada: Basic findings of the 2004 WALL Survey.* Toronto: Ontario Institute for Studies in Education.

Lopata, Helena Znaniecki. 1971. *Occupation: Housewife.* London: Oxford University Press.

Lowe, Graham S., and Harvey J. Krahn, eds. 1993. *Work in Canada: Readings in the sociology of work and industry.* Scarborough: Nelson Canada.

Luxton, Meg. 1980/2009. *More than a labour of love: Three generations of women's work in the home.* Toronto: The Women's Press.

Luxton, Meg. 1997a. *Feminism and families: Critical policies and changing practices.* Halifax: Fernwood.

Luxton, Meg. 1997b. The UN, women, and household labour: Measuring and valuing unpaid work. *Women's Studies International Forum* 20 (3): 431–439.

Luxton, Meg. 2006. Friends, neighbours, and community: A case study of the role of informal caregiving in social reproduction. In *Social reproduction: Feminist political economy challenges neo-liberalism,* edited by K. Bezanson and M. Luxton, 267–292. Montreal and Kingston: McGill-Queen's University Press.

Luxton, Meg, and L.F. Vosko. 1998. Where women's efforts count: The 1996 census campaign and family politics in Canada. *Studies in Political Economy* 56 (Summer): 49–82.

Lv, Nan, and Katherine L. Cason. 2004. Dietary pattern change and acculturation of Chinese Americans in Pennsylvania. *Journal of American Diet Association* 104 (5): 771–778.

MacKeracher, Dorothy. 2004. *Making sense of adult learning,* 2nd ed. Toronto: University of Toronto Press.

Maddock, Mandy. 2006. Children's personal learning agendas at home *Cambridge Journal of Education* 36 (2): 153–169.

Maher, J.M. 2004. Skills, not attributes: Rethinking mothering as work. *Journal of the Association for Research on Mothering* 6 (2): 7–16.

Malul, Miki, John Gal, and Miriam Greenstein. 2009. A universal basic income: Theory and practice in the Israeli case. *Basic Income Studies: An International Journal of Basic Income Research* 4 (1): 1–19.

Marini, Margaret Mooney, and Beth Anne Shelton. 1993. Measuring household work: Recent experience in the United States. *Social Science Research* 22 (4): 361–382.

Marshall, Gordon. 1998. Work. In *Oxford Dictionary of Sociology,* edited by G. Marshall, p. 706. Oxford: Oxford University Press.

Marshall, Katherine. 2006. Converging gender roles. *Perspectives on Labour and Income* 7 (7): 5–17.

McIntosh, W.A., and M. Zey. 1989. Women as gatekeepers of food consumption: A sociological critique. *Food and Foodways* 3 (4): 317–332.

Mederer, Helen J., and Laurie Weinstein. 1992. Choices and constraints in a two-person career: Ideology, division of labor, and well-being among submarine officers' wives. *Journal of Family Issues* 13 (3): 334–350.

Mennell, Stephen, Anne Murcott, and Anneke H. van Otterloo. 1992. *The sociology of food: Eating, diet, and culture.* London: Sage Publications.

Merriam, Sharan B., and Rosemary S. Caffarella. 1999. *Learning in adulthood: A comprehensive guide,* 2nd ed. San Francisco: Jossey-Bass.

Miller, John (Jack). 2002. Learning from a spiritual perspective. In *Expanding the boundaries of transformative learning,* edited by E. O'Sullivan, A. Morell, and A.M. O'Connor, 95–102. New York: Palgrave.

Morris, Jenny. 1998. Feminism, gender, and disability, (Journal, 2005 February 19), http://www.leeds.ac.uk/disability-studies/archiveuk/morris/gender%20 and%20disability.pdf.

Murcott, Anne. 1984. *The sociology of food and eating: Essays on the sociological significance of food.* Aldershot: Gower.

Nakano Glenn, Evelyn, Grace Chang, and Linda Rennie Forcey, eds. 1994. *Mothering: Ideology, experience, and agency.* New York: Routledge.

Newman, Jacqueline M., and Ruth Linke. 1982. Chinese immigrant food habits: A study of the nature and direction of change. *Journal of the Royal Society for the Promotion of Health* 102 (6): 268–271.

Ng, Roxana. 1998. Is embodied teaching and learning critical pedagogy? Some remarks on teaching health and the body from an Eastern perspective. Paper read at AERA Annual Meeting, April 13–17, San Diego, California.

Ng, Roxana, Guida Man, Hongxia Shan, and Lichun Willa Liu. 2007. *Learning to be good citizens: Informal learning and the labour market experiences of professional Chinese immigrant women.* Toronto: CERIS—The Ontario Metropolis Centre.

Noce, Mary Louise. 2005. Support networks and welfare state restructuring: The experiences of 40 Ontario households. Ph.D. dissertation, Department of Sociology and Equity Studies in Education, Department of Sociology and Equity Studies in Education, Ontario Institute for Studies in Education at the University of Toronto, Toronto.

Nolan, Peter. 1993. Work. In *The Blackwell dictionary of twentieth-century social thought*, edited by W. Outhwaite and T. Bottomore, 715–717. Oxford: Blackwell Publishers.

Nosow, Sigmund, and William H. Form, eds. 1962. *Man, work, and society: A reading in the sociology of occupations*. New York: Basic Books.

Oakley, Ann. 1974. *The sociology of housework*. New York: Pantheon Books.

O'Connor, Susan M., Alan G. Jardine, and Keith Millar. 2008. The prediction of self-care behaviors in end-stage renal disease patients using Leventhal's self-regulatory model. *Journal of Psychosomatic Research* 65: 191–200.

Oerton, Sarah. 1997. "Queer housewives?": Some problems in theorizing the division of domestic labour in lesbian and gay households. *Women's Studies International Forum* 20 (3): 421–430.

Oliver, Michael. (1996). *Understanding disability: From theory to practice*. New York: St. Martin's Press.

Olssen, Mark. 2006. Understanding the mechanisms of neoliberal control: Lifelong learning, flexibility, and knowledge capitalism. *International Journal of Lifelong Education* 25 (3): 213–230.

Organisation for Economic Co-operation and Development. 2006. *Starting strong II—early childhood education and care*. Paris: OECD Publishing.

Pan, Y.L., Z. Dixon, S. Himburg, and F. Huffman. 1999. Asian students change their eating patterns after living in the United States. *Journal of American Diet Association* 99 (1): 54–57.

Papanek, Hanna. 1973. Men, women, and work: Reflections on the two-person career. *American Journal of Sociology* 78 (4): 852–872.

Parreñas, Rhacel Salazar. 2001. *Servants of globalization: Women, migration, and domestic work*. Stanford: Stanford University Press.

Patterson, Charlotte J., Erin L. Fulcher, and Megan Sutfin. 2004. Division of labor among lesbian and heterosexual parenting couples: Correlates of specialized versus shared patterns. *Journal of Adult Development* 11 (3): 179–189.

Pettinger, Lynne, Jane Parry, Rebecca Taylor, and Miriam Glucksmann, eds. 2005. *A new sociology of work?* Sociological Review Monographs. Malden: Blackwell Publishing.

Polanyi, Michael. [1966] 1983. *The tacit dimension*. Gloucester: Doubleday.

Poole, Marilyn, and Dallas Isaacs. 1997. Caring: A gendered concept. *Women's Studies International Forum* 20 (4): 529–536.

Pratt, Geraldine. 2004. *Working feminism.* Edinburgh: Edinburgh University Press.

Pratt, Geraldine. 2008. Waiting, and some limits to transnational mothering. Paper presented at Southeast Asia Seminar Series, The Munk Centre for International Studies, Toronto, (Tues) February 12, 2008.

Pratt, Geraldine, and Victoria Rosner. 2006. Introduction: The global & the intimate. *Women's Studies Quarterly* 34 (1): 13–24.

Press, Julie E., and Eleanor Townsley. 1998. Wives' and husbands' housework reporting: Gender, class, and social desirability. *Gender & Society* 12 (2): 188–218.

Rager, Kathleen B. 2004. A thematic analysis of the self-directed learning experiences of 13 breast cancer patients. *International Journal of Lifelong Education* 23 (1): 95–109.

Reskin, Barbara F. 2001. Work and occupations. In *Encyclopedia of sociology*, edited by E.F. Borgatta and R.J.V. Montgomery, (Eds). (2nd edition, Vol. 5, pp. 3261–3269). New York: Macmillan Reference USA.

Ritzer, George. 1989. Sociology of work: A metatheoretical analysis. *Social Forces* 67 (3): 593–604.

Ross, Catherine E., and Marylyn P. Wright. 2001. Women's work, men's work, and the sense of control. In *Working in restructured workplaces: Challenges and new directions for the sociology of work*, edited by D.B. Cornfield, K.E. Campbell, and H.J. McCammon. Thousand Oaks: Sage.

Rothbard, Nancy P. 2001. Enriching or depleting? The dynamics of engagement in work and family roles. *Administrative Science Quarterly* 46: 655–684.

Ruddick, Sara. 1989. *Maternal thinking: Toward a politics of peace.* Boston: Beacon Press.

Ruderman, Marian N., Patricia J. Ohlott, Kate Panzer, and Sara N. King. 2002. Benefits of multiple roles for managerial women. *Academy of Management Journal* 45 (2): 369–386.

Sassen, Saskia. 2000. Women's burden: Counter-geographies of globalization and the feminization of survival. *Journal of International Affairs* 53 (2): 503–524.

Satia, Asongate Jessie. 1999. Diet, acculturation, and health in Chinese-American women. Ph.D dissertation, University of Washington.

Schmuttte, Timothy, Elizabeth Flanagan, Luis Bedregal, Priscilla Ridgway, Dave Sells, Thomas Styron, and Larry Davidson. 2009. Self-efficacy and self-care: Missing ingredients in health and healthcare among adults with serious mental illness. *Psychiatric Quarterly* 80: 1–8.

Schugurensky, Daniel. 2000. *The forms of informal learning: Towards a conceptualization of the field*. Retrieved from http://www.oise.utoronto.ca/depts/sese/csew/nall/res/19formsofinformal.htm.

Shilling, Chris. 2003. *The body and social thought*, 2nd ed. London: Sage Publications.

Shrestha, Mona, Steve Wilson, and Michael Singh. 2008. Knowledge networking: A dilemma in building social capital through nonformal education. *Adult Education Quarterly* 58 (2): 129–150.

Simpson, Ida Harper, and Elizabeth Mutran. 1981. Women's social consciousness: Sex or worker identity. In *Research in the sociology of work: A research annual volume*, edited by I.H. Simpson, 335–350. Greenwich: JAI Press.

Simpson, Ida Harper, and Richard L. Simpson, eds. 1983. *Research in the sociology of work*, vol. 2. Greenwich: JAI Press.

Skinner, Mark. 2008. Voluntarism and long-term care in the countryside: The paradox of a threadbare sector. *The Canadian Geographer* 52 (2): 188–203.

Solomon, Sandra W., Esther D. Rothblum, and Kimberly F. Balsom. 2005. Money, housework, sex, and conflict: Same-sex couples in civil unions, those not in civil unions, and heterosexual married siblings. *Sex Roles* 52 (9/10): 561–575.

Spitzer, Denise, Anne Neufeld, Margaret Harrison, Karen Hughes, and Miriam Stewart. 2003. Caregiving in transnational context: "My wings have been cut; where can I fly?" *Gender & Society* 17 (2): 267–286.

Stasiulis, D., and A. Bakan. 1997. Negotiating Citizenship: The Case of Foreign Domestic Workers in Canada. *Feminist Review*. 57: 112–139.

Statistics Canada. 1996. *1996 Census dictionary—final edition*, http://www.statcan.ca/english/freepub/92-351-UIE/92-351-UIE1996000.htm

Statistics Canada. 2008a. *Canada's changing labour force, 2006 census*. Catalogue no. 97-559-X. Ottawa: Minister of Industry, http://www12.statcan.ca/english/census06/analysis/labour/pdf/97-559-XIE2006001.pdf

Statistics Canada. 2008b. *Community highlights for Toronto.* 2006 Census of Canada, http://www12.statcan.ca.

Stehlik, Tom. 2003. Parenting as a vocation: Lifelong learning can begin in the home. *International Journal of Lifelong Education* 22 (4): 367–379.

Stephens, Mary Ann Parris, Melissa M. Franks, and Audie A. Atienza. 1997. Where two roles intersect: Spillover between parent care and employment. *Psychology and Aging* 12 (1): 30–37.

Stevens, Daphne, Gary Kiger, and Pamela Riley. 2001. Working hard and hardly working: Domestic labor and marital satisfaction among dual-earner couples. *Journal of Marriage & the Family* 63: 514–526.

Strazdins, L., and D.H. Broom. 2004. Acts of love (and work): Gender imbalance in emotional work and women's psychological distress. *Journal of Family Issues* 25 (3): 356–378.

Sumer, H. Canan, and Patrick A. Knight. 2001. How do people with different attachment styles balance work and family? A personality perspective of work-family linkage. *Journal of Applied Psychology* 86 (4): 653–663.

Taylor, P.G. 2000. Exploring the role of grief and grieving in coping with lifelong change. *International Journal of Lifelong Education* 19 (6): 525–534.

Thiessen, Victor, and E. Dianne Looker. 1999. Images of work: Women's work, men's work, housework. *Canadian Journal of Sociology* 24 (2): 225–254.

Thomas, Carol. 1993. De-constructing concepts of care. *Sociology* 27 (4): 649–669.

Thomas, Carol. 2007. *Sociologies of disability and illness: Contested ideas in disability studies and medical sociology.* New York: Palgrave MacMillan.

Titchkosky, Tanya. 2003. *Disability, self, and society.* Toronto: University of Toronto Press.

Titchkosky, Tanya. 2007. *Reading and writing disability differently: The textured life of embodiment.* Toronto: University of Toronto Press.

Torjman, Sherri. 2009. The three ghosts of poverty. *Caledon Commentary.* Ottawa: Caledon Institute of Social Policy.

Tough, Allen. 1999. *Reflections on the study of adult learning.* NALL Working Paper Series, Paper no. 8, 1999 (retrieved September 22, 2003), http://www.oise.utoronto.ca/depts/sese/csew/nall.

Tran, Kelly. 2004. Visible minorities in the labour force: 20 years of change. *Canadian Social Trends*. Catalogue no. 11-008:7-11. Ottawa: Statistics Canada.

Trotz, D. Alissa. 2006. Rethinking Caribbean transnational connections: Conceptual itineraries. *Global Networks* 6 (1): 41–59.

Twiggs, Joan E., Julia McQuillan, and Myra Marx Ferree. 1999. Meaning and measurement: Reconceptualizing measures of the division of household labor. *Journal of Marriage and the Family* 61: 712–724.

Vallas, Steven. 2001. *Research in the sociology of work: The transformation of work.* Oxford: Elsevier Science Ltd.

Vallianatos, Helen, and Kim Raine. 2008. Consuming food and constructing identities among Arabic and South Asian immigrant women. *Food, Culture & Society* 11 (3): 355–373.

Van Esterik, P. 1999. Right to food; right to feed; right to be fed: The intersection of women's rights and the right to food. *Agriculture and Human Values* 16: 225–232.

Viklund, Gunnel E., Susanne Rudberg, and K.F. Wikblad. 2007. Teenages with diabetes: Self-management education and training on a big schooner. *International Journal of Nursing Practice* 13: 385–392.

Wang, Lu, and Lucia Lo. 2007. Immigrant grocery-shopping behavior: Ethnic identity versus accessibility. *Environment and Planning A* 39: 684–699.

Wang, Shuguang, and Lucia Lo. 2005. Chinese immigrants in Canada: Their changing composition and economic performance. *International Migration Review* 43 (3): 35–71.

Waring, Marilyn. 1988. *If women counted: A new feminist economics.* New York: Harper and Row.

Waring, Marilyn. 1999. *Counting for nothing: What men value and what women are worth*, 2nd ed. Toronto: University of Toronto Press.

Watson, Tony. 1987. *Sociology, work & industry.* London: Routledge & Kegan Paul.

Wax, Amy. 2009. Basic income or caretaker benefits? *Basic Income Studies: An International Journal of Basic Income Research* 4 (1): 1–21.

Wayne, Julie Holliday, Nicholas Musisca, and William Fleeson. 2004. Considering the role of personality in the work-family experience: Relationships of the big five to work-family conflict and facilitation. *Journal of Vocational Behavior* 64: 108–130.

Welton, Michael R. 1998. The struggle of memory against forgetting. In *Learning for life: Canadian readings in adult education*, edited by S.M. Scott, B. Spencer, and A.M. Thomas, 35–45. Toronto: Thompson Educational Publishing.

Wendell, Susan. 1996. *The rejected body: Feminist philosophical reflections on disability*. New York: Routledge.

Wendell, Susan. 2001. Unhealthy disabled: Treating chronic illnesses as disabilities. *Hypatia* 16 (4): 17–33.

West, Candace, and Don H. Zimmerman. 1987. Doing gender. *Gender and Society* (1): 125–151.

Whyte, William H. 1956. *The organization man*. New York: Simon & Schuster.

Williamson, Bill. 1998. *Lifeworlds and learning: Essays in the theory, philosophy, and practice of lifelong learning*. Leicester: National Institute of Adult Continuing Education.

Windebank, Jan. 2001. Dual-earner couples in Britain and France: Gender divisions of domestic labour and parenting work in different welfare states. *Work, Employment & Society* 15 (2): 269–290.

Wipper, Audrey, ed. 1984. *The sociology of work: Papers in honour of Oswald Hall*. Ottawa: Carleton University Press.

Wong, Connie Ching-See. 2005. Power, gender construction, and interactional processes of family-to-work impact in married couples. Ph.D. dissertation, Adult Education and Counselling Psychology, University of Toronto.

Wu, David Y.H, and Sidney C.H Cheung, eds. 2002. *The globalization of Chinese food*. Surrey: Curzon Press.

Zukewich, Nancy. 2003. Unpaid informal caregiving. *Canadian Social Trends*, Vol. 70. Ottawa: Statistics Canada: 14–18.

Zuo, Jiping, and Yanjie Bian. 2001. Gender resources, division of housework, and perceived fairness—A case in urban China. *Journal of Marriage & the Family* 63: 1122–1133.

CONTRIBUTORS

PATRIZIA ALBANESE is Associate Professor of sociology at Ryerson University. She is author of Child Poverty in Canada (Oxford, 2010), Children in Canada Today (Oxford, 2009), and Mothers of the Nation: Women, Families and Nationalism in Twentieth Century Europe (U of T Press, 2006). She is co-editor (with Tepperman) of Sociology: A Canadian Perspective, 2nd ed. She is also doing research on child care in Canada, on the well-being of youth in Canadian Forces families (with D. Harrison, UNB); and on the intergenerational transmission of problem gambling (with L. Tepperman, U of T).

MARGRIT EICHLER is a Professor in the Department of Sociology and Equity Studies at the Ontario Institute for Studies in Education at the University of Toronto. Her more than 200 publications deal with women's and feminist studies, unpaid household work, environmental sustainability and social justice, family policy, feminist methodology and other issues. She is Vice President of BIAS FREE Inc, see www.biasfree.org and Secretary of Science for Peace.

SUSAN FERGUSON is a graduate student in the Department of Sociology and Equity Studies in Education at the Ontario Institute for Studies in Education at the University of Toronto. Working at the intersections of disability studies, feminist theory and anti-racism, Susan's research interests include the cultural work of pain narratives, decolonizing methodologies and the politics of health and healing. She has presented her work at Canadian and international conferences, designed and delivered disability equity workshops and co-authored (with Tanya Titchkosky) a chapter on disability in higher education. Susan currently works as a researcher, writer and educator and is committed to bringing embodied pedagogical practices into her teaching, scholarship and community work.

NICKY HYNDMAN is a PhD candidate at the Ontario Institute for Studies in Education, University of Toronto in the department of Sociology and Equity Studies in Education. Her PhD research examines the home/school relationship through the practice of elementary homework. Nicky lives in Charlottetown, PEI and is a sessional instructor in the faculty of education at University of Prince Edward Island.

LICHUN WILLA LIU is a PhD candidate at the Ontario Institute for Studies in Education, University of Toronto. Her doctoral research focused on Chinese immigrants, unpaid household work (food work, childcare, and emotion work), and lifelong learning. Her other PhD-related publications include two peer-reviewed journal articles, in Cuizine, 2009, 1(2) and in the Canadian Journal for the Study of Adult Education, 2007, 20 (2) two book chapters (one forthcoming), and over 20 conference papers/proceedings.

ANN MATTHEWS is a PhD candidate at the Ontario Institute for Studies in Education at the University of Toronto. Her research explores the ways in which learning through unpaid household work by women with disabilities challenges traditional discourses about the ways in which adults learn. Ann was a stay-at-home mother for her two daughters, has engaged in extensive volunteer work, and taught part-time at Seneca College (Toronto). She has several publications related to work and adult learning and has presented papers on the same topics at a number of Canadian academic conferences.

ACKNOWLEDGEMENTS

We are grateful to a large number of people without whom this book would not have been possible. First of all, we thank David Livingstone for inviting Margrit Eichler to conduct one of the case studies of the large-scale study on Work and Lifelong Learning (WALL) that he initiated and led, and the Social Sciences and Humanities Research Council of Canada for funding the research. A number of people, beyond the authors, were part of the research process: Our community partner, Mothers are Women (MAW) was represented by Kathryn Spracklin, who continued working with us even when MAW, as an organization, ceased to function. Doug Hart was helpful in a multitude of ways, especially with statistical analysis, but he gave good advice and support throughout the project's duration. A number of students participated at different times in carious capacities in the research: Robyn Bourgeois, Mary Bullen, Alexia Dyer, Lingqin Feng, Young-Hwa Hong, Gada Mahrouse, Carly Manion, Tracey Matthews, Gayle McIntyre, Thara Mohanathas, Sam Rahimi, Milosh Raykov, Susan Stowe, Carole Trainor, and Natalie ZurNedden – thank you for your hard work! Most of all, we thank the over 400 women and men who shared their insights and experiences – some of them painful – with us in a mailed survey, in focus groups, in individual interviews, or in front of a camera. We hope that we have been faithful in representing what you communicated to us.